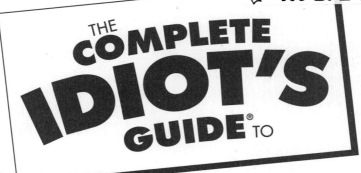

THE COMPLETE IDIOT'S GUIDE® TO

Raising Boys

*by Laurie A. Helgoe, Ph.D., and
Barron M. Helgoe, Esq.*

ALPHA

A member of Penguin Group (USA) Inc.

To Bjorn and Joshua, for whom we are forever thankful

ALPHA BOOKS

Published by the Penguin Group

Penguin Group (USA) Inc., 375 Hudson Street, New York, New York 10014, USA

Penguin Group (Canada), 90 Eglinton Avenue East, Suite 700, Toronto, Ontario M4P 2Y3, Canada (a division of Pearson Penguin Canada Inc.)

Penguin Books Ltd, 80 Strand, London WC2R 0RL, England

Penguin Ireland, 25 St. Stephen's Green, Dublin 2, Ireland (a division of Penguin Books Ltd.)

Penguin Group (Australia), 250 Camberwell Road, Camberwell, Victoria 3124, Australia (a division of Pearson Australia Group Pty. Ltd.)

Penguin Books India Pvt. Ltd., 11 Community Centre, Panchsheel Park, New Delhi—110 017, India

Penguin Group (NZ), 67 Apollo Drive, Rosedale, North Shore, Auckland 1311, New Zealand (a division of Pearson New Zealand Ltd.)

Penguin Books (South Africa) (Pty.) Ltd, 24 Sturdee Avenue, Rosebank, Johannesburg 2196, South Africa

Penguin Books Ltd., Registered Offices: 80 Strand, London WC2R 0RL, England

Copyright © 2008 by Laurie A. Helgoe, Ph.D.

International Standard Book Number: 978-1-59257-730-9
Library of Congress Catalog Card Number: 2007906891

10   09   08   8   7   6   5   4   3   2   1

Interpretation of the printing code: The rightmost number of the first series of numbers is the year of the book's printing; the rightmost number of the second series of numbers is the number of the book's printing. For example, a printing code of 08-1 shows that the first printing occurred in 2008.

Printed in the United States of America

Note: This publication contains the opinions and ideas of its authors. It is intended to provide helpful and informative material on the subject matter covered. It is sold with the understanding that the authors and publisher are not engaged in rendering professional services in the book. If the reader requires personal assistance or advice, a competent professional should be consulted.

The authors and publisher specifically disclaim any responsibility for any liability, loss, or risk, personal or otherwise, which is incurred as a consequence, directly or indirectly, of the use and application of any of the contents of this book.

Most Alpha books are available at special quantity discounts for bulk purchases for sales promotions, premiums, fund-raising, or educational use. Special books, or book excerpts, can also be created to fit specific needs.

For details, write: Special Markets, Alpha Books, 375 Hudson Street, New York, NY 10014.

Publisher: *Marie Butler-Knight*	**Cartoonist:** *Steve Barr*
Editorial Director: *Mike Sanders*	**Cover Designer:** *Bill Thomas*
Managing Editor: *Billy Fields*	**Book Designer:** *Trina Wurst*
Executive Editor: *Randy Ladenheim-Gil*	**Indexer:** *Tonya Heard*
Development Editor: *Lynn Northrup*	**Layout:** *Ayanna Lacey*
Production Editor: *Megan Douglass*	**Proofreader:** *John Etchison*
Copy Editor: *Nancy Wagner*	

Contents at a Glance

Contents

Introduction

This book is a continuation of the excitement and conversations that come before hearing "It's a boy!" The intense emotion that flows from the moment of birth—the compelling sense of thankfulness that parents feel at the arrival of a newborn son—is the wellspring of good parenting. In that moment of gratitude, a new parent finds the source of energy to decide to parent well. To accept the responsibilities, fears, and daily "to-do" lists demands the best of men and women. Parents need not work for perfection but rather dedicate themselves to the purpose of raising a healthy, happy, educated boy in a home that offers safety, kindness, and unbounded love.

If you have accepted the challenge and seek the rewards of "raising a son," we congratulate you. That you have chosen this book is a testament to your willingness to learn about boys. And there is much to learn.

How This Book Is Organized

This guide is broken down into easily readable portions. You may wish to read the book all the way through one time, and then keep it on the shelf to consult as your boy grows. Even if your son is in diapers now, what you read about older boys will allow you to be a keen observer. You'll come to appreciate the various stages of a boy's life and congratulate yourself on your ability to spot emerging behaviors in other boys around you.

Part 1, "Boy Gets Personality," addresses newborn issues, from the wishes of new parents to a decision about circumcision. We discuss boys at play, behaviors at the potty, and discipline for very young boys. This part also looks at boys "playing doctor" and "playing daddy." Finally, this section begins the explanation of gender identity, personality, and emotional and social interaction for boys.

Part 2, "Boy Gets Skills," discusses self-care, chores, games, and the creative opportunities of unstructured time. We help you get your son ready for his big adventure in the land of no-parents: school. Material in this section will help prepare you for the time when school calls, whether the call is for the gifted program, an individual plan for a boy with ADHD, or a disciplinary conference with the principal. We discuss sports at length, from how to get coached to how to be a team player. We look at solo activities, too, and the great tradition of outdoor sports, such as hunting and fishing. Brain competitions, the arts, and survival training are reviewed along with the social and emotional skills that will guide your son through to the middle school years. We take an extensive look at teasing, both what is bad and what is very good about teasing. Finally, we celebrate the joys and challenges of raising boys who want nothing more than to run and tumble in a large pack during middle school.

Part 3, "Boy Gets Hormones," is a guide to the sexual maturation of your son: puberty. We present a straightforward explanation of this long process, which involves body changes, sexuality, and his fears. We discuss the importance of image, the development of teen identity, and the reasons he strains under your authority. As his friends are very important to him, we help you understand his needs for companionship as well as safe and consistent boundaries. Girl smarts and gay smarts are explained, including how to have a real conversation about love, sex, and commitment.

Part 4, "Boy Gets a Life," discusses the challenges of raising a boy in high school. We help you get your son ready for his new life of more demanding classes, intense emotions, and the license to venture out into the world. You'll be ready for his first love and, no doubt, first heartache. The continued importance of family and ritual will be detailed, as well. Finally, we help you launch your son into adulthood, whether it is choosing and paying for college or managing a slower transition for the boy who remains at home.

Extras

We have included four different types of sidebars to break out special thoughts on a wide variety of subjects:

Boy Wisdom _____
These quotes offer brief insights into raising boys.

Keep Out! _____
These sidebars warn parents with sons of traps and pitfalls.

Toolbox

These sidebars pass along practical information that makes parenting boys in a particular situation easier.

Toy Box

Enjoy the humor of these sidebars—something a parent of a boy requires in large measure every day! You'll also find interesting tidbits of information here.

Acknowledgments

Laurie's acknowledgments:

To Bjorn: We called you the "Sparkler" because of the way your eyes—and your personality—sparkle, always drawing people to you. I love your quiet intelligence, the value you place on friendship, your kindness, your light-up-the-world smile, and your strong sense of who you are.

To Josh: If Bjorn is the Sparkler, you are the Firecracker, waking us up out of drudgery and reminding us to lighten up, make room for fun, and celebrate the events of our lives. I love your exuberance, the care you provide our dog, Coco, your concern for the environment, and your self-directed passion to create.

You have both taught us that knowing and loving a boy is a tremendous privilege. Knowing and loving the two of you is as good as it gets.

To Barron: I have admired and learned from your integrity, your strength, and your ability to laugh at yourself. You stimulate our minds, make us laugh, and bind us together as a family. You are the best kind of man, and I still revel in my luck to have married you. I love you.

To Jacky Sach, my agent: The day you called me changed my life, and the journey together has been great. Thank you for making this writer into an author.

To Beth and Cindy, Becca and Julie: Thank you for your friendship and loyalty through it all. I treasure you. To Carolyn and Phil and Andy and Sandy, for your amazing support and for the reminder that, with family, I am never alone. To Dad, for having so much fun being a dad; to Mom, for showing me how to respond to every emotion with love.

Special thanks to our boys' Aunt Jen and Grandma Beth, for the generous mothering you provide to the boys and to me.

To Alpha's team of outstanding editors: To Randy Ladenheim-Gil, a veteran New York editor who still knows how to be kind. Here's to our third book together! To Lynn Northrup, who moved us quickly and easily through polishing the text, proving that pain is not necessary for great gain. And to Nancy Wagner and Megan Douglass. Thank you all!

Barron's acknowledgments:

To Bjorn: Your bright eyes reflect the same as they did when we brought you home from the hospital. We especially cherish your insightful and critical thinking, your kindness, and your love of your friends and your brother.

To Josh: Your energy and desire for activity is a constant source of joy. Your perseverance in the face of frustration and your desire to challenge your older and stronger brother inspire us all to work harder and accomplish more.

This book is inspired by you both and offered in the hope that other parents will read it and find additional wisdom and strength to raise sons who are equally strong, kind, and loving.

To Laurie, my wonderful wife. Twenty-five years down and several decades to go with a brilliant, gorgeous woman who sees through my shortcomings. I am truly a lucky man.

To my mother, Beth. Your love and devotion to family are my first touchstones for raising our sons.

To Bernie, my father. Thanks for teaching me that honest men sleep well at night, that true success is found in good friends and family, and that few things are more enjoyable than a good game of poker.

To my sisters, Carol, Caf, and Jen. I send you my heartfelt thanks for your love and constant encouragement over the years.

To my brother-in-law and law partner, Matthew. Your warrior spirit, knowledge of the law, and devotion to our clients, so many of them lost boys, is a real inspiration.

Trademarks

All terms mentioned in this book that are known to be or are suspected of being trademarks or service marks have been appropriately capitalized. Alpha Books and Penguin Group (USA) Inc. cannot attest to the accuracy of this information. Use of a term in this book should not be regarded as affecting the validity of any trademark or service mark.

Part 1

Boy Gets Personality

You look into your son's eyes and meet for the first time. This very special moment prompts parents to simply say: "Hello." Hello, indeed!

Part 1 helps you connect with your son before and after he grows too big for his crib. It discusses your wishes and fears about boys, and the meeting that takes place when he arrives.

His exploration of his new world is a focus, as well. From bathroom to playground, adventures and challenges await. By reading these chapters you can understand the reason for and answer the inevitable question: "Why can't I marry you, Mommy?"

1

It's a Boy!

In This Chapter

- ◆ What a boy means to you
- ◆ Fear of boys?
- ◆ Society's view of boys
- ◆ Telling *his* story
- ◆ Testing four common assumptions about boys

He's here! Whether you meet your boy in the hospital, fresh from mommy's belly, or later down the road, you already have desires, fears, and expectations about who he is and who he will become.

At the beginning, you have very little to work with. A mother feels the baby in her womb, and an adoptive parent gets a sketch through the child's records. Maybe you've even met the boy because he's the son of the partner you are planning to marry. Even so, we usually know very little and imagine much more. That's why we make so much of one concrete piece of information: "It's a boy!"

When we hang our "It's a boy!" banners and share the news of having a son, we are saying much more than we probably realize. In this chapter, we look at the complex mix of expectations and assumptions that come with a boy, work to understand the purpose these ideas serve, and help you clear the way to see the unique human being entering your life.

Boy Wishes

When you wish for a boy, you probably aren't even aware of all that goes into your desire. Maybe another little boy has captured your heart already, and he forms your model of a child you could love. Or you already have a girl and want "one of each." Maybe you like sailor suits and overalls better than frilly dresses. Regardless of the reasons, it is helpful as parents to look at what we project onto our boys. That way, we can enjoy the fantasy for what it is, while getting ready for the fulfillment as well as the surprises to come. Let's look at some common wishes associated with the one in blue.

The Family Name

We once heard a comedienne joke about how "liberating" it was to live in a country where she got to choose whether to take her husband's name or her father's. For better or for worse, we still tend to trace family lines through sons and see boys as continuing the "bloodline."

It's not unusual for parents to feel some relief that the male child will carry on the family name. Along with this awareness, parents might imagine that the son will remain more connected and identified with the family. Dad especially may imagine an inherited legacy that will be fulfilled through his son. These wishes can provide a sense of importance to this new life. The boy is automatically given a role in a larger story and will not have to decide what his name will be when he enters a committed relationship. His identity may seem stronger and more continuous, helping him feel more grounded and confident.

Toolbox

We need only look at names such as "Johnson" ("son of John") to see how family names are made.

On the other hand, the wishes related to family name can become a burden when the son's individual identity conflicts with the family identity. It is also important to remember that the family identity is more than that of Dad and his family. Sometimes the challenge is to transcend the limitations of family name and help your son know that, with his birth, he has changed the family. He has invented something entirely new.

Assuming Competence

As we anticipate having a boy, we may imagine him as being more self-sufficient and less "emotional" than a girl—in other words, easier. We may feel relief at the thought that he's not going to share a play-by-play of every drama that goes on with his friends and that he won't have menstrual periods and the emotional rollercoaster that comes with the turf. We also tend to see boys as tougher and more solid than girls, as more able to hold their own, take a tease, and get dirty. A boy can seem more like a buddy or partner, someone who can be strong for his parents.

Believing your boy is strong and competent is a wonderful gift you can give him. As he sees you seeing *him* that way, he'll probably feel stronger and more capable. Your confidence in him can spur him on to face and overcome risks and challenges.

However, belief in his competence won't feel so good to him if it becomes a source of pressure or a cause for neglect or when it clouds the reality that you are his parent. As tough as he may be, he enters the world fully dependent on you. First boys, in particular, are often considered older and more skilled than they actually are. And as fun as he may be, he still relies on you to teach him how to get along and to provide him structure and safety.

Boy Wisdom

#1

Used to be we all wanted to be firefighters and police officers. But no longer. Saddled with more expectations than ever before, today's young men seem as if they'd come out of the womb with a burning desire to pursue careers in law, medicine, and high finance.

—John Nikkah, *Our Boys Speak*

Parents of even the most capable boys remain parents—the ones who rein him in, settle him down, push him when he needs it, and sometimes spoil everything. The very fact that a boy can be easy challenges us to be present for him as much as we are for the chatty girl. And when he's difficult, he'll give us a workout. But while we are raising him, he'll be raising us, too. By challenging and resisting us, boys make us stronger. And when that happens, everyone gets to be competent!

Fear of Boys

In addition to our boy wishes, we may harbor fears. A mother who has suffered abuse at the hands of a male can unconsciously fear her boy's natural aggression. A father who was neglected by his dad may worry about his ability to be present for his son. We all have "boy baggage" of some kind, even if it's a light load. The good news is that when we consciously separate past experience from this fresh relationship, a son can motivate us to deal with and heal old hurts. In addition, a healthy relationship with the boy we know so intimately can be wonderfully healing.

Unfortunately, the very expectations we set up for boys can promote fear of them. We push boys to be independent and then feel intimidated when they act aloof and detached. We tell them not to cry, then wonder why they only seem to express anger.

To some extent, boys need to develop a "posture" to function in society. But it's crucial that we don't confuse the posture with the boy. If we are intimidated and controlled by our sons, *they* have good reason to be afraid. A boy needs to know that he can be strong *and* safe—that his parents have the courage to disappoint him, if necessary, to provide what he needs.

What's in a Boy?

In addition to personal expectations for boys, we can be influenced by societal definitions. Societal definitions are ideas about boys that become so popular we start to see them as facts. These definitions, which tend to linger even when they become outdated, combine with our personal expectations as we envision who this new arrival will be.

History and Boys

History has a way of influencing our beliefs even when, or perhaps especially when, we are clueless about the past. Feelings about having a son provide an apt example of this carryover. The widespread European tradition of *primogenitor* instilled the belief that a son was more valuable than a daughter. In this tradition, the firstborn son got everything—all the land, all the money. The other sons had other options: priesthood and spiritual power or battle and the power to conquer. The social and economic value of a girl child was tied to the man she would marry.

So that's in the past. Or is it? In my (Laurie's) family, the eldest son had an honored place at the table: at the end opposite my father (Mom sat in the chair closest to the kitchen, of course). Though this tradition may be fading away, weddings are still steeped in the primogenitor model. Dad "gives away" the daughter, and the husband "takes her." Depending on the religion, he may be asked to take care of her while she submits to him.

Although your son may carry on the family name, he's not likely to get the whole pie of your "fortune"—that is, unless he's the only child. Today, daughters also inherit fortunes and companies and take over family businesses. But boys continue to inherit the responsibility to be in charge and provide. Consider the fact that boys are still expected to pay the tab on a date, as well as initiate the kiss. While we hold on to the belief that boys "have it all," they actually no longer get it all.

But boys do still inherit a sense of their value and potential, something every individual deserves. The challenge as parents is to separate history from *his story*.

Equality and Boys

Today, another cultural trend—gender equality—influences our feelings about boys. Though we have been challenging gender-based limitations for some time now, boys have only recently become the focus of its concern. An outpouring of popular literature has brought attention to the neglected needs of boys due to the limitations of stereotyped gender roles.

Up until recently, we have viewed boys as the winners in the gender gap and have focused on the neglected rights of girls. In this context, we have become conscious of the need to teach boys to respect girls and see them as equals. Who could argue with that? Mothers and fathers contribute to society when they pledge to raise their boys to respect and value women. (We'll look at "girl smarts" for boys in Chapter 16.)

Yet our perspective remains limited when we sell equality to boys for the sake of girls alone. We are now advocating broader role definitions for the sake of boys as well, and we've become keenly aware of how boys have been ripped off in what seemed like a sweet deal. We want our boys to have access to the emotional and social freedom girls enjoy. We want them to feel less pressure to be strong and in charge. We'd like them to feel more comfortable with their vulnerabilities.

But let's not throw the "Y" chromosome out with the bathwater! Qualities such as competitiveness and toughness are real—and attractive—in boys. We enjoy watching our two boys playfully sparring, creating balance by challenging each other, smiling all the while. They add a dimension to our home that we would miss if they toned down the action.

Toy Box

Henry VIII could have saved himself a lot of trouble if he had known simple genetics. He threw aside woman after woman—and murdered one—because they were unable to provide him a male heir (he murdered the other because she was unfaithful). Had he realized that his sperm was the culprit, he could have simply fallen on his own sword. Or he might have just relaxed: Anne Boleyn's daughter ended up with the throne anyway.

If we mistake equality for sameness, we risk seeing boys as less than girls, perhaps simpler, and work to "catch them up" with their feminine counterparts. A boy is not an unfinished girl. Boys are constructed differently than girls, and their bodies and brains grow at a separate pace. The true spirit of equality is to allow differences to thrive, side by side—equally.

So when you anticipate a boy entering your life, don't worry so much about being boy-centric. Today's boy can be fully boy *and* move beyond old gender roles. In other words, he gets to be who he is.

Meeting Him

The world changes the moment you first look into his eyes. In that moment, expectations dissolve and you see a real human being. This can be a powerful and even scary transition because there is no guide to exactly who he is and what he'll need.

This moment of pure potential is a helpful reference point as you seek to understand your boy. As much as this book and others can say about boys, he is ultimately the one who will show you what describes him.

As parents, we can benefit from thinking the way scientists do: they don't claim to know the answers but carry around educated guesses and test them out. We invite you to approach this book in that spirit. We'll give you our best educated guesses, based on the current literature and the experience we've gathered while parenting and counseling boys. But it's up to you to test things out with the real boy in your home.

But before you get him home, you'll need to deal with a very sensitive issue. *Circumcision* is the surgical removal of the skin covering the tip of the penis. The decision of whether to circumcise your boy or not is probably the first "boys-only" issue you'll face, and you'll need to sort it out without his input.

The practice of circumcision began as a religious rite, in Islamic and Jewish traditions, to affirm and celebrate a boy's relationship with God. Concerns about boys' hygiene popularized the practice, and hospitals now routinely offer the procedure to parents of boys. When circumcision is a part of your religious practice, the decision can be very straightforward. But when this factor is removed, what's the right choice?

The bottom line is that it is just that—a choice. The American Academy of Pediatrics has concluded that the medical advantages of circumcision are not sufficient to recommend routine use of the procedure, so the decision remains a personal one. We have listed some pros and cons in the following table for your consideration.

Pros	Cons
No pain	Pain (the anesthetic helps)
Looks like Dad	Alteration of natural anatomy
Slightly easier to clean	Surgical risks
Slightly lower risk of STDs	Cost (insurance may not pay)
Looks like most boys in U.S.	
No surprises for sexual partner	
Lower risk of urinary tract infections*	
Reduced risk of penile inflammation and penile cancer*	

These problems are quite rare.

As you do your own research, you'll find that some sources passionately advocate one perspective. Gather facts, but let the values come from you.

Testing Assumptions

As you get to know the real boy in your life, you'll have the chance to learn what fits him and what doesn't. Let's look at four common assumptions about boys and what we've learned about boys in general.

Boys Are More Aggressive

Yes, boys are generally more aggressive than girls. There are always individual differences, but a boy's biology gives him extra equipment for initiating and competing in the world. Specifically, he's got bigger amygdalae—the areas of his brain that determine reactions to emotional stimuli—and he's got more of that aggression potion called testosterone. His aggressive edge not only helps him compete but also allows him to solve problems and assert his needs.

Boys Are Less Sensitive

Yes and no. Boys are less *sensory*, less tuned-in to input from their senses in comparison to girls. Girls hear more acutely, are better able to see rich colors and textures, and can more easily identify emotions in others. But there is evidence that boys may actually be more *emotionally* sensitive—more impacted in emotionally stimulating situations. They are just less likely to show their feelings.

Boys Are Less Emotional

No. Boy babies have been observed to be more emotionally expressive than girl babies and, as noted previously, boys tend to get more worked up when their emotions are tapped. In addition, boys' brains are less equipped to read emotional cues and process feelings. So contrary to stereotype, boys tend to be more emotionally vulnerable than girls. Because girls wear their emotions more openly and comfortably, we assume they are more "emotional." The reality is, the girls are *handling* their emotions, while the boys often try to manage the overload privately or express it through aggression. When boys have safe avenues for expressing feelings, they have much to share.

Boys Are Slower Than Girls

No, boys can't really be considered slower because they are on a completely different developmental *track* than girls. Boys are generally slower to develop verbal and fine motor skills (talking, reading, writing), but they are quicker to develop a knack for spatial relationships and abstract problem solving (math, mapping, construction). Though boys and girls both reach the finish line of adulthood with fully developed brains, they get there by different routes.

Boy Oh Boy!

As parents, we love capturing our boys through photographs and video footage. But it's the pictures in our mind that provide the most delight. This is the time to take those pictures, and not just the ones of him cleaned up and smiling. We love the advice to take pictures of babies when they cry or pout—those times are a big part of the story!

When we run through our inner picture books of our boys, we think of toddler jeans, hoards of boys coming in for drinks, a fistful of dandelions, trips to the ER for stitches and sprains, lots and lots of hugs, tons of laundry, and even more laughter. It's the mix—the whole story—that makes a boy.

Use this book to enrich the picture book of your boy—to help you look at him from different angles, to cast some light on what he's going through, and to help you step back and see him more fully. Boys are not always easy to see, but when we get the picture, helping them grow is not that hard. Let's get started!

The Least You Need to Know

- ◆ Your relationship with your son starts as you prepare for his arrival.

- ◆ Beliefs about your boy's competence are good for him as long as they don't undermine his childhood or his true identity.

- ◆ Separate your real-life boy from any fears of boys and you'll find an opportunity for healing.

- ◆ Like parents, society has expectations for boys, and knowing these expectations will help you make informed decisions about parenting.

- ◆ Look at boy advice as "educated guesses" that you and your boy test out.

Chapter 2

Growing at *His* Pace

In This Chapter

- ◆ Allowing his tears
- ◆ Toys for boys
- ◆ His roundabout route to the potty
- ◆ Getting him to listen and other disciplinary issues

If you read the Sunday comic *The Family Circus*, you are accustomed to following Billy on his many-detoured routes from point A to B. Billy has to investigate everything along his path, but we know he'll eventually get there. It may be helpful for us to keep little Billy in mind as we see our boys through the stages of early development. He'll get there, but his route may be a bit different than what you had in mind.

Boys Do Cry!

Any parent of a baby boy can tell you that boys do cry—and cry and cry. Crying is a very effective form of communication! Studies show that the grating cry of an infant arouses physiological responses in parents, preparing them for action. We will do *anything* to silence that cry, and that's how we figure out his complex needs and effectively respond.

As he grows, he discovers new ways of expressing himself, which is good for everyone. He learns to point and speak, and we don't have the burden of figuring it all out. When we say, "use your words," we are helping him develop a language for his emotional life. Even so, sometimes all he needs is a good cry and a comforting hug.

Unfortunately, we can start to see crying as "feminine" and become uncomfortable when our boys cry. Sensing this discomfort, boys can quickly learn to "stuff it." Then we later wonder why our boys don't talk to us!

Boys can also conclude that "boys don't cry" when they miss out on the emotions of the men in their lives. If your son sees Mom up close and personal, while only hearing a summary of Dad's day, he will naturally see Mom as more emotional. Many dads today face the challenge of becoming more emotionally accessible to their sons without having had that kind of help from their own fathers.

Boy Wisdom _____

In our study, fathers who could give their sons even a small portion of the kind of caring, time, and love they had longed for from their own dads—but often did not receive—got a great personal emotional boost of self-esteem. They were giving something to the next generation of boys—a legacy—and repairing something from their own boyhood simultaneously. It was a second chance for male-based caring and love.
—William Pollack, *Real Boys: Rescuing Our Sons from the Myths of Boyhood*

Another concern for parents is how society will view our boys if they cry more freely. We don't want some playground bully calling him a crybaby! Besides, kids of both genders can manipulate with tears, and that's a real turn-off. Here are some ways to teach your boy how to have his tears and protect him, too:

◆ **Investigate.** Crying happens for all kinds of reasons, and it is helpful to approach his tears without assumptions. Take him seriously; gently try to retrace what happened, and read his nonverbal cues. As you respond with calm curiosity, he learns to be calm and curious about his feelings, too.

◆ **Teach him.** When he's a baby, you naturally teach him emotions by mirroring back his facial expressions. By looking at his "reflection" in your face, he gets feedback about what his inside feeling looks like on the outside. As he starts talking, you can use crying spells as an opportunity to teach him to distinguish "mad," "sad," "glad," and "scared." When a boy is quickly shushed from crying, he misses out on important learning about his feelings.

◆ **Let him feel.** A boy may learn to brush off a bruised knee without much fuss, but say "no" to him and you're probably in for some waterworks. He'll do everything he can to convince you that you are mean and that he will not survive unless you relent. And he's good at it! As much as you want him to stop, hold your ground. Giving in to his intense emotions tells him you are scared of his feelings. Instead, give him permission to feel by saying, "I know you'll be mad for a while, and that's okay, but I'm not changing my mind."

◆ **Let him see you feel.** Watch the tendency to hide from your son when you're sad, thinking that you're protecting him from your "weakness." Instead, in an age-appropriate way, let him see your emotion and tell him what you're feeling. Not only do you teach him that feelings are okay, but you give him the opportunity to learn empathy and provide comfort.

◆ **Dads, be around.** This simple advice is the first of "five keys" in *Father to Son: Life Lessons on Raising a Boy* by Harry H. Harrison Jr. (see the Resources appendix). Just being around helps him know you through your ups and downs and accept his own range of emotions. Moms, when there is no dad in the home, help your son connect with a male family member or friend who is willing to hang around for more than just the ballgame.

◆ **Teach him where it's safe to cry.** To receive a compliment from another parent that our sons are "so easy to have around" is gratifying, but we know there's another side to the story: they aren't always "easy" at home! When home is a safe "container" for difficult emotions, boys are better able to protect feelings in situations where more give-and-take is expected.

Toy Box

Bill Keane is a father who is around. The creator of *The Family Circus* (www.familycircus.com) drafted the cartoons right at home, amid the chaos of a young family of five. The first *Family Circus*, published in February 1960, showed Mommy in a room full of toy clutter, greeting a survey taker at the door who asks, "Any children?" Today, with his nine grandchildren providing inspiration, Keane's *The Family Circus* is the most widely distributed cartoon panel in America.

Boys at Play

In addition to the joy of loving our boys, they provide us a great deal of entertainment. Boys have a way of pulling us out of our heads and into the present. They help us take ourselves a little less seriously, let go, and get a little dirty. Let's look at the way boys like to play and how we can join the fun.

Wheels

Do boys like trucks because we teach them to like trucks or because they just prefer trucks? To find the answer, researchers have looked at choices babies make before they have any idea of their gender. When offered an array of toys, baby boys generally pick trucks (or trains, balls, or cars), and baby girls generally pick dolls. In addition, the boys' preference for "boy toys" was stronger than the preference girls showed for dolls.

In his book *Why Gender Matters* (see the Resources appendix), Leonard Sax explains that boys like moving things because they *see* movement better than texture and color, and this is reversed for girls. Boys and girls see through different eyes—literally! The male retina is mostly made up of cells (*M cells*) that record location, direction, and speed, while the female retina is dominated by cells (*P cells*) that identify color and texture.

Sax ties this finding to research of children's drawings. Boys tend to draw action from a distant perspective; girls draw people (or animals, trees, or flowers) facing the viewer. Boys use just a few colors at the "cold" end of the spectrum (i.e., blue, silver, black); girls use a wide variety of "warm" colors (i.e., red, green, brown). Similarly, when babies are given the option of looking at a young woman's face or a dangling mobile, girls tend to gaze at the face while boys prefer the mobile.

So when your boy draws rockets and explosions and speeding cars, he's drawing what his eyes are *drawn* to. And when he races around and throws balls and zooms his trucks, he's not being oppressed by an old stereotype—he's stimulating his brain! And he's having fun at the same time. Instead of rolling your eyes at his antics, get into the action! See if you can top his activity level, and notice how alive you feel.

Parenting trends tend to move like a pendulum: we go to one extreme and then correct the imbalance by going to the opposite extreme. This is certainly true of our attitudes toward boys and play. The assumption that boys "should" play with trucks was corrected by an assumption that preferences are programmed, which has been corrected by the assumption that boys prefer trucks. While research supports the latter assumption, we also know studies can only tell us about generalities.

Let's try to see beyond the trends. Exposing our boy to a variety of play experiences helps him reveal what he uniquely enjoys and also helps him get along with friends who have different preferences. At the same time, it is helpful to know that a boy who is bored playing "house" is not deficient—he is probably just less stimulated by the colors of the dishes and the soft skin of the baby doll. Let him add a little action to the plot, and he might get hooked!

Mom's Fun Clothes

Just when you've gotten used to all his "boy stuff," he might surprise you by his delight with Mommy's clothes or accessories. It is not uncommon for boys to be curious about Mommy's clothes, shoes, and jewelry, and to even want to try them on.

By age two, boys are exploring their world through imaginative play. They learn by trying it out and trying it on. Mommy is a natural target for his curiosity: he is learning that she's a separate person and he wants to know her. Our boys had a particular fascination with Mom's shoes, and our youngest still enjoys sliding one on and then flinging it off across the floor. This mom has learned to put her shoes away!

Understand that his curiosity does *not* imply some deep-seeded conflict over his identity as a boy. He is healthy and normal. If he does feel uncomfortable with his gender, he will let you know in more obvious ways—he'll insist that he is not a boy or that he does not want to be a boy. If this happens, you'll want to observe what he's responding to. Is he worried about separating from Mom? Is there something about Dad he's afraid to identify with? Is he opposing everything right now?

If he truly seems uncomfortable with his gender, you can reassure him that boys and girls can do a lot of the same things. Help him develop his identity as a *person* and not only as a boy.

Toolbox _____

Play therapy is an approach used with toddlers and preschoolers in place of the verbal psychotherapy commonly used with adults. The technique draws on the idea that children naturally use play to work through their experiences and feelings. A skilled play therapist can help your boy express his struggle through play and provide a professional perspective on what is going on. The therapist has a diverse selection of toys available, and the child gets to use them as he wishes. Play becomes the language of communication between child and therapist.

"He's Shooting Me!"

Don't be surprised if your little guy starts shooting at you—even if he's never seen a gun! Boys have been known to create guns out of sticks, sandwiches, or whatever's handy—and a pointed finger will do in a pinch. Parents often struggle with the dilemma of whether to let a young son have a toy gun. Though toy guns are associated with an increase in aggressive play—big surprise!—the question is whether this is a problem.

Studies have shown that playful aggression helps boys bond. A good game of cops and robbers leaves them smiling, not hostile. But we do worry about him becoming desensitized to the danger of guns. Consider these factors as you make your choice:

◆ Does it look like a real gun? A brightly colored squirt gun is clearly in a different category than a toy gun that looks like an AK-47.

◆ Does it have "bullets" that could hurt him or a friend? The soft bullets of a Nerf gun shouldn't do much damage.

◆ Can he limit his "shooting" to willing victims? My husband couldn't care less if the boys shoot him, but I feel uncomfortable with even a play pistol pointed my way—and I told them so. They were happy to turn their fire on Dad.

When our youngest used his allowance money to buy a toy gun, I made a comment that revealed my anxiety about his choice. He said to me in a reassuring but slightly patronizing tone, "Mom, it's not *real*."

Boys and the Potty

If you do a quick Internet search under "potty training boys," you'll find plenty of offers on the "secrets" to training him in three days *or less*—as if you didn't feel enough pressure already! Pressure is the enemy of effective potty training, especially for boys.

Though we don't completely understand why, boys take longer to learn to use the toilet. Some practical realities do make the transition more challenging for boys: first, the primary trainer is usually Mom. She may feel less comfortable toileting with her son, and he will have a little more trouble imitating her. For example, while Mommy's pee goes straight down when she sits, his needs a little guidance. In addition, toileting for boys is a two-step process involving sitting training and standing training. Finally, toddler boys, who tend to be more active than girls, find it hard to break away from the action to sit on the potty.

What we do know is that your boy will not be trained until his muscles and nerves are able to hold bladder and bowel contents. His timing has nothing to do with how good a parent you are or how high an achiever he is. The American Academy of Pediatrics recently revised their estimate of "toilet readiness" from a range of 18 to 24 months to a range of 22 to 30 months, with boys being at the higher end of that range.

So relax, and get ready for a sometimes frustrating and often comical ride, as he trains to become a real "Captain Underpants."

Ready, Set, Go (or Not!)

If there is a secret to smooth potty training, it's to wait until he's ready. Generally (and fortunately!), his interest increases right alongside his body's growing capacity to pull it off. These signs might show that he is ready:

◆ He expresses discomfort when his diaper is wet or dirty.

◆ He gives cues, such as grimacing, squatting, or crossing his legs, when he's about to go.

◆ He has learned that things, such as toys and clothes, go in certain places.

◆ He can pull off his clothes.

◆ He can imitate you on the potty.

◆ He is not going through a major transition like a move or birth of a new sibling.

◆ He can say "no" if he does not want to try but is not at a stage where "no" is the only word in his vocabulary!

◆ He has dry spells of three hours or more.

◆ He is curious about the bathroom and about his body.

If he asks you questions about the way you pee or poop, this is a great opportunity to teach him without pressure. Talking about and showing him what you do in the bathroom will arouse his interest more than focusing on what you want him to do. You can plant a seed by telling him, "When you're ready, you can learn to use a potty, too." When you go to the store, you can show him what a potty his size looks like. Let him know that you will have a special shopping day to pick out his potty when he's ready.

Experts generally recommend starting boys on a potty chair, as bowel training tends to come first and he is likely to urinate in close proximity to his bowel movements. However, "toddler urinals" are now becoming available to allow boys to practice their aim. Parents who have employed the little urinals from the start notice that their boys find it fun to stand and seem more motivated to use the bathroom.

Previewing what he'll be doing "when he's ready" helps him cognitively prepare for the new adventure while giving him power over the timing. But even when he says he wants to try it, don't be surprised if he quickly gets bored or changes his mind. Though you may be accustomed to "sticking out" a challenge, let this one go. You'll get much further if you cheerfully give up and try again later.

Accept that your job will be to offer opportunities but he's the one in charge of his body. It's hard having so much responsibility with so little control. Find a supportive place to vent—and, hopefully, to laugh it off!

Toy Box

The only time I get "penis envy" is when my husband gets to sneak in an easy pee outside the car. Your son will enjoy the privilege as well, and this is an advantage to capitalize on in training. Let him "draw" in the snow or aim at a toilet paper target in the potty. You can even purchase fun "toilet targets" for him!

Boys Still Bedwetting—Normal!

Just when you see visions of diaper-free days, some parent at daycare will have the gall to brag, "Molly is already dry at night—and it was *so* easy!" Relax, for your sake and his. Boys take their time night training, too, so step out of the fast lane and wait until he's ready.

Most boys learn to stay dry at night somewhere between the ages of three and six. Unless he's begging to get up and use the toilet at night (yeah, right), don't even start night training until he's at least three. And don't start just because he's three or even four. In fact, don't start at all. Let *him* start. He will let you know. He'll start staying dry at naptime, and he'll express an interest in staying dry at night. Peers his age compare notes, and he'll want in.

Because boys are socialized to keep distress inside, they can start to harbor feelings of embarrassment and shame over the wet bed. Of course, we can save everyone a lot of grief by just keeping him in a diaper until he's ready. But nobody gets through nighttime training (okay, except for Molly) without some wet beds.

So where do shameful feelings come from? Unfortunately, they usually come from us. To some extent, we all regress with our children, and our own painful memories of bedwetting can get stirred up. Add to this any "concern" our parents or friends might express about him, and we get a rerun of old failure feelings. Our shame becomes his shame, and we catch ourselves feeling pity for the *absolutely normal* boy waking to a wet bed. We might even feel tempted to "cover up" the "problem."

The good news is, we're smarter than our parents (at least on this topic). As a society, we are learning that little boys deserve a chance to be little boys and that we should observe boys' development in relation to *boys*.

Still, when you're in the middle of it, you may wonder if he will *ever* get up to go. As you watch him sleep even harder than he plays, it's difficult to imagine how he will get there from here. So much of his growth is out of sight. We don't get to observe his bladder developing or to track his brainwaves during sleep. But these things *are* changing inside him, naturally preparing him to get up in response to bladder signals. Reminding him of this inner process can spare him a lot of unnecessary guilt.

> **Boy Wisdom**
>
> A six-year-old boy once looked at me pleadingly in my office and said, "Will I *ever* be able to do it?" "Doing it" meant staying dry at night and pleasing those around him. His eyes contained a look of defeat and hopelessness—at six! Bedwetting may not start as an emotional problem, but it can surely become one.
>
> —T. Berry Brazelton, *Touchpoints*

Do we say "boys will be boys" while rolling our eyes and shrugging our shoulders or while smiling with pride? Take pride in him through it all—pride when he knows he is *not* ready, pride when he tries, pride when he takes a break—and Molly won't have anything on him.

Little Boys and Discipline

Discipline is the part of parenting we tend to like the least. And yet, when provided thoughtfully and consistently, discipline helps our little boys stay safe and get along better in the world. So let's look at what we need to consider when teaching boys the rules.

"Tougher Love" for Boys?

We have come a long way to understanding what works and what doesn't when we discipline boys. For example, we know that abusive punishment instills aggression, not "good character." We have developed more creative and effective ways to discipline our children. Why is it, then, that boys sometimes "just don't seem to listen"?

First of all, it could be that he didn't *hear*. Not only do boys see differently than girls, but we are finding they also hear differently. As a group, baby boys are less likely to be soothed by lullabies, and school-age boys don't always hear the teacher. Girls are more sensitive to sounds and may feel "yelled at" when a strong voice delivers a command. Boys generally do not hear as well as girls and are more likely to respond to firm, clear, and louder communications.

This could possibly explain a surprise we had with our newborn boy. He was crying inconsolably, and after trying everything we could think of to calm him, we flipped in a tape someone had given us. Travis Tritt's twangy song "Country Club" blared out. The song got our baby's attention, and he forgot about his tears! When he turned 15, testing revealed the first evidence of a mild hearing impairment—inherited from his father. Coincidence?

Secondly, little boys do not pick up on emotional cues as well as little girls do. A groundbreaking study of parent-child interactions, published as "Speak Roughly to Your Little Boy?" in *Social Development* (August, 1999), revealed that girls are much more responsive to their parents' emotions and benefit from a gentler approach to discipline. By contrast, boys actually did *worse* when the "kinder, gentler" approach was used! Boys responded best to nonabusive but strict and authoritarian discipline.

This difference makes sense if we think of the time baby girls spend studying people's faces. When a girl does something wrong, she's probably analyzed everyone's feelings by the time the parent speaks. Meanwhile, boys, who have been busy watching things that move, need you to get their attention and move things along, too. Our youngest boy called me on an unclear communication common to parents: I *asked* him to get something, though I meant it as a command. He smiled, said "no," and then added, "It's not really a question, Mom. Why don't you just *tell* me to get it?"

He was right. While I would prefer to have someone ask *me*, even knowing that it was a command, he wanted me to be direct and clear and felt manipulated by my question.

As a society, we have rightly reacted against the abusive punishment of boys. But being clear is not the same as being abusive. In fact, child abuse is everything but clear, often happening in the context of a parent's rage, drunkenness, or embarrassment. Perhaps we have focused so much on concerns about abuse that we have left boys confused in a new way. The study published in *Social Development* found that, contrary to our stereotypes, parents were stricter with their girls than they were with their boys! So the girls, who already "got it," were getting more discipline, and the boys, who needed it, were getting less discipline.

Time Out!

The simple act of having a boy take a breather, or a time-out, is a life-saver for parents. We can yell and reprimand and "teach him a lesson" all we want, but pulling him away from his activity is what will speak loudest.

Giving him excessive attention for bad behavior—the yelling and reprimanding—can actually be *rewarding* for him. As we flip out, he can sit back and enjoy the show—secretly satisfied with the spectacle he was able to create. After all, he likes to make things move! On the other hand, having your boy *sit* takes him away from the action and serves as an effective punishment. As a bonus, the breather helps him. He gets time for the intensity of his emotions to settle down, as well as an opportunity to reevaluate his behavior.

A common rule-of-thumb for the length of a time-out is one minute for each year of age, up to 5 minutes. Use a kitchen timer and apply the time-out immediately after the unacceptable behavior. Provide a consistent place for him to sit, such as a chair that's placed away from toys and distractions. If he yells and complains, act as if you can't hear him. If he gets up, sit him back down and reset the timer. He'll eventually learn that sitting still will get him moving again more quickly. Finally, when the time-out is over, welcome him back with a smile and a hug.

Parenting experts recommend running through the time-out procedure *before* he acts up, so he knows what to expect. Also, when you sit him down for a real time-out, clearly state why you are doing so.

When disciplining boys, keep in mind that the purpose of punishment is to provide safety and to help our boys get along in the world. Remember when he was a newborn, crying and flailing about, and the nurse pulled him together with the help of a tightly wrapped blanket? The red-faced, anxious baby suddenly felt safe and calm. We are doing the same thing when we provide and enforce boundaries for our sons—simply and clearly.

The Least You Need to Know

◆ Emotionally accessible fathers raise emotionally intelligent sons.

◆ Boys like toys that move, and they bond through aggressive play.

◆ Don't push him to use the potty until he's ready—he will let you know when he is.

◆ Boys respond best to firm, nonabusive discipline.

Chapter 3

Mommy, Mine Is Different!

In This Chapter

- ◆ Your son's exploration of his body
- ◆ Telling him what he wants to know
- ◆ Comparing body parts
- ◆ Helping him through the "Oedipal Phase"
- ◆ Setting boundaries

"Mommy, what dat guy doin'?"

Our son was pointing at a sculpture at the art museum. He wasn't satisfied to just stand and look; he wanted to *know* this man and what his purpose was.

Your boy has emerged from the cocoon of immobility—that place where everything was connected. With mobility comes the realization that he is separate: he can move away and he can come closer. He can reach and touch and taste and hold and throw, and this is how he learns about the amazing world around him.

It is at this stage of exploration that your boy also learns about himself. "Me" and "mine" become very important words in his vocabulary. And his body, like everything else, is a curiosity. Let's look at this marvelous stage of his development—the time when he first recognizes his identity as a boy.

Body Exploration

As early as the age of two, a boy begins to explore his genitals. The penis is particularly interesting to him. He will pull on it, hold it in his little hand, and may even rub it in a way that looks like masturbation. Add this to the fact that even baby boys can have erections, and it's easy to assume that your toddler is pursuing sexual pleasure. Don't be fooled. He's exploring this body part the way he explores everything in his world. At this stage, his penis is mostly just a cool squishy part that sometimes changes shape.

Treasure this time when he is so openly curious and free of shame. He'll leave the Garden of Eden soon enough. Yet, even when we know it's healthy, his openness and candor can be disconcerting. After all, we've undergone years of training to keep spontaneous feelings and questions to ourselves. The challenge is to celebrate his good feelings about his body while separately managing our own anxieties. Who knows, maybe he'll teach us to lighten up a little.

Do These Parts Have Names?

Your boy is at a crucial stage of language development and needs you to help him name things. This includes his "private parts." You may want to practice saying "penis" calmly and with a straight face to overcome our programming to be embarrassed. Telling him the thing between his legs is a penis need not be any more significant than telling him the thing in the middle of his face is a nose.

While boys may make up their own labels, it is important that parents provide accurate answers to his questions about his parts. This way, he not only acquires correct information, but he also learns that his body is not mysterious, shameful, or worrisome. In his mind, if there's a name for it, it's supposed to be there.

You don't need to have any big sit-down meeting to talk about his genitals or sex or how babies are made—these formalities can put the topic into the "big deal" category. When he asks a question, simply answer him. Maybe he'll want to have a conversation, but chances are he just wants precisely what he's asked for. Here's an example:

Boy: Where did I come from?

Parent: You came out from Mommy's belly (a photo of pregnant mom can help). (Conversation may stop here.)

Boy Wisdom

A 3-year-old's brain is twice as active as his pediatrician's.

—Dorothy James, family life specialist

Boy: How did I get in there?

Parent: You were made from two things: a tiny egg that was already inside Mommy and something called a sperm from Daddy. Once you were made, you grew inside Mommy until you were ready to come out. (Conversation may also stop here.)

Boy: How did Daddy get the sperm thing in Mommy?

Parent: The sperm comes out of Daddy's penis. Daddy's penis fits into an opening in Mommy and the sperm squirts into Mommy's body. (And so on …)

Playing Doctor

As your boy explores himself and his world, he'll begin to notice his differences from his girl friends. Little boys and girls sometimes mimic what the doctor does to check them, but "playing doctor" usually involves a particular kind of checkup: the one that helps them see how their bodies are similar and different.

Playing, Not Player

It is so important that we regard such play for what it is: his desire to explore and learn about his world. Boys and girls may even mimic Mom and Dad with awkward kisses and "flirtatious" behaviors they have observed.

No, while your boy may do a decent preschool imitation of Don Juan, he is not a player. He is contending with the startling realization that he belongs to a tribe of people called "boys," and that he is different from another tribe called "girls." Not only is he trying to figure out what "boy" means, but he also wants to know what boys are supposed to *do*.

Boys don't only compare notes with girls; they also may show each other what they've got. They have not yet associated guilt or shame with their bodies, and it's our job to try to keep it that way.

Handle with Care

Finding your boy showing his parts and/or observing those of a little friend can activate all kinds of parental fears, but most likely the situation is *very* benign. Stay calm and navigate things sensitively. You can affirm the discovery they are making by saying, "Boys and girls have different private parts, and that's what makes you both special. Let's put your clothes back on and we can talk some more!" By having them dress and talk more, you are responding to their curiosity while encouraging healthy boundaries. As you encourage and answer questions, you can explain the "private" part of "private parts" in a matter-of-fact way.

It is only fair to let the parents of the friend know about the play, but again, communicate this without alarm or concern. If you do observe behavior that reflects knowledge beyond what is appropriate for a child, you will want to share your concern with the parents. In the rare situation where you suspect the parents of sexual abuse, you can call your county's child protection agency and speak with a caseworker. You'll get help sorting out whether what you observed is cause for a formal report, and you'll get the peace of mind of knowing that the matter is in protective hands.

Can I See Yours?

As your son explores his own body, he'll be curious about yours as well. He'll want to know if you have a penis like his, and he'll be curious about Mommy's breasts. Don't worry, you don't have to give him a live presentation, just answer his question. If he asks to see or touch it, you can tell him that those parts are private. Add that he also gets to keep his parts private, except when Mommy or Daddy or the doctor needs to check his private parts to make sure he is healthy. The trick is to teach him privacy without shame.

Bathroom Visits

Boys have a natural way of learning about their parents' bodies when they go to the bathroom together. He may see Daddy's penis and wonder why his is so big or he might get worried that Mommy doesn't seem to have one. Again, these are "teachable moments" when simple answers go a long way. Maybe he won't say anything, but you notice him staring or looking distressed. At these times, you'll want to ask if he's worried about something.

Toolbox

Some boys question everything; others absorb things more quietly. We needlessly stress ourselves out when we expect sensitive topics to come up in a certain way at a certain time. Be ready for anything, and you won't be disappointed.

Bedroom Visits

For a scared little boy to want to crawl into bed with his parents is not uncommon, and we often have mixed feelings about how to respond. As with many parenting issues, the question of whether to share sleeping quarters with him is a "hotbed" of controversy.

Advocates of the *family bed* concept argue that today's children are prematurely forced to sleep alone and that "co-sleeping" is good and natural. The idea is, rather than waiting for him to get scared, just have him sleep with you every night until he's ready for his own room. This practice is practical for nursing moms, who appreciate having baby close by when feedings are frequent. Advocates of co-sleeping emphasize the intimacy that develops between parents and children as well as the benefits to the child's (and parents') sleep.

Still, parents generally prefer to keep their bedroom to themselves, especially when the boy is no longer a baby. Parents choosing this option like to keep their bedroom for their intimacy needs and to help the baby adapt to sleeping in his own space. This doesn't mean that parents choosing the family bed have to give up sex. In fact, advocates of this approach talk about spicing up their sex lives by finding new times and places for romance.

Whatever your choice, it's much easier to make in the light of day, and it's essential that you as parents make the decision together. We recently saw a movie in which Mom couldn't bear to part with her toddler boy and Dad, who was wanting to be intimate, reluctantly slid in beside the sleeping boy. Our boys do need the assurance that they have access to us at night, but they also need parents who take care of their adult relationships. It is easy enough for busy parents to set their love life aside. What happens when you limit the option of spooning, nighttime nudity, or "sleeping together" in the Hollywood sense?

> **Toy Box**
>
> What if he finds you in a compromising position? Do you need to start saving for his psychoanalysis? Comfort yourself in knowing that he is clueless about what you're doing. Think of the boy who walked in on his parents and said, "I want to play wheelbarrow, too!"

Talking about your bedroom policy and coupling needs *after* a good night's sleep will help you clarify your mutual desires, values, and boundaries. Your boy may be in the middle of your bed, but if he's in the middle of your relationship, you may be repeating a very old story.

Oedipus Lives!

During ages 3 to 6, your son starts to comprehend that Mommy and Daddy—or parent and stepparent, parent and partner, parent and adult friends—have a relationship separate from their relationship with him. Understandably, his worldview gets rocked a bit. This phase of adjustment was termed the *Oedipal Phase* by Sigmund Freud (1856–1939), the founder of psychoanalysis. Freud named the phase after Oedipus Rex, an abandoned prince in Greek mythology who inadvertently killed his father and married his mother. Freud theorized that, as a boy recognizes that he is the third in a triangle with his mom and dad, he works to regain his "kingship" with his mom. Although the theory did not include the prediction of murder, Freud indicated that boys typically become competitive with Dad for Mom's favor and may have primitive wishes to marry Mom. Because the boy does not want to lose Dad, however, he successfully resolves the crisis by becoming *like* Dad (rather than killing him off). This resolution then forms the basis for the boy's male identity.

Toolbox

In the myth, Oedipus Rex kills his father accidentally while trying to escape the prediction that he will kill his father. As he's fleeing town and the man he believes to be his father, he unknowingly meets his biological father, who also happens to be a king, "where three roads cross." His father blocks and challenges him, a duel ensues, and Oedipus wins. The victor proceeds to Thebes, where he performs an act of heroism and wins the hand of the widowed queen—his mother.

When taken out of context, the myth and the theory can seem far-fetched, antiquated, and irrelevant. That is, until you have a boy. The central action in the myth takes place "where three roads cross," and your son is at a crossing as well. Let's look at how you can help him through this time of his life.

"Flirting"

You'll feel it. One day he's your baby, and the next day he's "flirting" with you! When your son suddenly wants to be your man, it is common to feel a bit intimidated. He may assert that he is going to marry you or want to play house and be the daddy. He might even take on a pseudo-sexual air as he mimics the way Daddy approaches you.

Although normal experiments for your boy, these behaviors can feel very out-of-place for you. Here's what's happening: when your son flirts with you, he is mimicking what he sees between you and your partner. He wants you back, and he's smart enough to study the adversary! He'll also be very ready to earn points by sticking up for you when you're mad at your partner. Finally, he may become clingy and protest any time you spend time with someone else.

Because he has become aware that Mommy and Daddy have something that he is not a part of, this worries him. He does not yet understand the distinction between adult love and parent-child love, and it is your job to help him. He needs to learn that the love his parents share does not threaten the love they share for him.

His concern may not be only directed at Mom: he may also be jealous that Mommy gets more of Daddy, and express a desire to marry Daddy rather than Mommy—or he may want to marry Mommy one day and Daddy the next. The dynamic is not dependent on the parents' gender—gay parents can feel the same pulls for an exclusive relationship. Your son has found himself in a triangle and, naturally, he wants to be king.

"Competing"

In the Oedipus myth, Dad is the one who is threatened. He sees his son as a rival and makes every effort to do away with him. It is common for a father to feel displaced by his new son as his partner's attention shifts toward the baby. Then, just as Dad is getting back in the game, the preschool boy pulls at Mom in a new way. Sure, he can be obnoxious, and we all regress a little along with our children. So if your little buddy treats you like an alien intruder, keep one thing in mind: *he's your son!* He needs your love and protection as much as his Mom's.

Again, the roles can easily flip with Mom cast out as the third wheel. But either way, he only loses if he successfully banishes one of you.

Note that a first child or only child tends to be more sensitive to his parents' relationship. When there are siblings involved, he adapts to sharing earlier and experiences less of a "fall from grace" when he learns of parental partnerships.

Helping Him Through

As much as your son may want to displace your adult love interest, winning a partnership with you is his loss. An adoring little boy can certainly be a comfort to a parent who's mad at the other parent, but it is unfair to put him in the middle. He needs you both whether you are madly in love or in the middle of a cold war.

So what if you are single or divorced? In the case of divorce, your boy can take credit—much to his harm—for the dissolution of the marriage. After all, he wanted you all to himself, didn't he? Even with the trauma of divorce, your son may feel that his wish was granted when he gets one of you *all to himself*. But just as Oedipus couldn't really see his future, little boys have no idea what a burden it can become to be a parent's partner.

Use these ways to help him accept you as parents while knowing that his love is secure:

- **Don't buy his act.** If you misinterpret his flirtations as sexual, you are likely to become uncomfortable and defensive, focusing on your own comfort rather than the important crisis he is negotiating. He is still your little boy, and he needs you to be ahead of the game.

- **Keep your relationship with your partner at the center.** He needs to know that *someone else* is caring for your adult needs and that he gets to be the kid. If you have no partner, you still should make time for your adult needs. Meet up with friends; go to a day spa; or even take a little excursion by yourself while your son is enjoying the attention of another trusted caregiver. Your job as a parent is not just to care for him but also to teach him how to care for himself and his relationships.

> **Boy Wisdom**
>
> I don't think everything beautiful has to be exploited. Some things can be beautiful and left beautiful.
>
> —Rick Schroder, former child actor and father of three boys, *Parade Magazine* interview

- **Let him know that you haven't gone anywhere.** When he flirts, tell him how wonderful he is and that, yes, you'd marry him for sure if you weren't his mommy (or his daddy). Explain to him that, if you married him, you'd have to stop being his mom, and that you would never do that. Tell him, when he gets big, he will find somebody very, very special, and then he can get married and be a daddy. But even then, you'll still be his parent.

◆ **In addition to family time, give him special mommy-son time and daddy-son time.** Show him that there is enough love for all the relationships in the family.

◆ **Don't withdraw from him physically.** Over and over, experts are challenging our culture's tendency to pull sons away from their mothers. As long as we are clear about our roles as parents, there is no harm in showering him with hugs, kisses, squeezes, compliments, and love, love, love. He is looking to you to help him decide if he is an attractive male. *You can assure him that he's "got it"—that special magnetism that makes people want to be with him—without exploiting it.*

Boundaries, Not Shame

As your son begins to recognize himself as a boy, the world becomes more exciting as well as scarier. He needs safe boundaries to protect him from overstimulation and to assure him that the world around him is stable even as his internal world is changing.

When parents don't provide adequate boundaries, he may feel gratified at first, but he'll also experience guilt and shame. Let's say, for example, that you and your partner are leaving for a date and your son has a tantrum. You then decide that you can't possibly leave him with someone else when he's so insistent on having you stay. So you stay with your son, and you and your partner become irritable because you "had" to cancel your plans. Your son has successfully intruded on the boundary for your time together. This may feel good for him at first, but he learns that what he did was hurtful. Now he is burdened, and something good is tainted.

Though this is a benign example and one that could happen to any of us, it reveals the reality that "giving in" is not always "giving." Boundaries may make him mad, but they also leave him free to push without fear of harming the people he loves.

The Least You Need to Know

◆ The exploration of his body as a toddler is not sexual.

◆ Respond to his questions with accurate, but age-appropriate, answers.

◆ "Playing doctor" is nothing more than your boy's desire to explore and learn about his world.

◆ Have a love life or social life separate from your son, so that he can remain free to be a kid.

◆ Setting appropriate boundaries around what is private and what is "adult" may frustrate your son at first, but it will protect him from guilt and shame.

Chapter 4

My Gender, Myself

In This Chapter

◆ Hero worship

◆ Strong mind, strong body

◆ Fostering your son's first friendships

◆ Parentification: too much, too soon

Men. Men. Men. The echo of *Monty Python* sketches rings in the head for any man over the age of thirty. The boys from England made great fun of parodying life and stereotypes of men in particular. And we define the popular image of the modern man from his birth to his death from our culture.

In this chapter, we explore the constellation of male archetypes and characteristics: heroes and superheroes, rock stars and athletes, and loving dads. These polestars guide our understanding as well as lesser stars of equal and even greater power.

Using these images, let's take a journey that helps define men and boys and in the process inform ourselves of the underlying strengths of the male identity, images your son will draw on to grow strong and confident.

Having a Hero, Being a Hero

Hero with a Thousand Faces is a seminal book on the hero mythology. The author, Joseph Campbell, describes the hero's journey: from accepting a call to adventure, to the inevitable clash with and victory in a supreme ordeal, often over supernatural forces, and the return home, where the hero uses what he has learned to better the lives of others.

Boys and men draw sustenance from the old myths, and modern storytellers recreate these myths with wonderful effects. From *Star Wars* to the latest movie release, tales of not just daring, but of men confronting their fears, surviving, and thriving surround us.

Superheroes

Imagine a simple walk to the park for a five-year-old. The cars and trucks are monstrous; the dogs that seem meek to parents appear to a boy as dangerous as a caged lion when they growl and snap. If your son is going to the park, he's going to need some help.

Toy Box

Boys in Canada grew up with additional superheroes little known in the United States. *Johnny Canuck* and *Commander Steel of the International Police Service* helped defeat the dreaded Nazis, too.

Thank goodness, he has Superman along. Boys, who love action more than girls, are particularly enamored with heroes who can fly, climb skyscrapers, and hurl a badman with a gun into outer space.

Your son's infatuation with superheroes is mostly healthy and will likely fade well before he reaches middle school. Making sure his hero is on board for every trip to the store may be annoying, but try to remember the purpose of Superman's presence. Superman and you are a team, protecting your son from the dangers of the real world and calming the fears that naturally arise in the active imagination of your son's fast-developing mind. If Superman goes missing, recognize your son's fears and simply state that you will keep him safe.

And you will.

Reading Adventures

Some superheroes last generations while others just several years. I (Barron) grew up in an era when society still sought healing from World War II and was rising to fight another war in Vietnam, and found great entertainment in reading *Sergeant Rock* comics. Reading about Easy Company confronting the dreaded Nazis not only passed the time but also provided a framework for understanding forces much greater than teachers, parents, and schoolyard bullies.

Reading adventure stories can start as soon as a boy can focus on pictures. Few joys are greater than reading to a small boy on your lap. Three- and four-year-olds relish hearing the same story read over and over again. As boys of this age are sponges for language, reading together lays the building blocks for language. Whether it's the *Little Engine That Could* or the story of Frodo's adventure in the *Lord of the Rings* trilogy, time spent traveling through a heroic tale with your son will leave a memory that will last.

Toolbox

Raising a boy who reads can be challenging. Boys read less, value reading less, and take longer to read than girls, maybe because girls' language skills develop faster than boys'. Encourage his reading of all types: nonfiction, newspapers, comic books, and so on. Find a book series he likes. Boys like to collect things; he might as well collect books he enjoys.

Rock Stars and Athletes

As your son grows, he will look to more contemporary heroes to develop an appreciation for what it means to be a man. Rock stars seem to be a dime a dozen these days, with a few stars known for being talented and others who seem to be famous for being, well, famous. This may be why teenagers still seem drawn to The Beatles, Jimi Hendrix, and the past generation of stars.

If your son loves music of a particular artist, take the time to read the lyrics for his favorite tunes. Parents can view these on several lyrics databases online, for example, music.yahoo.com/lyrics. Listen to the songs, and ask him what he likes about the music. If you consider it too objectionable, say so and take action. If absolutely necessary, you can prohibit your son from listening to a particular song or artist. Just realize that doing so may merely entice him to listen to this music when you are not around. Listening to a tough rap song on occasion does not mean your son has decided to be a gangster. It will be helpful for him to hear what you like and don't like about his choices in music and pop icons.

Your son will likely encounter many "heroic" everyday people as he grows. One memorable teacher can have a profound effect on a boy. We discuss the value of teachers who love boys in Chapter 7.

Most professional athletes, fortunately, do not sing. Some have bad habits, which are more easily discussed (drugs or drunk driving). Your son's adopting a favorite player is a fun and healthy way to participate in professional or college sports teams. Ron Santo, the great third baseman for the Chicago Cubs, is one of my (Barron's) childhood heroes. Of course, not all hero draft choices work out so well in the end. I remember writing an eighth-grade essay extolling the virtues of a talented NFL running back. Yep, it was O.J. Simpson.

You just never know.

My Dad

One popular country music singer has helped fans embrace the heroic father with a song called "Watching You." In the song the boy learns to swear and pray by watching his dad, something almost every father can appreciate. Boys watch us at all times, and not just noticing what we say. Sons absorb lessons by watching how early or often we get up to go to work and how we temper our emotions (or not) when frustrated. When Ralphie uses the "F" word in the movie *The Christmas Story* while helping his father fix the spare tire, he explains he learned it from his father.

Boys pay special attention to how we treat our wives, and that is why the parents of boys who hope to instill in their sons a healthy love and appreciation for women will make time for their own relationship. Dad's heroic actions in being there, trying, loving, and providing create the everyday family mythology that turns boys into heroic men.

Fortunately, dads do not need perfect physiques or even tempers 100 percent of the time to parent boys well. Boys can discern between a loving father who may have some imperfections and a striving father who announces the beginning of "quality time" and then offers little meaningful attention or concern during a forced engagement.

Modeling is often the word therapists use to describe the learning that takes place as boys observe men. However, this term is perhaps a little too demanding. After all, models have no flaws, and parents have very real flaws. Yet, parents of sons who sincerely try to do better, and, who at the same time forgive themselves for not quite meeting the model standard, show their true loving nature.

The "Watching You" father's plea—"Lord, please help me help my stupid self"—speaks volumes about the heroic nature of men as fathers. Heroes recognize their shortcomings, ask for help, and improve.

Your son and future hero is watching. Even if he can't talk or crawl yet, he is watching and learning.

A Hero at Home

Young boys love to help their teachers; after all, they have the power, and acting on their behalf allows the boy to bask in the reflected glory. Around the house, parents have the same opportunity to select age-appropriate tasks to put a boy in the position of acting the hero. A simple act of having a son pick up an item dropped by a neighbor hauling in groceries or having the boy return an extra penny given in change at a store can be a delightful access to power for a boy.

The essence of heroic action is self-sacrifice for others. Yet laying the moral foundation in boys of valuing service to others can start very early. Few of our sons, thank goodness, will be placed in mortal danger during their lives

Toy Box

A 2007 Coca-Cola commercial displays the theme of acting heroically. The hip urban Coke drinker, while walking down a city street, nabs a purse snatcher, returns the purse, helps a homeless man into a car full of beautiful women, and ends up in a parade, all without missing a beat.

by diving in front of the speeding bus to save a kindergartner or fending off a robber who is assaulting the elderly neighbor. But we want our sons to appreciate that they are capable of acting heroically.

There is a good chance you picked a name for your son from a list of popular heroes of the past. So look up the origin of it. You can teach your son the story of his name and look for chances for him to resurrect these adventures in your daily lives.

I Am a Strong Boy

Men are strong. This quality, strength, defines men in society. Men used to pull strong bows or carry heavy burdens and served the family by their physical brute strength. With a man around, things got done. Today, men use less physical strength and thankfully rely on machines, but, of course, need the same quantity of emotional and moral strength to succeed in their relationships.

What does it mean for a boy to be strong? A boy's challenges come from confronting the tying of shoes, reading the alphabet, making a new friend, and so on. These efforts seem commonplace and, sometimes, trivial to an adult. Yet, they can appear Herculean to your son's developing mind. So let's explore the concept of strength in boys.

Physical Strength

My (Barron's) father announced that he could defeat me with the strength of one finger. After he wrapped his index finger around my fingers and twisted, the match was over and the boast was proven true. I never tried that again!

Boys also love to compare biceps with their fathers (and sometimes mothers). Their toys come with muscle groups that appear to have been steroid induced, as well. Big muscles loom in a boy's mind as an attribute of an iconic man.

You can emphasize your son's physical strength as he takes on new challenges. Carrying laundry or picking up big toys provides an opportunity to comment on your son's strength. This works well in younger boys, the three-to-seven-year-old crowd.

To help older boys develop an appreciation for their physical strength, call on them when you have hard work to do. Carrying boxes that aren't too heavy, clearing out the garage, or shoveling anything are great chores for boys to engage in to help them prove to themselves they are strong. A simple "good job" expressed in a way that tells him you knew he was up to the task solidifies for a boy the idea that he can do the work of a man.

Ego Strength

Common understanding of ego is the sense of self. Most often, use of the word ego is made in the negative, such as he's got a big ego or he's an egomaniac. Nevertheless, we would not want our son to be raised without any sense of self-worth. A healthy image of self is important, as so much of what makes life enjoyable is the ability to sustain daily bruising. Persevering with the knowledge that he is secure and safe, or at least strong enough to withstand temporary setbacks, is very important to your son's development.

In the more classic, albeit very abbreviated Freudian sense, a boy develops ego after he realizes that he cannot supplant his father. Rules of behavior become the super-ego, the desires and impulses are found in the child's unconscious id, and the ego rides in the middle balancing the mind and making sense of the world. A well-developed ego is one that can derive power from the primal drives of all men (for Freud, principally sex) and venture out while abiding by the known rules of engagement. In short, a boy with a healthy—but not overinflated—ego is one who is driven by ambition and goals and who risks going out into the world to succeed, while educated about and following the rules of society and his own well-developed set of ethics.

For men, however, ego strength fails quite often when emotions are not seen as temporary but appear hopelessly fixed and devastating. Boys externalize and mask to themselves and others these inner emotions.

Grown men who struggle in life frequently blame others for their problems. These men often don't recognize that they are depressed. They are impulsive and break rules. Yet, when *other* people break rules, they get wildly angry. These men don't possess the calming presence of a healthy, balancing ego.

Look for everyday ways to encourage your son, and teach him that negative emotions fade. Insincere or wildly disproportionate praise is not helpful, but too many parents do not praise enough. They criticize instead of catching their son doing something well. If you need to inject criticism, do so in a calm voice, provide instruction that is helpful at the same time, and avoid humiliation. Value yourself, and be willing to laugh at yourself when you make a mistake. Show the strength and emotional maturity you desire in your son.

> **Boy Wisdom**
>
> Train up a child in the way he should go, and when he is old he will not depart from it.
>
> —Proverbs 22:6

Broadening the Definition

It's easy to marvel at the father-son photos in the newspaper that show a family business being carried on, the young adult son looking like a cookie-cutter image of the older, grayer father. Your son may very well have the same strengths as you. He may look like you, walk like you, and hit the ball just like you did.

But on the other hand, he may not.

One of the joys of parenting a boy is discovering his true gifts, not just his capacity to learn, but something more natural and innate. I (Barron) vividly recall puzzling over a puzzle piece, only to have our four-year-old son, Josh, snatch it from my hand and place it quickly, while glancing back with a look that said "dumbass." Now much older, Josh excels at lateral thinking exercises, chess, and other mind-bending games. If you're an extrovert, your son may very well be quieter. If you're an introvert, your bookish ways may not transfer to the next generation, and your son may seem more destined for a career as a disc jockey. Whatever his natural or acquired talents, recognizing his strengths and nurturing them—even if they grate on your preset expectations—is an important attribute of raising your son. Valuing his strengths will also help him avoid the risk of identity foreclosure, where he chooses to equate his desires with yours; that is, he chooses to be *you* instead of *him*.

I Have Buddies

For young boys, a sense of who they are will also arise in play with other children. It is no great insight to say boys play with other boys. Since familiarity breeds a sense of security and comfort, and shared activities breed fun, your son will likely befriend other boys. Preschoolers develop friendships, and some believe even infants can attach to friends.

The quality of the parent-child relationship also has implications for friendship development. Behaviorists define a relationship as a series of interactions between two people occurring over time. While a quality relationship between a parent and a child is related to the skills or traits of a child, the same relationship also correlates with how well the child develops healthy relationships with others. Let's look at your son's first friends and consider how you can foster these early relationships.

First Friend

Our firstborn brought home a preschool buddy. They sat quietly on each side of me (Barron) as I read them a favorite book. This first experience embodied in form the majority of interactions our son would have with his future friends, an expression of a desire for company, a welcoming into the home, and a shared activity.

Your son can develop meaningful attachments to friends at a very young age. While the jumble of picking a child up from daycare doesn't lend itself to conversation, try to make a point of asking whom your son played with that day. Many preschools will even hand out a quick daily report identifying how well and what a boy ate, who he played with, and how long he took a nap.

Your son's forays into the toddler world of friends will come with a few bumps, too. One young relative of ours announced after a day at preschool: "I don't like her (referring to a playmate). She tried to be the boss of me, and I wanted to be the boss of her!" Children who have difficulty forming early attachments should be examined for the condition known as *autism*. Parents typically notice these problems in the first 18 months.

Keep Out! _____

The most recent statistics indicate that autism strikes boys three to four times more than girls. A couple symptoms of autism, among many, are that a boy uses repetitive motions and does not meet a parent's gaze. Early diagnosis and treatment can help these boys tremendously. If you have any concerns at all, ask your physician.

Boy Interactions

In most cases, boys' friendships, whether as toddlers or adults, are defined by the activities they share, whether it's playing with trucks, shooting hoops, or sizing each other up at a poker table. For men, activities *are* the relationship.

Women seem mystified by this reality. Mothers lament the lack of feelings expressed by boys and seem confused that their sons want to *do* things all the time. Yet their sons will likely interact with other boys as countless generations have done before—with less language and more action.

If your son is having difficulty making friends, help him brainstorm on some activity he can do with his potential friends, and avoid the impulse to dig into his psyche. He may open up during this conversation, but in the meantime you'll be working toward a practical, boy-centered solution to gathering new friends.

Toolbox _____

If you put up a playset with a good climbing wall or build a tree fort, neighborhood boys will come running. Playsets offer lots of choices. For two- to five-year-old boys, think plastic. For older boys up to age 12, build a larger set with some climbing apparatus. Use a deep and wide ground cover like pea gravel to prevent injuries from falling. Also, avoid buying a used wooden playset built prior to 2005 because the wood may contain a preservative since phased out, chromated copper arsenate (CCA), considered harmful to humans.

Small Talk for Small Boys

Boys tend to not use as many words as girls or even think of as many words as girls. Compared to girls, boys have fewer vocal centers that are activated in the brain. Researchers report that worldwide, men use fewer words than women and their relationships are more dominated by activity.

Some boys, of course, may be very verbal, just as some girls many tend to love activity as much as boys. A recent report showed similar word frequency for young adult men and women. So the tendency for less talk by boys may diminish as boys mature.

I Can Take Care of You, Too

Mom and Dad's little hero may have to feed the hungry cat by making sure the food bowl is filled or help Dad out by handing him the right tool at the right time. In each of these interactions, your son is developing empathy and showing, by his own conduct, that he can display loving emotions in a concrete way.

However, one of the developmental risks associated with boys is *parentification*. That is, boys who naturally wish the best for their parents will attempt to fill adultlike roles in families. Parents who are too busy or too consumed by personal crises will permit a child to take on these roles: frequently feeding themselves and siblings, dressing, bathing, or disciplining siblings, and so on.

Women, in particular, who do not have a stable relationship with an adult male, may allow their "little man" to take on a surrogate friendship role with his mother. Unwittingly the boy grows up too fast and skips developmental phases important to balanced and healthy adult relationships.

The Least You Need to Know

◆ The world is a big, scary place to a young boy. Superheroes help boys feel safe.

◆ Boys admire their parents, and regard parents as their first heroes.

◆ Look for everyday opportunities to teach your son he is strong in body and mind.

◆ Friendships for boys center on activities, not talking.

◆ Your son can be your hero, but he shouldn't be your "little man."

Chapter 5

Confidently Me

In This Chapter

- ◆ Discovering his natural gifts
- ◆ Setting aside your own expectations of success
- ◆ Recognizing unhealthy behaviors
- ◆ Instilling confidence
- ◆ Seeing him beyond stereotypes
- ◆ Tools to help him build his personality

As parents of boys, we often feel pulled in two directions at once. On the one hand, we are encouraged to be *gender-sensitive* and understand the ways boys uniquely develop, think, and learn. On the other hand, we are asked to be *gender-blind*, so that the identities of our boys are not limited by male stereotypes. The arguments for both perspectives are passionate and convincing.

What's a parent to do?

This chapter suggests ways you can help your son become who he really is—and feel good about that person. This is not a simple task, but we can use a simple guideline—*confidence*. When we lead him toward who is he, he'll puff up and feel good;

when we lead him away from who he is, he'll feel inadequate and small. Simple? Let's see.

Confidence Has No Gender

When we think of a confident person, we may imagine someone with head held high, chest puffed out, walking with pride, and speaking up—a person who is unapologetic and bold. Although this may be the visible side of confidence—or of an attempt to *look* confident—the key to this desired state is less visible and comes in the form of *trust*. A confident boy trusts himself.

> **Toolbox** _____
>
> Confidence is not the same as arrogance. A "show-off" usually *lacks* confidence; he constantly seeks approval to build himself up. A truly confident boy feels solid inside and, while he may have much to share, he has nothing to prove.

We instill trust in our boy when we affirm his natural gifts—what comes easy for him. His gifts may or may not be what we consider "boy strengths," and they might even be seen as problematic, i.e., his preference for being alone or his ability to take things apart. Rather than looking beyond him for his star quality, look at what he does to the point of annoyance, what he does *not* do, and what everyday qualities you associate with his name. *These* are his gifts, and they are extraordinary.

Hand-Me-Down or Custom-Fit Me?

As parents, we want our boys to be successful. But what is success? Our definitions are often based on what society values, as well as what worked—and what did not work—for *us*. If your confidence came from your outgoing nature, you may worry about a son who is more quiet. If you think athletic boys have it easier, you may worry about a son who prefers to read. And because there are so many different definitions of success out there, almost any quality he reveals or lacks can be a source of worry.

It's not easy to wipe the slate clean and see him through fresh eyes. A parent's vision is often clouded by his or her own past. You want him to be like you in the ways that helped you, but you also hope that he'll do better than you in other ways. If you were scolded or teased for something you liked to do or were good at, you'll probably be concerned if your son reveals the same qualities. So not only do we "hand down" our best qualities, but, without knowing it, we also hand down *restrictions* on who he can be.

Here's where embracing who he is can help us, as well. Think of natural tendencies of yours that you were criticized for (or criticized yourself for) as a child. Write down a label that captures how each of these tendencies was seen. Next to each negative label, write down the advantage of having that style. Here are a couple of examples:

◆ "The Terror" High energy; willing to shake things up

◆ "The Dreamer" Rich inner life; imaginative

As you label these qualities differently, you'll see that it was the *label* that was the problem, not you. You'll also probably notice how your gifts became a part of your success as an adult. Think of how life might have been easier for you if a loving spin had been put on these qualities.

Your son will probably be like you in some ways and completely different in others, and just when you think you understand him, he'll surprise you. The more we can shed our own baggage, the better we'll be able to see that he is living a brand-new reality. Then we can sit back a little and enjoy the show!

What If His Style Is Unhealthy?

It may be "natural" for your son to sit on the couch and watch TV all day, but you know this is not healthy. Beating on a younger sibling may be fun, too, but you don't want to encourage this form of self-expression. Your job as a parent is to help your son channel natural desires in healthy ways so that his personality does not become a problem.

Some behaviors, such as excessive television viewing, can actually *conceal*, rather than reveal, his natural gifts. "Canned" entertainment is fine for what it is—it's just very limited as a form of self-discovery. Television and video games can also be easy fillers for boredom and interfere with his motivation to explore more creative ways of enter-taining himself. But if he really loves his "show," take care to channel, rather than squelch, his enjoyment. Rather than criticizing his desire, set appropriate limits and help him be more selective about what he watches. Identifying what he prefers to watch and why *can* help him learn more about himself. And rather than just watching someone on TV do something he might enjoy, you can help him explore these options more directly.

Similarly, beating up on a sibling is not okay, but tackling an equal opponent in a football game is good fun. The heart of his desire is usually healthy—he just has not developed the judgment and self-control to always *keep* it healthy. From you, he can learn to listen to his desires and figure out safe and healthy ways to express them.

Not Just for Girls

We know that some boys can be especially sweet, graceful, cuddly, dependent, sensitive, or emotional. When our boys reveal gifts that we tend to put in the "feminine" category, how do we respond? Do we give as much attention to these gifts as we do to his rougher qualities? Do we feel uncomfortable and discourage him out of worry that he might become a "wimp" or a "mama's boy"?

Keep Out! _____

If being a "mama's boy" means that Mom uses her relationship with her son to meet adult needs, it's a problem. If "closeness" with a son means neglecting your responsibilities to him as a parent, it's a problem. But a lack of closeness is much more of a concern. Today's parenting experts warn that we have pulled boys away from their mothers too soon, to the detriment of boys. A mother's affection helps her son feel attractive and confident. In addition, mothers often serve as the moral compass for their boys and can have a powerful influence on the choices they make.

Again, the labels we use are more of a problem than the behaviors our son may be exhibiting. When we use words like "wimp," we focus on the *lack* of something. If a boy isn't big on confronting things head-on, he may be quite skilled at working things out in a more indirect, agreeable way—a talent that will take him far socially and professionally. Let's look at some other gifts that are not just for girls.

Caring About Relationships

Those of us who parent boys see evidence everywhere for their concern about relationships. Our younger son is the one who tunes in to anyone who might be neglected in the family, including the dog. Our older boy clears his schedule if a friend is in need, and also relies on his friends for support when he is down. Girls may *talk* more openly about relationships, and society gives them permission to want and need relationships. We just have to look a little closer to see the way our boys relate.

It is interesting to note that, contrary to the stereotype of the relationship-hungry woman and the aloof man, studies have shown that men are generally more devastated after a divorce, while women often feel happier. Men also remarry much more quickly than women. Men seem to be the "hungry" ones, probably due to their tendency to neglect other friendships once they are married. Women are more likely to maintain close friendships throughout their lives.

Notice the way your son attends to and values relationships now, and help him embrace this part of his identity. If he doesn't let this part of him become invisible, maybe he won't let the friends disappear either.

Gentleness

Testosterone and gentleness would seem to repel each other, yet boys can be amazingly gentle and kind. When Laurie witnessed the death of her ill mother, her two-year-old boy was the one who comforted her the most. Even at his young age, he sensed intuitively that this was a time to give; he spoke in a soft voice; and he knew what to say. His gentleness was in him all along, but this was a time when his gift was particularly visible.

Our son's story is not unique. In fact, telling and writing stories about your son is a great way to identify his gifts, as well as to help him build confidence in his identity. Watch how your son interacts with a pet or a younger sibling or how he tucks his stuffed animals into bed with him. Notice how he responds to you when you are sad or comforts a hurt friend.

It is interesting to note that we use the word "gentle" very commonly in regard to males. A term of respect for an adult male is "gentleman"!

Creativity

Do you ever find it curious that a boy might be teased for wanting to stay inside and help Mom cook, but then later gains status when he becomes a chef? Young people see the adult version of male artists and writers as "free spirits" and male actors and musicians as cool—not bookish, weird, or "band camp" geeks. Interestingly, the most accepted avenue to popularity for boys—sports—is rarely a career option for them.

To help our boys feel confident about their creative gifts—*now*, not just later—let's start with ourselves. A truly cool person is unselfconscious. He is oriented to who he is, more than what society expects. We help our boys when we also set aside "what people might think" and just enjoy who he is. When he's having a good time, people will naturally be drawn to him. "What people think" may turn out to be, "I want what he's got!"

Another way to bolster his confidence is to connect him with people who will support his desire. If your son prefers drawing or painting to playing ball, show him that he is not alone. Take him to a local art center where other creative kids draw and paint and sculpt, or enroll him in an art camp. Introduce him to some cool male artists. Your television can even be a resource: boys have more exposure than ever to creative men, including celebrity chefs, home and landscape designers, and fashion consultants. Television's not just ESPN anymore! Help him know that every gift comes with a community.

While we want to provide opportunities for our boys to explore their creative passions, we need to watch the temptation to take over. For example, Laurie worked with an adult man who was experiencing performance anxiety as a professional musician. As a boy, he was a prodigy, playing his trumpet for hours at a time—and he truly was at play. His parents began taking him around to performances and competitions, and instead of feeling free and joyful, he began to feel pressured and anxious. He described himself as being a happy, well-rounded kid, popular with friends and athletic as well as creative, but *losing* his confidence and social comfort once his parents took charge of his gift.

His gift did take him to the heights of his profession, but he wasn't having much fun. And by the time he came in to see Laurie, he was *dreading* his performances. Much of their work together involved taking the seriousness away from his performing and putting the *play* back in playing. He also started paying attention to other areas of his life, and even took the time to fall in love!

Toy Box

It is always fun to see somebody transform a quirky talent into a career. Artist Julian Beever has done just that. He creates sidewalk art with chalk! Is it hard to imagine someone getting paid to do this? Seeing is believing. Beever's chalk creates the illusion of "tearing up" a section of concrete to make room for a swimming pool, river, or even an underground city. He has added dimension to sidewalks in Europe, America, and Australia. Check out his creations at users.skynet.be/J.Beever.

Most boys do need structure when they are learning a new skill—because it's usually boring at first. But a boy who is gleefully learning on his own needs adults to stay out of his way. He'll let you know what he needs. Our older son took piano lessons until he had the basics down and had no interest in going further. It was a good education for him, and we had him stick with it until he could truly evaluate whether he was into it. Our younger son required no structure—we haven't had to remind him to practice, and he plays so much we are tempted to suggest he practice *less*. He even reminds us when we need to schedule his lessons!

Studies have demonstrated that, when a person begins to receive external rewards for something that is *intrinsically* rewarding, the activity provides less enjoyment and the person becomes more dependent on the external rewards. Your son's best motivator is his own desire—recognize it and support it, but don't take it away.

Building a Personality

When we talk about *personality*, we are usually referring to the person's signature style, his or her most natural way of being in the world. Personality theorists talk about the importance of developing an identity, a sense of self, to provide feelings of safety and continuity in a changing world. In this sense, your son's personality is like his home, the place he feels most comfortable and safe. As he grows, he'll venture out and explore new sides of himself, but home is always there for him.

As a young boy, your son is still discovering his personality. You can help him build a firm structure by teaching him where he comes from—your values and heritage—and by reinforcing his natural gifts. Use the following "Personality Playsheet" as a discovery tool.

You might want to make copies of this blank playsheet and have your son answer the questions at different stages of his life. His personality will go through growth spurts just like his body, and it can be fun to watch his story evolve.

Personality Playsheet

I am (his full name): _____

My Foundation

I was named after: _____

The people in my family are (list names): _____

_____

Way back, my family came from these places: _____

_____

Our religion is: _____

We celebrate: _____

_____

Every year, we (annual rituals/traditions): _____

_____

Every week, we: _____

_____

Every day, we: _____

_____

My Style

My nicknames are: _____

_____

I am happiest when: _____

_____

My favorite toys are: _____

_____

I am like Mom in these ways: _____

_____

I am like Dad in these ways: _____

_____

I am completely different than my parents in these ways: _____

_____

I am naturally good at: _____

_____

I really don't like: _____

_____

When I am alone, I: _____

_____

When I am with friends, I: _____

_____

A silly thing I like to do is: _____

_____

Words that describe me are: _____

_____

From Part to Whole

Personality has been compared to the tip of an iceberg that sticks up out of the water—there's a lot more underneath. The iceberg image can be a helpful way to look at gender differences. Boys bring qualities to the world that are different than the ones girls show. There are also differences in what society asks of boys and girls, and these factors likely influence what we see above the surface. But these influences in no way define the *potential* of boys and girls. In school, boys and girls start out with different intellectual specialties but perform more similarly as they develop.

Having a specialty is helpful, as long as it's *his* specialty. When a child is pressured to play out an assigned role, he may develop a *false self*, a term psychologists use to describe a personality that covers over the authentic, or real, personality.

When you look at what he brings to the world, don't forget to appreciate his quirks, too. In the movie *Signs*, the children's unique "problems"—the boy's asthma and the girl's obsession about contaminated drinking water—came in handy against alien invaders. Though your son may not save the world from aliens, he will be a stronger, more confident person when he embraces the "weak and weird" aspects of who he is. A boy who can accept, and even laugh at, these quirks actually comes off as more confident than one who gets defensive about any suggestion of imperfection. And, as in the *Signs* story, we don't always know when a quirk that seems like a problem may actually turn out to be a strength.

When your son becomes the best version of himself that he can be, he offers the world a real gift. Personality theorist Carl Jung said that whatever we show on the outside has its opposite on the inside. It's exciting to think that, even when his specialties are developed to their fullest, there's another world of possibility for your son to explore. One pair of opposites Jung talked about was introversion and extroversion.

Introvert or Extrovert?

When we refer to someone's personality, we might call the person introverted or extroverted. These terms refer to two different ways that people draw in energy for living:

◆ An *extrovert* is energized more through interactions with people than by private reflection.

◆ An *introvert* is energized more by private reflection than by interacting.

Most people use both ways to energize at different times, but usually one style feels more natural than the other.

A boy who prefers introversion can become overstimulated if too many people are around, and a more extroverted boy might feel stressed if he has too much time alone.

People often mistake introversion for shyness, but many introverts are actually quite outgoing. The key is what he needs when he's *stressed*. Watch your son. If he wants *just one friend* over when you're listing names, if he seems drained after a group activity, or if he does well by himself, he might be an introvert. An introverted boy needs time away from people to refuel. Our youngest, who loves hanging with his friends, will come home haggard and often sick if we let him do consecutive overnights with friends. And this is a boy who didn't get sick when he spent two weeks in the Amazon rainforest!

Toolbox _____

If your son is spending a lot of time alone, should you worry? The easiest way to know is to observe him. Is he engaged and enjoying himself, or does he seem lonely and sad? A shy boy may *want* to have more friends but feel hesitant. An anxious boy may fear embarrassment or social attention. For a scared or hesitant boy, *desensitizing* him by gradually introducing him to social situations is most helpful. An introverted boy may be taking an enjoyable and needed retreat. Applaud his wisdom!

The more introverted the boy, the more he can thrive on solitude and nonsocial activity. His gift is his ability to draw on his rich inner resources for guidance. He needs generous doses of space and time and prefers fewer close friends to lots of acquaintances. He keeps his best stuff inside and lets it out thoughtfully and often profoundly. People are drawn to introverts because they *don't* talk so much and seem to have "something more." But because we live in an interactive, competitive society, introvert qualities can easily be overlooked and even labeled negatively. When you "worry" about your self-directed boy, think Bill Gates!

If your son can't get enough time with his friends and seems to feel healthier after a social marathon, he's probably an extrovert. An extroverted boy is fueled by interaction. His gift is in his ability to think on his feet and engage in back-and-forth conversation and play. He puts his best effort right out there and takes in the good stuff others have to offer. He's a "more the merrier" type and feels happiest around people. He needs social outlets and activities that involve interaction. Team activities are great for extroverts.

The Least You Need to Know

- A boy's natural gift is what comes easiest for him.

- Shedding your own baggage helps you see him more clearly and support him more fully.

- As a parent, it's your job to help your son channel natural desires in healthy ways.

- Help your son build his personality by teaching him where he came from, observing his style, and supporting his desires.

- His personality style helps him feel at home in the world but does not have to limit him.

Part 2

Boy Gets Skills

"Girls only want boyfriends who have great skills," said the infamously awkward teenager Napoleon Dynamite from the 2004 movie of the same name.

In this part, we focus on the many skills boys can develop to engage in and enjoy their widening world. We cover the spectrum from chores, to computers, to adapting to school. We help you sort out his gifts and challenges, such as ADHD. We help him suit up for team sports and take a run on his own. We also draw a picture of skill sets boys enjoy beyond sports, from brain competitions to Boy Scouts. We cover the important skill of teasing and the special treat that middle school boys bring the family, too.

So step up to the plate, and let the pages swing away.

Chapter 6

Skill-Building at Home

In This Chapter

- Practicing daily self-care
- A member of the home crew
- The challenge of the game
- Caring for pets
- Teaching money skills
- Why a little boredom can be good

"How do we do that?" was the question one of our sons asked when he was told he was going to help build a long wooden rail fence along the driveway. The answer he got was: "We'll figure it out." And we did, spending many hours digging the postholes, cementing the posts straight and true, and placing the rails. The end result was handsome and accompanied by the realization by two boys that they could, indeed, build a fence, even though they had never seen one built before.

For parents who do repairs around the house—which is most of us—a willingness to learn by doing is an important character trait. Home repair is just one skill set among many. In this chapter, we look at how parents can foster skill development in their sons, starting with the basics: self-care at home.

Self-Care Basic Training

Make your bed; brush your teeth; blah, blah, blah.

Boys lament the tasks assigned to them and often act as if the Commander of the French Foreign Legion had demanded they scout the Algerian desert before dinner. As parents, we need to realize the task of requiring self-care-related chores is not simply a way to get the housework done, but is instead, a way of building a path for our children to follow.

The quality of your son's life depends on his making good and consistent choices about his body and his environment. Valuing the self by practicing daily self-care is an integral component to a healthy and happy life.

Toy Box

In one of our favorite *Cheers* episodes, Cliff threatens to let his personal hygiene go after suffering yet another setback in his life. The response of the bar patrons: "How would we know?"

Showing your son pictures of dirty and rotting teeth may frighten him into brushing, but, then again, it may not. The scare-the-crap-out-of-them approach is common, even revered; unfortunately the long-term effects of such tactics are not well understood. Remember the famous egg-frying-in-a-pan public service announcement, "This is your brain; this is your brain on drugs"? Those ads did not work and were replaced.

Federal boot camps for young criminals did not work, either, because there was no consistent family or community support network for these offenders after they were released. These programs did not succeed like military training, which provides employment, housing, food, and so on after boot camp.

So if scaring does not work, how do you instill self-care? Let's take a look at how to get your son to do some simple self-care chores.

Teeth-Brushing

I (Barron) recall vividly a visit to the dentist at the age of nine in Springfield, Illinois. The dentist still used an old, slow drill and was not too gentle at the chairside. In the dentist's defense, I walked in with nine cavities as a result of poor teeth-brushing habits and ignoring my mother's admonitions. I did not enjoy this visit to the dentist and made my point by intentionally biting very hard on the dentist's finger as he jammed yet another painful bitewing x-ray film into my mouth. "You little son of a bitch!" cried the dentist, while the nice, pretty assistant exclaimed, "Doctor!" The dentist and I had a contemptuous relationship, to say the least, most of which could have been avoided had I actually listened to my mother.

To encourage your son to brush his teeth, let him go to the store and pick out his own toothbrush and toothpaste. God knows there is way too much marketing of this stuff because it all pretty much works the same. Encourage him to choose a soft bristle brush, and you can refuse the $100 electric sonic model.

As for the toothpaste, since the point is for him to willingly go to the bathroom and brush his teeth, let him choose the paste that has a Blue's Clues character label or whatever he likes. You will have less chance of success if you insist he use the baking soda paste you like.

Teeth are healthier these days, so much so that traditional dentists are spending much more time on optional treatments as opposed to filling cavities. However, boys have worse oral health habits than girls. Instilling daily dental care habits in your son will pay dividends long after he has moved out of the house. Make teeth-brushing a ritual.

Wearing a Retainer

A boy who has had braces may need to wear a retainer. Fortunately, by the time he needs one at age 13 or so, he will likely have developed habits that will support his consistent use of the retainer. Feel free to mention that his beautiful smile costs $4,000, but casually check to see if he's wearing his retainer when you tuck him in, if this is still your ritual.

Retainers are nothing like those worn in the 1970s, either. There is no metal wire in front of the face attached to a hideous elastic band around the back of his head. Retainers are see-through or come in other colors. They are still important to retaining the smile corrected by braces, and putting them in should follow along after nighttime teeth-brushing.

Showering and Bathing

The joy of bathing seems to be a distant memory for most adults as showering is quicker and more economical. But many parents of boys still relish the preschool years when bubble baths make bath night a fun event.

Teaching your boy to clean himself properly starts in these early years when he is not modest and will let you clean him. Teach him to use a washcloth and scrub from head to toe; taking time to reach all the places filth accumulates.

NO GIRLZ ALOWD! Keep Out!

Never leave a young boy in a bathtub unattended, as water is dangerous. While you may not be hazarding his life by grabbing the phone and bringing it back, the risk is you'll forget he's in the tub or get distracted too long. Then comes the ominous silence that has you racing back to the tub with your heart in your throat. Stay with your son as he bathes to avoid these life-shortening shocks to your system.

Show him how to use the shampoo—massage with your fingers—and buy a brand that he likes. Some shampoos that moms like smell way too flowery. A mild fragrance is fine, but no boy wants to leave a toxic lavender cloud behind him at school. Conditioners are fine, too, but the goal here is to get him to appear presentable, not necessarily ready for his next model shoot.

Also, buy several combs and brushes. Give him a few, and store the extras. Boys are notorious for losing these items and will frustrate parents to no end by appearing for departure to a social event with their hair resembling an abandoned bird's nest. Save the mad scramble, and buy a bag of combs.

Bed-Making

Teach a boy to make his bed every day, and you'll teach him real discipline. Resist the temptation to permit a messy bed. You can let him leave his toys on the floor for a few extra days, even ignore some dirty clothes for a bit. But try to draw a line in the sand about the bed.

A made bed will make a room look much, much better. Completing the task of making a bed will make your son realize that he *can* get something done each day. If he cares enough about himself to make his bed, he'll care that much more about how he looks and how he works, etc. Teach him to care about his property, and he'll care for himself.

Shoot for substantial compliance here. One hundred percent compliance is unlikely, but you can expect and enforce regular bed-making. If your son shoots off to school and forgets, direct him to make his bed when he gets home. Firm directions, unaccompanied by shouting, will work. Also, if you let him pick out his own sheets and comforter, he'll likely make his bed more often simply because he'll take pride in the way it looks.

Picking Up Dirty Clothes

A laundry chute is a real boon to parents of boys. Boys seem to enjoy the physics of dropping the clothes down the chute. If your residence requires you to carry your laundry, buy your son an inexpensive clothes hamper without a lid for his room. You can make picking up his floor fun by installing an over-the-door basketball hoop above his hamper. These laundry hoops are available online and at stores like Wal-Mart. You can also find a collapsible laundry basket with team colors that he can use for shooting baskets.

Family Work Crew

In an age of suburban living and car rides to the store, city boys know little of what boys who grow up on a farm or ranch experience. Out in the country, chores are a daily part of life. The ranch can't operate without the horses being fed or the stalls being mucked. Manure happens, as they say, but kids who grow up around animals don't much mind. They learn quickly that their work is valued and valuable. They become part of a cohesive family unit where all members are expected to contribute.

For city boys, the challenge is for them to realize the value of their help. They must see the family work crew as that: a group dedicated to the daily working of a social unit of which they are an important part. We are not suggesting that you burden boys with the worry that if they don't take out the trash, the family is endangered. We are suggesting that it is imperative for boys to know that what they do is important.

Their chores are important because the family works as a team, with the leaders being the parents. Parents, of course, must start the game off right by getting up and doing their chores. A boy's labor is valuable not only because it helps relieve the parents of additional tasks but also because the boy comes to realize that through his efforts he is learning to care for others and himself.

He realizes dinner gets on the table faster for everyone when the cook isn't slowed by having to take out the trash. His favorite jersey is available to wear on Friday night because he unloaded the dryer and hung up the clothes. The lawn looks great because he mowed and trimmed it before he took off with his buddies.

When it comes to nonroutine tasks like washing windows, cleaning baseboards, and so on, posting a chore chart is helpful. Put it on the refrigerator where no one can ignore it. Along the top of the page in a row, list each room in your residence. On the left side in a column, list the chores you want done. You can use a spreadsheet if you want, but paper and pencil work just as well. Where the rows and columns intersect, have your boy put his initials and the date he completes the chore.

This is a simple but highly effective idea. There are way too many tasks to carry around in your head. Also, a to-do sheet that includes dates helps you gauge how much time you need to get things done.

As for compensation, our recommendation is to not compensate boys for routine chores. Your son is not a paid laborer, he is a part of the team. An allowance can teach financial management and the benefit of delayed gratification, but avoid tying an allowance directly to the completion of chores. If you want to "hire" your son to do some special work, such as updating your website or painting the mailbox, that's fine. (See "Money Skills" later in this chapter for more on paying an allowance and handling money.)

Toolbox _____

Reward your crew for the extra effort required in nonroutine work: dinner at McDonald's, a trip to the amusement park, something to celebrate the end of the labors. Teach your son to work hard, and teach your son to relax and reward himself, too. The old saying is true: all work and no play makes Jack a very dull boy.

Puzzles and Games

Skills come in all varieties. Instead of pigeonholing these categories for your son (athletic, academic) look for skills that are harder to define.

One recent and very large study from Norway of 241,310 children, including some 60,000 pairs of brothers, indicated that firstborn children are more dutiful, make better students, and have slightly higher IQs than second children. Researchers theorize, though, that second children adapt and distinguish themselves in other areas, such as social skills, music, and so on. Secondborn sons are more likely to engage in adventurous lifestyles. Where firstborns have won more Nobel prizes, they have done so by advancing current understanding as opposed to overturning the worldview.

Whatever the birth order of your son, take the time to step back and observe his skills. Often children at a young age display advanced skills, or what might be referred to as a natural ability, to complete certain tasks better than others.

Jigsaw puzzles and games are two activities that can help you identify and nurture both natural and learned skills. Simple board games, such as *Candyland*, teach color and counting. *Chutes and Ladders* teaches frustration tolerance. "Stupid slides!" Games with other children, to be fun, require a willingness to "play along" as well as being patient while awaiting a turn.

Boggle teaches words; *Monopoly* teaches about money and risk; and so on. Stop by the local game store, and ask what games are the most popular today. Except for a few classics, games go in and out of popularity, driven by a collection of serious players who love to try new games.

Try to incorporate games that are cooperative as well as competitive. When the boys were in the early elementary grades, we created a treasure hunt game for parties by hiding a prize and hand-drawing clues in the form of pictures. Each clue would be a drawing of the location where the next clue would be found.

Puzzles improve spatial orientation and demand that the mind hold many images at once. Start with simple puzzles made of wood and work your way up quickly to larger puzzles if your son is bored. Puzzles are a great way to occupy a child's time and to free up Mom or Dad for other tasks. They are also an excellent holiday pastime, allowing every family member an opportunity to participate at his or her own pace. Puzzles are also an inexpensive way to pass the time. Consider buying some inexpensive glue, like Modge Podge, to glue the puzzle together for framing once you complete it.

Also keep in mind age appropriate crossword, maze, mystery, and lateral thinking books. Kids love these mind-benders because they can take on the challenge without fear of embarrassment—the answers are in the back. And they can revel in the glow of having solved a difficult challenge. Check them out at any bookrack; they don't cost very much.

Computer Time

You have two choices concerning your son's learning of computer skills. You can teach him now, or you can teach him later.

Today, computers are everywhere. Soon the flat-surface computers will be released, and touch-sensitive computer screens will replace sections of walls and counters. Boys who wish to excel in school and at work need to be not only familiar with computers but proficient as well.

Fortunately, the video gaming industry has made computers fun. Boys gravitate toward video games and learn computer commands to run and install the games. The prevalence of the Internet has kindergartners developing web pages. How best, then, do you manage this component of learning that did not exist when many parents were growing up?

For the computer to be interesting to your boy, you might want to start with what interests you. Pick a subject you find interesting, and show your son how you enjoy researching the topic, such as the Chicago Cubs: visit cubs.com or the news: stop by nytimes.com. Your excitement and interest will power a hunger for learning in your son while he observes. Then ask him what subject he wants to learn about, perhaps a type of dinosaur. Find a website, and let him look around.

Toy Box

Trust your son to do right, but verify the sites he is viewing by looking at the file history. In a computer with a Microsoft operating system, go to Start, then Control Panel, then Internet Options, then Browsing history settings, to finally, View Files. The Internet addresses listed will show you where your son has been exploring on the Internet.

Kids love to play with Paint and other drawing programs and can amuse themselves with a word processor, too. Write a letter to Grandma, and let him dictate while you type. Then play with the fonts and colors. You can even show him how to make a spreadsheet of household chores to post on the refrigerator.

For a boy who wants a more immersive experience, he can try the paid site clubpenguin.com. For around six dollars a month, he can live and play with other kids in a virtual world with an alter ego penguin personality.

Webkinz is a line of stuffed animals. Each animal comes with an online personality and plays, shops, and sleeps online. You've never heard of them? You will. Some 100 factories in China are making them, and there is a severe shortage. If you can't find one for your son, take heart. This fad may fade quickly, too, just as adults migrate to different social networks on the Internet.

Runescape is a free (and paid) fantasy game that boys over 12 would enjoy the most. Take a look at www.runescape.com. If your son likes *Lord of the Rings*, this may be the thing for him.

The LEGO *Mindstorms* products are very boy-oriented as boys compete in robotics competitions at a seven-to-three rate over girls. Check out www.usfirst.org and www.mindstorms.lego.com. These robots can be built by hand and then manipulated by computer.

Once your boys are using a computer, always monitor their usage. Keep them safer by using parental control software like netnanny (www.netnanny.com). Make sure your computer has spam and pop-up blocking software as well. Check out www.pcworld.com for info on the latest security software, much of which you can download for home use for free.

Place the computer in an area viewable by adults, not tucked away in a bedroom. Impose a time limit to prevent repetitive motion injuries and decrease the real risk of addiction. Require your children to do their chores by certain times. Turn off the computer a half hour or more before bedtime, to allow them to unwind and check in with you.

Pay *close* attention to the Entertainment Software Rating Board system. Video games are labeled as follows:

- Early Childhood, "EC"
- Everyone, "E", is for boys six years and older
- Everyone Ten+, "E10+", is for boys ten years and older
- Teen, "T", 13+
- Mature, "M", 17+
- Adults Only, "AO"
- Rating Pending, "RP"

The tolerance for violence and language increases as you go up the scale. Mature in this context does not mean well-considered adult behavior. Depending on the game, a Mature rating can mean free of any morality whatsoever. The notorious game series Grand Theft Auto allows a player to kill the police, have sex with a prostitute, and then rob her—all in living color.

Caring for a Pet or Sibling

Pets have comforted us for centuries. The pharaohs of Egypt had cats and dogs, and your son will likely yearn for animal companionship, too. Tending to an animal teaches many things, and you should seriously consider getting a pet for your son to nurture at the proper age. Gauge your son's interest *before* you bring home a pet. If he sounds excited and willing to take on the responsibility, feel free to forge ahead. If he is lukewarm to the idea, set the thought aside for the time being.

Toy Box

Your son may not see health concerns that could prevent your buying an animal as an insurmountable barrier. This conversation occurred during a car ride many years ago:

Bjorn (age 4): "Can I have a cat?"

Mom: "No, your daddy is allergic to cats."

(pause)

Bjorn: "When my daddy dies, can we get a daddy who's not allergic to cats?"

School-age boys are capable of handling dogs in the house or on the property. You are going to be responsible for much of the dog's care, but a boy can learn to feed a dog dry food. Water is harder to handle because it is heavy and creates a big mess when spilled. Some boys, though, may relish the task of watering. If he wants to try, let him.

Cats require less attention and may be easier to manage in a busy or smaller household. Hamsters are not readily affectionate (they may bite at first), but they are entertaining to watch and usually warm up with frequent and careful handling. Keep in mind that cages and fish tanks require regular cleaning, something an eager child may not consider and later resent. Rabbits, birds, snakes, mice, and guinea pigs are available, too. As they all need to eat, any animal can teach a child some measure of daily nurturing and empathy. Dogs and cats prevail in popularity, though, for the simple reason they can be very affectionate. Dogs are called man's best friend for a reason.

Your son can also learn valuable skills by caring for a sibling. A three-year-old can grab a diaper; a five-year-old can help make sandwiches; and a thirteen-year-old can baby-sit. By caring for another human being, your son will learn that humans are vulnerable and need each other. He will also learn that he is capable of helping and protecting a vulnerable person, and valuable simply because he interacts in a caring manner.

Sibling rivalry, while natural, is tempered when boys learn to care for a sister or brother. Caring for a sibling teaches the concept of humanity in the close sphere of family. A boy who can learn to care for a brother or sister may eventually venture out to care for friends and neighbors. A caring boy will mature into a caring adult.

Money Skills

If you ask your son to take out the trash and he says, "Give me a dollar," feel free to say "No." Boys need to contribute unpaid chores to sustain the family. At the same time, you may want to give him a weekly, age-appropriate allowance; perhaps 25 to 50 cents per year of age, depending on *your* budget, starting at age five. Give him a bank to store his money in, or help him keep a ledger to show him how money accumulates. Teach him about compound interest, too. But the best teacher is hands-on. When a boy has his own money, he learns to be more discriminating about what he wants. He'll probably blow it all at first, then learn that if he wants something bigger, he has to wait—something many *adults* take a while to figure out! Some parents have children save half of their allowance to a certain point before spending it, and some teach their children to tithe (give 10 percent to charity) from the start. Having an allowance increase with age allows children to take on more responsibility for purchases as they grow.

Take the time to discuss family money issues with your boys. Speak frankly and kindly with them about difficulties the family is facing. Of course, measure the amount of information you give to your son based on his age. Boys can be very understanding. Share with your son when you are making a choice *not* to buy something because you cannot afford it, at least right now. Show your son that budgeting and delaying gratification are the hallmarks of a less stressful and more manageable life.

Also, show your son that you can find happiness even with less money. Modeling for your son the ability to find joy even in times of trouble will instill in him the sense that he has power over money, not the other way around. At the same time, help your son appreciate that money is an important tool that allows you to provide for the family.

Especially, teach your son about debt and the very real hazards and long-term costs of borrowing money.

Let your son make mistakes with his own money. If you're conflicted about buying a nonessential but desirable item for your son, stop and ask him if he wants to pay for it himself. You'll be surprised how many times he'll say, "No" and then walk away completely content with not having the very thing he needed just a minute earlier.

Unstructured Time

"I'm bored." Parents hear this lament time and time again. If you've spent very little time with your son, this may be an invitation to jump-start the fun by thinking of a game you could play together. More likely, though, your son is just unwilling to tolerate the dormant state of his mind—the state, which, if you let him be bored, will bloom with creative ideas. In other words, let your child be bored. Boredom is not fatal. Boredom is good. Boredom precedes creation.

To encourage your son to create his way out of boredom, buy toys that allow him to build, draw, and paint. There is no end to the fun that arises from fort-building with the assemble-at-home large cardboard bricks you can buy at any toy store. Buy a lot of them, and then stand back in wonder at the castle he makes. Ask other parents and teachers for ideas.

> **Boy Wisdom**
>
> Ironically, it is a lack of external stimulation and solitude that facilitates creative play.
>
> —Steven Perry, M.D., Ph.D., child psychiatrist

If you like to schedule your son's time, remember to schedule unstructured time: no class, playdate, lesson, or enriching activity. Leave him alone in his playroom or bedroom.

Some parents just tell their kids "there is no such thing as boredom." Make your own choice about this, but make it clear that entertainment is not offered on the hour at your house. Certainly spend much time with your son; you'll love it and so will he. When you're done spending time together, be strong enough to let him live through the frustration and tedium of time without you. He'll emerge on the other side with a "skill" all boys need in full measure: an active imagination.

The Least You Need to Know

◆ Practicing good self-care skills, such as brushing teeth and bathing, will last a lifetime.

◆ Chores solidify family unity and should be an expected part of family life.

◆ Games and puzzles identify and nurture both natural and learned skills in boys.

◆ Computer competence can be acquired through fun, but always monitor your son's usage.

◆ Caring for a pet teaches nurturing and empathy.

◆ A bored child will use his imagination if given the time.

Chapter 7

Helping Him Be Cool with School

In This Chapter

- His first schooling
- His first day at school
- Qualities of a good teacher
- Moving to a new school
- Alternatives to public schools

Making school cool begins with a home that includes learning as a part of everyday living. While "school" invokes many thoughts, helping your son understand that learning for you as a parent has never stopped, and will never stop, is the first step in showing your son that he can learn anyplace, anytime.

His stepping away from you to the embrace of a teacher, though, is a big step toward maturity. It's hard and exciting at the same time for both you and your son, but you can help increase the chances that your son will do well in school.

Let's look at school issues, from home to elementary schools. Much has changed in the last 20 years.

School at Home

Your son's first school is his home. Your interests will drive how you teach. Dad, while readying the golf bag, can take this simple moment to show his one-year-old the golf balls. He can teach "ball" and "round" or can drop the ball and teach "down" and "up."

The point is that everyday experiences are, to your son's developing mind, school for all intents and purposes. As he is observing you talk softly or yell, hold your fork, or hug and kiss your spouse, your son is learning. He drinks in these experiences like water.

Toolbox

Boys love to build and like action. Good toy choices are anything they can stack, ride-on toys, Little People villages, and so on. Check out toydirectory.com for some new ideas.

Provide a place for your toddler to play that you can observe. A separate play area that doesn't have to have the toys put away all the time will benefit your son and put less stress on you. Your home "school" should be fun and inspire creativity. Having a parent who insists that every toy that is touched be put away immediately, takes more than a little fun out of the equation.

Preschool Options

Preschool options for parents will largely hinge on the costs to parents of staying home versus working. Many parents choose to stay home and raise their son until he is school age and then return to work. For these parents a shorter preschool program of half-days or alternate days may work better. Other parents are unable to stay home full-time and seek out full-time providers. Even if relatives or neighbors are available to watch their boys, parents often still choose preschool for perceived social and developmental opportunities.

Whether part-time or full-time preschool works for you, choosing a preschool requires much more than choking up the astronomical costs. According to one recent article in *The New York Times*, preschool expenses for one child for a full year exceed the cost of yearly tuition at a state university in 49 out of 50 states. Parents with two children need to take a hard look at such high costs before choosing to remain at work and place children in preschool.

If you are considering a particular preschool for your son, visit the potential site at a time you can observe the children being taught. Don't go after work when most kids are gone. You may need to schedule an initial visit. You also might want to "drop by" for a quick second look even if you cannot be accommodated with a second tour at that moment. If your second look does not confirm your initial favorable impression, think hard before enrolling your son.

When you arrive, take a look around and listen. Do the kids look happy or bored? Are teachers asking the children individual questions in an encouraging way? Are the children involved in different activities (better) as opposed to all doing the same thing? Do the kids have enough room to play? Boys prefer activity, so the more room the better. Do they get time to be alone? If the children are working on a sheet of paper, is each doing his own project or copying someone else's? Is there at least one adult for every ten children? Also find out what the teacher's educational background is. The lead teacher—prefer-ably all teachers—should have a Bachelor's degree in early child-hood education.

Toolbox

Maria Montessori (1870–1952) was an Italian educator who developed a very hands-on, child-focused approach to teaching young children. *Science* magazine reported in 2006 that, among five-year-olds, Montessori-method students performed better in reading and math than non-Montessori students. If a "Montessori" preschool or school is in your town, check it out.

A desirable preschool concentrates on child-initiated and varied activi-ties, including free-choice and small group, active times and quiet times, short activities as well as longer story-telling times. The presence of pretend stores, pretend cars, and so on reflect that the preschool is providing the children with an understanding of the world around them.

Follow your instinct here, too. If something doesn't feel right, pay attention. We once had a negative experience with a temporary placement. The woman ended up being too high-strung to enjoy active boys, despite her friendly demeanor. She was definitely in the wrong profession. On the other hand, we were able to finally place our two boys with a wonderful, and highly recommended, preschool.

Don't just accept one recommendation, though. Every parent wants to think they've made the right choice. Ask around. Especially ask parents whose boys are now in school. They can provide a wealth of information. The preschool we sent our boys to had a llama on-site.

Llamas are a good sign.

Kindergarten and "Redshirting"

At some point, your son will venture into the brave new world of kindergarten. Education policy changes in the early 1980s as well as recent federal legislation means teachers in early elementary grades are *pushing down* curriculum. This means that in many schools kindergarten boys now must know what their parents were learning in first grade many moons ago.

Boy Wisdom

According to the apple-or-coin test, used in the Middle Ages, children should start school when they are mature enough for the delayed gratification and abstract reasoning involved in choosing money over fruit.

—Elizabeth Weil, *The New York Times*, June 3, 2007

The important date to know is the birthday cutoff date for admission to kindergarten. The most popular deadline for state policies says that a boy must be five years old to start kindergarten and his birth date must fall before September 1. Other states have dates that range from July 1 to as late as January 1 of the middle of the kindergarten year. According to the National Institute for Early Education Research (NIEER) at

Rutgers University, the fact that cutoff dates have moved back from December and January over the past 30 years suggests that educators have perceived a readiness problem for kindergartners.

The kindergarten your boy will attend will be an *academic kindergarten*, not one wholly devoted to play and socialization. By the time they complete the year, kindergarten boys must know how to read and write two complete sentences.

If your boy was born near the cutoff date for kindergarten, the question then becomes whether to keep him in preschool for one more year or send him ahead to kindergarten. In general, a boy can start kindergarten late, but he cannot start it early.

In sports, a first-year athlete who plays on a college team is called a *true freshman*. A student who attends classes his first year and starts playing sports his second year, but still retains four years of playing eligibility is a player who has been *redshirted*. The same goes for kindergartners. A boy held back, or retained, in preschool an extra year has been redshirted. Boys are redshirted more often than girls.

Early research showed little advantage over time to redshirting, but more recent research shows that redshirting has positive effects. Many parents believe redshirting is the preferred choice. And it may very well be, provided parents can afford it.

Students older than their classmates perform better in academics and in sports and are more likely to take a college entrance exam. The main advantage may be that skills "snowball" as do negative experiences, and sending your son to school when he is older will simply give him a better chance to enjoy and succeed in school.

While many American schools use an academic model for kindergarten, not all countries do. In Finland, students start school at seven years of age and spend the first year playing. Yet compared to other European students, Finnish students excel academically and the advantage of relative age for these students is diminished.

A boy who must sit and do little for a year, with no preschool to attend or no playmates, may bloom spectacularly once in school. A gifted boy who has a birthday near the cutoff date may be bored out of his mind waiting for school to start. Each boy is an individual, and you must consider him individually when deciding whether or not to send him to kindergarten.

Are you unsure of what to do? Ask your school to perform a brief readiness test on your son. Not all school districts routinely do these tests, but most will likely make this available upon request. Kindergarten teachers perform this brief test at the school. Meeting with the teacher and observing your son during the test and in the classroom will help you feel more confident in your decision.

Elementary Joys for Boys

As the "big day" approaches, help your son understand that his adventure into school is something he is ready for. Reassure him by stating that you know he can handle it and that if he does not like something, he can come and tell you after school. If he has younger siblings, point out that he will be able to come home and tell his brother or sister what school is like. In other words, he can serve as a guide. This may add a little cachet to stepping out of the house.

At the same time, you don't want to oversell his start at school, either. Point out plainly that "school" is something that boys attend and now it is his turn to go to school. Like anything new, teach your son that school is something he can handle with relative ease, and he will be more confident when his first day arrives.

Toy Box

The wise kindergarten teacher of our youngest son offered cloth squares for students to carry around in their pockets. These squares were like the blankets many of the children loved at home. Joshua, who up to 10 minutes before kindergarten began was deeply devoted to his blanket, shook his head as if to say, "Blanket, I don't need no stinking blanket!"

He may be quite flushed with excitement or he may be quiet when he returns. Avoid the temptation to immediately drill him for info when he steps off the bus. He should open up in short order.

He will soon be sharing his pride in his accomplishments, so buy lots of magnets for the refrigerator. School can indeed be very cool. He is separate from Mom and Dad, yet he is not only surviving but also thriving.

Pay attention to his significant behavioral changes during the first weeks, changes beyond a few grumpy days. For a few boys, the transition to school does not go well at all. Your son may not be ready for kindergarten, or bullies may be verbally or physically abusing him. Address your concerns with the teacher and principal immediately.

Identifying Teachers Who Love Boys

Teaching boys requires patience and an appreciation for energy that sometimes explodes like a firecracker. Veteran teachers put boys in the front of the classroom because they know boys do not hear as well as girls (see Chapter 2). Teachers who do well with boys recognize the fact that boys may speak fewer words but that does not signal an attention deficit. These gender-aware teachers know that boys recharge in rest and need time to drift away. They also know that boys need to *move*. One kindergarten teacher we read about had a running track circling her classroom! And *creative* writing teachers who know boys do not prohibit "killing" the bad guy.

While almost all teachers express a sincere love of children—few teach only for the modest pay—the best understand that boys will make different demands on them. They don't accept stereotyping; they know boys have feelings that can be hurt and that boys need to be shown the same degree of love and caring as girls. They perhaps discipline boys in a more firm way and with fewer words because boys will react better, but they do not seek to humiliate. These quality teachers use maps and similar techniques that utilize boys' developmental strengths.

Meet with your son's teachers. If your boy tells you he is having a problem with a teacher, do not dismiss his concerns. Some school districts pass around bad teachers because they are too timid to fire them. If your boy gets stuck with a bad egg, express your concerns in a polite but direct way to the principal. You can ask for your boy to be moved to another class.

Ask other parents of older boys who their boys liked for teachers. For our two sons, their favorite teachers were two women who co-taught fifth grade. When we see either of these women around town, they express affection for our sons that is genuine and heartwarming. When one stopped teaching many years later, our oldest son made a point to attend the teacher's retirement party. These two teachers were the very ones other parents had raved about.

New Boy in School

No one particularly enjoys moving, but for a boy who has to start all over again making new friends and meeting new teachers, moving can be particularly stressful. Ease the transition by planning ahead. If you can, visit the new location before you move. Take your son to visit his new school right at dismissal time, so he can see the kids, meet his teacher, and find out where he will sit. Do not take him in the middle of a school day so he has to walk in cold to a room full of kids.

If possible, try to meet a boy in the neighborhood/church who can befriend your son before he goes to the school the first day. Get your son signed up for an activity (soccer) in your new location before you move so he has something to look forward to. If you have a choice, move early in the summer. This will give him a few months to make new friends, that is, find a pack to run with that will offer him companionship and protection.

Depression, anxiety, and compulsive behaviors are flagged by close observation: in particular, notice sleep disturbances (more than to be expected), marked behavioral changes, frequent crying/tantrums, and in young children, changes in toileting.

Go for a walk with your son. You may have to wait, but he will eventually start talking or move the casual conversation to what's going on inside. Try to let him lead and tell you about his feelings at his own pace. The main relationship/activity here is walking. It may lead to talking, but parents—moms in particular—need to avoid rushing to fill the quiet walk with talk about feelings. If you must talk, talk about something innocuous or silly, something unrelated to school. He'll likely open up to you soon enough.

Not-So-Public Options

The concept of school has changed over the centuries—from home instruction, to church education, to large public entities. Depending on their location and resources, parents have choices for their son's education beyond public schools.

Homeschooling

Homeschooling is the preference for parents of over one million students in the United States today. This concept became popular in the 1990s and has continued to grow with slightly more boys being homeschooled than girls. The rise of the Internet has no doubt made teaching children from home easier. Even regular schools use Oasis programs and computer connectivity to teach children who must stay at home. Families with three or more children are much more likely to homeschool, as well.

Teaching boys at home requires the same awareness of boys that in-school teachers must possess. Boys need to be able to work off steam. Because they develop more slowly at reading, they may not progress at the same pace as a sister.

Field trips are not a twice-a-year treat for homeschoolers. Any day can be a trip day. To stay on track, make full use of a calendar. Do not try to replicate a school environment in your home. It is not school in the home; it is homeschooling. Boys do not need to sit forever, boxed in by a clock and a lecture.

Ask for help when you need it. Both parents should expect to share a part of the load. There are families in which both parents work who still homeschool. Such a challenge, however, requires an additional measure of coordination and scheduling. For a good jumpstart to learning about homeschooling, check out homeschooling.about.com.

Public vs. Private Schools

When choosing to place your son in a private-school setting, don't place too much emphasis on your own experience as a child. Your sample size of one is not big enough to form any conclusions without a bit more effort. In this age of school choice, you may have quite a few more options to choose from.

Public schools used to be assigned by residence location. You went to the neighborhood school. Even today, many homeowners build or buy in a neighborhood because of the quality of the local schools. This is a very valid consideration. You're paying the taxes anyway, so you might as well put your hard-earned money to use for your son.

If you haven't preselected your son's school by moving into the district, you have many other options. Some public schools permit a student to choose the school he wishes to attend, and provide a menu of curriculum options from arts, to foreign language, to magnet schools for science, and so on. Even on an elementary level some schools offer variety in curricula.

Private schools require quite a bit more effort. The first thing a private school requires is money. While many offer scholarships to many children, if you want your boy to attend a private school you will need several thousand dollars for each year. A private, nonreligious school will set you back around $15,000 per year, per child. A religious, or parochial, school will likely be much less, around $4,000–7,000.

Private schools can be highly selective. Your son may need to take an admissions test; you will need to fill out an extensive application and possibly be interviewed. Identifying potential schools, on-site visits, applications, interviews, and final selection may take nine months to complete.

When considering a school for your son, make an appointment to visit the school when classes are in session so you can look at several factors:

◆ What is the teacher-student ratio?

◆ What is the educational level and experience of the teachers?

◆ Because boys respond well to male teachers, how many male teachers are on the staff?

◆ What is the quality of the facilities? Are the bathrooms clean? Is there an abundance of graffiti or disrepair?

◆ When you visit a classroom, do the boys look like they are engaged with the teacher? Do the boys look reasonably happy or bored? Are they all permitted to sit at the back of the classroom? If so, choose another school.

- ◆ Do the classes have maps, models, and other teaching tools that boys respond well to?

- ◆ Will this school nurture your son's unique abilities?

Compare your answers to these questions for each candidate school. Then make a choice that feels right for your son. For additional resources, check out he National Association of Independent Schools (nais.org) Parent's Guide and the helpful index at privateschoolreview. com, and consult with your house of worship for parochial listings. Almost all faiths have faith-based schools. Large metropolitan areas offer the most parochial school options, particularly at the elementary level.

Since there is so much variation among schools, it is hard to say which is better—a public or a private school. Some private schools are well-funded while others are run on a shoestring. There is, though, a popular perception that private schools are better than public schools. Even if this perception were true, you are only sending your son to one school at a time. You can't conclude private school would be better until you've examined your son's particular private and public school options. Case in point: we live near an excellent public school, one that is ranked academically in the top 3 percent in the nation. Had it been ranked in the bottom 3 percent, we would have chosen to live somewhere else.

> **Keep Out!**
>
> When visiting a school, take a look at the schoolyard. Is there room to run and play? Do they *let* boys run on the playground? If they don't, choose a different school.

Special needs boys may thrive in a public school because the special education resources may be more available to the average household. Parents who simply want to surround their son with the embrace of a faith-based education will look to the local parish school. Families with a strong military tradition may favor a military academy, although these are often seen as an option for unruly boys. Parents who desire a college-prep-only curriculum may look to rigorous private schools as well. In Southern California, *Chinese Christian Schools* is a college-prep,

Christian, Chinese-culture-based association of schools (ccc-rams.org) that advertises that 100 percent of its graduates go to college. Now, that's specialized.

A 2006 report from the United States Department of Education indicated that students at public schools hold their own against students from private schools in achievement, at least in elementary school. Public-school kids did better at math in fourth grade than private-school students. Private-school students did better in reading than public-school students by the eighth grade. If you really want to know much, much more, go to nces.ed.gov and search for "Comparing Private Schools and Public Schools Using Hierarchical Linear Modeling." Unfortunately, this large report does not break out results by gender.

The Least You Need to Know

- Parents can ease the transition to school by matter-of-fact talk and on-site exploration.

- Benefits of preschool must be substantial to outweigh the large cost.

- Keeping your son in preschool an extra year may be a very good idea.

- Veteran teachers are gender-aware and can make a world of difference in your son's education.

- Ease your son's move to a new school with thoughtful planning and a visit.

- The correct choice between a private or a public school depends on the actual schools your son would attend and his unique needs.

Chapter 8

When His Teacher Calls

In This Chapter

- ◆ Problems at school
- ◆ Ways to make school work better for him
- ◆ Can boys be boys?
- ◆ Handling aggression
- ◆ Does he have Attention-Deficit/Hyperactivity Disorder (ADHD)?
- ◆ From exceptional teachers come exceptional boys

On January 26, 2006, the cover of *Newsweek* featured a group of young boys in a schoolyard along with the boldfaced caption: "The Boy Crisis." The magazine's cover story discussed the growing evidence that boys have unique academic needs and that these needs are not being met in our schools. The article reflected a shift from our gender-as-learned thinking to an understanding of boys as fundamentally different from girls. Who hasn't had the thought that unruly boys just need more attention to their feelings? Or that, "If only he were nurtured more, he wouldn't be so aggressive." As empathic as these sentiments may seem, they reflect an association between boys and *lack*.

Unfortunately, the idea of boys as lacking can get reinforced in our schools. And when we get a call from the teacher, we worry. "Is he slow?" "Is he ADD?" "Is he misbehaving?" And just when you're ready to sound an alarm, a new headline appears. In the August 6, 2007, issue of *Time*, an article boldly states "The Boys Are All Right." Author David Von Drehle acknowledges the "alarming decline" in boys' academic performance that has prompted concern, but finds a new picture emerging. He concludes that our attention to boys is paying off and they're doing better—socially and academically—than ever. Let's capitalize on our progress and take a closer look at the problems that can arise for *your boy* in the school setting and the responses that will help him *thrive*, and not just survive.

To Be or Not to Be "Gifted"

When our son was in grade school, I recall his telling me in a matter-of-fact way, "I'm not gifted. My friends who are gifted have a lot more homework." His statement stopped me in my tracks. I had seen him master jigsaw puzzles as a toddler, and he was now learning piano at a rate that amazed his teacher. Not gifted?

Before I had a chance to protest his comment, he made it clear to me that he did not *want* to be gifted. He wanted his free time, unlike his "gifted" friends who had extra assignments.

Our conversation revealed to me the tricky dilemma that gifted programs set up for our boys and for us as parents. Gifted classes can feed the minds of boys who would otherwise be bored and understimulated, and they can be fun. The problem for many boys is that to be gifted means more *school*. And we are finding that school itself is often a problem for boys. Ask a grade school boy what his favorite class is, and he's likely to respond, "recess!" To transition from the freedom of home or preschool to the structure of school can be an excruciating adjustment for boys. Our son had a habit of racing home from the bus and attending to his homework right away so that he could run free as soon as possible.

Our son didn't need more academic input; the kind of extra stimulation *he* needed was the kind he found through spontaneous exploration. But, as with many boys, his preference did not come under the heading of "gifted," which is limited, depending on the school, to students whose test scores fall in the top 3 to 10 percent of the school population. This limitation may explain why some schools are adopting the concept of *multiple intelligences* into their gifted programs and including students who have exceptional skills in nonacademic areas.

Toolbox

In 1983, Dr. Howard Gardner, Professor of Cognition and Education at Harvard, published a theory of multiple intelligences. He challenged the idea that intelligence is limited to the narrow categories assessed by an IQ test. He has since identified eight forms of intelligence: linguistic ("word smart"), logical-mathematical ("number/reasoning smart"), spatial ("picture smart"), bodily-kinesthetic ("body smart"), musical ("music smart"), interpersonal ("people smart"), intrapersonal ("self smart"), and naturalist ("nature smart"). He indicated that schools and IQ tests typically only emphasize the first two.

In elementary school, girls have tended to outnumber boys in gifted programs, though this trend reverses when a boy reaches tenth grade. This sequence is consistent with the boy literature, which emphasizes the initial, but temporary, lag in school performance for boys in relation to girls.

Because boys frequently get bored with school, the trick is to tune in to the kind of stimulation *he* needs. If he's bored in school, is it because he needs more challenging study material or possibly because he doesn't understand—or is it simply because he needs a break? If you observe and listen, he'll probably show you.

If he's really unhappy, you can also request testing to find out if alternative programming makes sense. If he qualifies for your school's gifted program, check it out. A meeting with you, your son, and the gifted teacher will help you assess if the *more* provided by the program excites him or overwhelms him. But whether he's deemed gifted by the school or not, it is up to us as parents to affirm and build on what *he* brings to the world—even if that gift is simply his joyful spontaneity.

Falling Behind

Just as we refer to the basics as "reading, writing, and arithmetic," in that order, schools and parents tend to push reading and writing first and math later. Reading used to be something we *started to* learn in first grade; now kids are often mastering books before they start kindergarten!

These early readers, however, are more often girls. Research has revealed that the brain regions involved in reading and writing mature about *six years earlier* in girls than in boys. Boys, on the other hand, are first to develop a sense of how things are arranged in space—or *spatial relationships.*

As we've discussed, these differences are evident from infancy. Girls, who have been studying people since birth, enjoy the *interpersonal* world and are natural storytellers. Boys, who have been moving and crashing their trucks, enjoy working out *impersonal* relationships—like the relationship between numbers or between points on a map.

When we push our boys to read before they are ready, we risk turning them off to reading altogether. Meanwhile, the blocks and puzzles that stimulated their growing brains are getting pulled away sooner (remember when we just *played* in kindergarten?). So boys, who are just developing differently, are easily flagged as "slow." And a boy who is expected to be slow may very well live down to the label.

So how do we help our boys stay clear of the asserted "crisis"? As unfair as it may seem, we need to bridge the gap. This means investing energy in his education rather than leaving him to "sink or swim." Here are some ways to make school work for him:

- **Advocate for reform.** Some schools have started to offer same-sex classes to provide realistic norms for boys as well as girls. Educational innovators are working to broaden the narrow definitions of intelligence that can hurt boys. Just educating your son's teacher on who *he* is can make a difference, and taking charge provides a good model for his own approach to learning.

- **Take advantage of school resources.** If your son is struggling, engage his teacher and school counselor in some detective work.

Request testing to find out his individual strengths, weaknesses, and learning style. And ask for individual programming for any special needs that may be identified. In today's schools, kids get pulled out of class for a variety of reasons, so it's not likely he'll be teased or labeled for getting additional help.

◆ **Don't give up.** Humans are complex, and figuring out the reason for an academic setback may take some time. Getting what you want from a school system also takes time and persistence. Resources are limited, and you'll have to wait your turn. To seek out a private evaluation by a child psychologist is always an option—and your health insurance can usually help with the costs.

◆ **Build him up and love him up.** Affirm that he is exactly who he is supposed to be. Help him develop pride in *his* preferences and skills.

Keep Out!

For boys, poor school performance and disruptive behaviors can be a sign of depression. Boys tend to *externalize* pain, to "be a pain," while girls are more likely to *internalize* these feelings. Girls get more empathy and help for depression; boys can drive away the very help they need. Asking him how he's feeling will probably stop the conversation. Instead, translate what he's doing "out there" to what's happening inside him. If he points out everyone else's "dumb mistakes," assume that he yells at himself for missing the mark.

"Behavior Problem" or Boy Behavior?

Boys like to move; classrooms are for sitting still. Boys don't hear so well, *and* they like to sit in the back; their female teachers don't talk loud enough. Boys avoid getting friendly with teachers because it's uncool; teachers may see "cool" boys as aloof. Boys internalize stress rather than asking for help; teachers rely on children's questions as indicators of whether they're "getting it." Boys enjoy relating to each other aggressively; female teachers and female classmates may not "get" or appreciate the sparring.

These clashing trends explain why natural boy behaviors, when put into a classroom, are sometimes hard to distinguish from "behavior problems." In addition, concerns about violence in schools and "zero tolerance" policies have resulted in restrictions on playful activities formerly seen as benign. I recall being shocked when my boys told me that their elementary school had eliminated the annual Halloween party and were replacing it with a "Fall Harvest Party." But to top that, our youngest son came home in tears one day to report on a new policy forbidding—get this—*running on the playground*. No wonder he couldn't wait to get home!

Zero Tolerance—for Boys?

In June 2000, The Civil Rights Project of Harvard University released a national report titled "Opportunities Suspended: The Devastating Consequences of Zero Tolerance and School Discipline Policies." The report discussed the tendency of school officials to enforce these policies more broadly than intended: "harsh arbitrary rules are zealously applied to suspend and expel students—some as young as four years old—for trivial misconduct and innocent mistakes." In one well-publicized case, a six-year-old boy was suspended for 10 days for taking a plastic knife home from the school cafeteria. He was apparently excited to show his mom that he'd learned how to spread butter on his bread.

As in this case, boys are the consistent targets of these fear-based and harmful reactions. A number of examples report suspension of young boys for pointing a finger and saying "bang." In one of these cases, four kindergartners were suspended for three days for playing a make-believe game of cops and robbers during recess.

So here we have boys discharging their aggression in a natural and *healthy* way—through fantasy—and the school's response turns the play into a truly dangerous game. The Harvard report discussed how this kind of reaction can start a pattern of criminalization. "Kids often interpret suspension as a one-way ticket out of school—a message of rejection that alienates them from ever returning to school."

Boy Behavior 101

Though we may be appalled at these examples, they illustrate a broader problem with our responses to boys: we consistently misinterpret and mismanage their aggressive behaviors. Boys generally use aggression as a way of connecting—ask my husband, who is the daily recipient of punches on his arm. Aggression between boys is associated with increased intimacy, whereas aggression between girls is likely to be hostile (hence the term "catfight").

Boys do need to learn to limit and channel aggressive behaviors, but who is going to teach them?

We need to teach them by *teaching* them, not suspending them. When we reject a boy for his playful aggression, he learns either to distrust himself or to distrust authority.

We also teach boys by *loving* boys, as they are, not as what we want to make them. Here are some ways you can help his "boy behavior" become a source of pride rather than a problem:

◆ Give him clear feedback. If the aggressive play is fun for you, go ahead and play. If you don't like it, say "I don't like this. Let's do something else." I recall interrupting rough play on various occasions to show one of my boys: "hold on, he's not having fun." His brother's blood-curdling screams apparently seemed like part of the action.

◆ Teach him how to keep aggressive play fun by knowing when to stop. "Stop" should mean *stop*. Use consequences and limit play when necessary until this principle is engrained.

◆ Give him healthy outlets for his aggression, such as competitive sports or martial arts, and be sure he has regular "recesses" from sedentary activity.

◆ Notice when you give him attention. It's easy to pay attention to boys when they are causing problems and, even though it's negative attention, he knows he's getting you to respond. Instead of reacting emotionally, provide him an impersonal "economic" system, such as giving or deducting points that he can save toward rewards.

◆ Compliment and reward him when he uses aggression appropriately, and schedule time with him to do what he wants to do. This teaches him that he can be in charge in healthy ways.

◆ If he's getting into trouble at school, help your teacher help him. In *Your Defiant Child* (see the Resources appendix), Russell A. Barkley and Christine M. Benton advise parents to give teachers simple "behavior report cards" to complete and return each day. The incentive for the teacher is that you are the one who sets up and enforces consequences for your son. Barkley provides templates of these "report cards" for parents to duplicate.

◆ While you don't want to overreact to aggression, you don't want to overlook or minimize his power, either. Affirm that he is strong, but help him take responsibility for how he uses that strength.

> **Boy Wisdom**
>
> Tony Hawk was an active boy. He was a "troublemaker" from an early age, but got focused when he discovered the adrenaline rush of hurtling into the air with a skateboard. Can you imagine being *his* parent? When Tony sheepishly told his dad—and basketball coach— that he'd rather skate than play basketball, his dad responded, "Fine by me." Tony became a professional skateboarder at the age of fourteen and by sixteen was the best skateboarder in the world.
>
> —Susan Strong, *The Boldness of Boys*

Help him manage his aggression rather than extinguish it, and you'll help his behavior without hurting his identity.

"Taking Out" Feelings

Most boys pick up pretty easily on when, where, and how aggression can get them into trouble. Remember, "trouble" can provide him the attention and stimulation he is craving. Persisting in making trouble can also be his way of showing you that something's wrong.

A middle-aged man recently shared a burden of guilt he had carried since childhood. For years, he had relentlessly bullied his younger siblings and never understood why. He talked of being rightfully "chastised" by his mom and continued to chastise himself as we talked. Then he shared something that gave him his first glimpse of empathy toward himself. His family doctor spoke with him privately and said, "It's impossible to love others until you love yourself." He immediately recognized that he didn't love himself. The wise doctor's words stuck with him as something he needed to explore, though it was decades before he formally asked for help.

So how do you talk to a boy who is "acting out" what's inside? Try saying, "I bet you talk to yourself that way, and that probably hurts." Even if he doesn't respond, you are teaching him how to see his feelings in the mirror of his actions. And your attention to *him* will be a breath of fresh air. A boy in trouble is like a porcupine hoping for a hug: we have to get past the protruding spines!

Is He ADD?

Perhaps your son is doing poorly in school. He's a smart kid, but he's disorganized and keeps losing points in class due to forgotten home-work assignments. His teacher gets annoyed with him because he doesn't pay attention. At home, he promises to do his work but gets distracted and ends up forgetting. Is he ADD?

Attention-Deficit/Hyperactivity Disorder (ADHD) is the actual term for the diagnosis considered when a child has these difficulties, though the older term "ADD" continues to be used. ADHD is much more common in boys than in girls, so you may wonder if he's just getting lumped into a popular category.

Are All Boys ADHD?

ADHD is the most common psychiatric disorder among children, and 60-80 percent of the kids diagnosed are boys. We all probably know someone with ADHD, and at least one or two children in every class-room have the diagnosis. A great deal of controversy has arisen around ADHD, particularly because the treatment involves the use of strong medications.

It's easy to wonder if ADHD is a catchall term for active, energetic boys. After all, boys are drawn to movement and the classroom is a pretty still place. What boy wouldn't want to look out the window at a passing airplane rather than at a teacher standing and talking? Critics of the diagnosis suggest that the problem is a social and educational one and that we need to change our approach to boys rather than to medicate them to fit in.

Experts don't know for sure why ADHD affects boys more often than girls. Some suggest that girls may be more inclined to blame themselves for the problem and become depressed, thus escaping proper diagnosis. Others suggest that boys may have a genetic vulnerability to the disorder.

While critics worry about the *overdiagnosis* of ADHD in boys, professionals who treat ADHD are concerned about another problem: when boys with ADHD are *not* diagnosed, they can be mislabeled as lazy, defiant, or even stupid. As much as they try, these boys suffer real barriers to performing as well as they could and, if undiagnosed, risk seeing themselves as failures and giving up.

> **Toolbox**
>
> Though symptoms may be evident earlier, parents don't usually suspect ADHD until school problems emerge.

It's helpful to note that, while boys are in the majority of ADHD sufferers, the actual percentage of boys who are diagnosed with the disorder is fairly low. Estimates of the prevalence of ADHD among all boys ranges from 3 to 8 percent, and studies estimate that fewer than half of the children with ADHD are diagnosed or properly treated.

So how do you know if he's got it?

ADHD Defined

According to author Russell A. Barkley, ADHD is "a developmental disorder of self-control." What is helpful about this description is that it clearly distinguishes ADHD from laziness, poor motivation, and parental failure. A boy suffering from ADHD has an impaired ability to keep future consequences in mind. That's why he may say, *and truly mean*, that he "has to" get an assignment done, only to seem oblivious to that fact moments later.

ADHD has two major sets of symptoms, which define three diagnostic subtypes: inattentive, hyperactive/impulsive, and combined. Boys with ADHD are more likely to display hyperactivity and impulsivity, whereas diagnosed girls are more likely to only have symptoms related to inattention. Examples of hyperactivity include continual fidgeting, inability to stay in his seat, and difficulty being quiet or resting from activity. Examples of impulsivity include interrupting, failing to wait his turn, and blurting out answers prematurely. Inattention is the symptom most associated with forgetting and losing things: his attention is constantly shifting, so he can't "keep track."

Boy Wisdom _____

Lots of kids who have ADD also have something else, something we don't have a name for, something good. They can be highly imaginative and empathic, closely attuned to the moods and thoughts of people around them, even as they are missing most of the words that are being said. The key is to make the diagnosis early before these kids start getting stuck in school with all kinds of pejorative labels. With some help, they can really blossom.

—Edward M. Hallowell, *Driven to Distraction*

Most boys will occasionally display these symptoms, but ADHD is only diagnosed when the symptoms are far beyond the norm. Other parents will report problems in his play behaviors; kids may be starting to avoid him; caregivers and teachers will note behavior problems; and you'll be exhausted—consequences seem to have no effect on him, and you don't know how to slow him down.

Parenting Power

If you suspect your son has ADHD, you're the ones who will need some energy. But then, what's new about that? Parent resources on ADHD emphasize being the "case manager" of your child's educational and psychological needs. This starts with the diagnostic testing, which draws on the expertise of medical, psychological, and educational consultants. Thankfully, great guides on the topic are available, often developed by experts who have ADHD themselves (see the Resources appendix). In the meantime, here's what to expect:

- **Medical checkup:** His doctor will rule out medical conditions that could explain your son's symptoms and will check his hearing and vision.

- **Psychological assessment:** This usually includes detailed interviews with you and your child and interpretation of behavior rating scales completed by parents and teachers. Intelligence and achievement testing may also be employed to provide a more comprehensive picture.

- **Treatment:** Recommendations usually emphasize behavioral management, and that involves you. Therapy is often recommended for helping him cope with the challenges of ADHD. His pediatrician or a child psychiatrist can prescribe medications to help him focus.

- **School accommodations:** You'll be learning some acronyms as you work with the school. IDEA, the *Individuals with Disabilities Education Act*, and "Section 504" assure educational provisions for your child's disorder. IEP is short for the *Individualized Education Program* that you and school personnel will set up for your son.

A key to parenting an ADHD child, and to parenting boys in general, is acceptance of the way he is wired. It's time to stop judging our boys against models that don't include him. When we ground ourselves in feelings of love and respect for boys, our very presence will be a form of activism.

Exceptional Adults, Exceptional Boys

Now it's time for the good news. Boys are in the limelight in the educational field. As educators attend to the unique gifts and needs of boys, schools are getting better. We have been heartened to see the immense amount of research being conducted on behalf of our boys. We've seen educational innovators and teachers dedicated to making a difference. Our boys' fifth- and sixth-grade teachers stand out in my mind because they loved boys, and our boys felt that. One was a tough and funny woman who could match any boy with her teasing skills, and the other was a nurturing goddess who every boy fell in love with. Our boys still talk about both of them and light up when they see them from time to time.

In discussing what helps kids overcome adversity, psychologist Julius Segal wrote: "one factor turns out to be the presence in their lives of a charismatic adult—a person from whom they gather strength. And in a surprising number of cases, that person turns out to be a teacher." When your teacher calls, open yourself to the amazing collective resources available to your boy. He'll feel the love.

The Least You Need to Know

- Normal boys can start out "behind" in academic areas like reading because their brains develop other specialties first.

- Zero tolerance policies are unhelpful and often misused against boys.

- Fear of his aggression can hurt him; showing him how to manage aggression helps him.

- ADHD is a disorder of self-control, and early diagnosis protects affected boys from being mislabeled as lazy, defiant, or stupid.

- Parents of boys need the strength and confidence to guide rather than extinguish "boy behavior."

- One exceptional adult, often a teacher, can rock his world.

Chapter 9

Sports 'R Boys—or Not?

In This Chapter

- ◆ The sporting news
- ◆ Keeping the focus on staying fit, not having one
- ◆ Playing on a team or going solo
- ◆ The call of the wild

"I rule at Mastodon hunting!"

No doubt our male ancestors delighted in glorying over their accomplishments on the field of play. Naked Greeks organized to launch the Olympics eons later. Today, we spend billions of dollars and hours reveling in sporting events, events that feature mainly very large *boys*.

Hopefully fitness and fun come with sports participation. Parents who become involved in sports with their sons increase the chances that their sons will continue to pursue healthy organized physical activity.

However, participation by parents, while important, is not enough. Parents need to model emotional stability and guide their sons through the wins and the losses. So let's take a look at what's sporting and not-so-sporting about boys and sports.

The Value of Sports

There is plenty of value in sports. While practicing fundamentals, a boy's body teaches itself. Muscle memory instills fundamental skill and a sense of grace. A trained athlete really does "make it look easy." At their best, sports produce healthy minds and healthy bodies. At their worst, sports reduce boys to statistics, crushing some boys and inflating the egos of others. It is up to parents to emphasize what is truly valuable about sports.

Getting Coached

If your son is a high school sprinter, he'll want to begin the race crouched down with his feet resting against starting blocks. How far should his feet be apart in the blocks to run the fastest race?

Sixteen inches.

Coaches know this. Parents have no clue. And since the goal of the race is to win, the boy with the best coach has a distinct advantage. Listen to Olympic athletes after they win a gold medal. After God and maybe their parents, the coach gets the credit. "Thanks, Coach, I couldn't have done it without you."

While a few aspire to be up on the latest sports scholarship, most coaches of youth sports don't read the *Journal on the Philosophy of Sport*. They do, however, work a long day at home or the office and then drop everything to throw the equipment into the van to make it, just in time, to the field. Youth coaches are, for the most part, kind-hearted parents who remember the joys of growing up when some kind-hearted parent coached them.

With the advent of the Internet, they have also become much better coaches. A video of teaching the in-step soccer kick to kids is very popular, as is a video on the importance of core body training in golf.

In the end, a good coach knows (or learns) the sport, wants to teach, and understands and empathizes with boys. To be the most effective, a youth coach needs to be aware of the differences and capabilities of boys at different ages.

You can educate a boy on how to take instruction, that is, "to get coached." The first thing to help your boy recognize is that all coaches deserve *respect*. Coaches are not getting paid anything or very much. They are volunteering their time. They are adults; they are leaders; they are not servants shepherding your son's imminent ascent to glory.

Toolbox

The YMCA guides rookie basketball coaches with several directives, including: teach the skills and tactics of basketball to the best of your ability; help your players learn the rules and traditions of basketball; and so on. The final directive: make it fun.

Respect means listening when the coach is talking and hustling when the coach calls a huddle. Having said that, boys are there to have fun, and fun includes acting goofy, so there's a fine line between "goofing off" and just having fun. He can join the Marines later if you want him to learn to march.

Assuming your son is polite enough, then, the boy needs to learn to share the coach. Time for personal instruction is limited. Encourage your son to learn on his own, too, and help him between coaching sessions to reinforce what he is learning. It's amazing how a simple adjustment can reap huge rewards for boys in sports.

One summer night, our younger son was playing baseball in a fifth-grade league and I (Barron) was helping coach the team. I gave a boy on the other team who had a truly tortured swing a couple good tips. The boy swung, connected with the ball (somewhat), and ran toward first. He was safe. It was apparently the first time the boy had ever hit a baseball in a game. For me, the look on the young boy's face, the pride in the way he took a breath and held his chest out to the world, was the reward. As the commercial says: priceless. Coaching kids after a

Toolbox

If there is one tool that has advanced communication between coaches, boys, and parents, it has to be e-mail. No more shuffling off to the game to see if the rain really did cancel the game. Parents of athletes: *check your e-mail!*

tough day at the office is an excellent remedy for cynicism and age-related grumpiness.

Also, help your son by encouraging him to *ask* for help. The coach might be able to meet you early or stay late at the field provided he has enough advanced notice. Boys do not ask enough, either because they are too embarrassed or they literally do not understand they that can *approach* a coach and ask.

Physical Identity

There is no getting around the fact that popular culture celebrates athletes. A boy who excels at a sport using superior coordination and ability receives plenty of praise. Conversely, boys with average or worse ability observe this praise and can and often do feel diminished or ignored.

To lessen the impact of this reality, continue to praise your son's other abilities while honestly acknowledging that some kids are better (at least right now) at the sport he is involved in. While your son may roll his eyes at the "You know, Michael Jordon got cut from his basketball team sophomore year" line (It's true!), parents need to continue to emphasize fun *and* practice, practice *and* fun. This will help your son make incremental and steady progress. Chart his statistics if they are improving to show him how.

Naturally, of course, many boys "catch up." In my (Barron's) family, males run slight in build at least until middle teen years, when they really fill out. As adults, the males run heavier than average. A 40-year-old family album looks like an early advertisement for people in need of heart medicine and a high colonic. (You can skip your own depressing family history while pointing out to your son that he is actually bigger, stronger, or faster than you ever were as a kid.)

Your son has only known you as a *giant*. Show him pictures of you as a boy. From that he'll be able to picture himself as a man and draw comfort from the knowledge he won't always be the shortest or least coordinated kid on his team.

Keep Out!

Cal Ripken Jr., who played shortstop for the Baltimore Orioles, holds the record for most consecutive games played by any major league baseball player: 2,632. He encourages parents of young athletes to give the games back to the kids and not to add pressure because there is already enough pressure on kids. Sandwich mild critical pointers for your son, if you are offering any, between more emphasized positive comments.

Yes! We Won!

Many younger sports teams do not keep score. These no-score leagues, often played by early elementary-aged boys, emphasize fundamentals and the joy of playing. Parents justifiably pat themselves on the back for trying to reduce the pressure on the kids to *win, for the love of God, just win!* Who wants to dump that on the shoulders of a seven-year-old?

The thing is, the kids know *exactly* who won and who lost the last game. Does this mean we should keep score in these leagues? No. Just realize this: your son already understands "winning" to a great extent. He does *not* understand proper batting stance, blocking patterns, or how to steady up while facing the basket, but he does know who won the last game he played.

If your son says, "We won!" in a no-score league, tell him. "Yes, you did." Then—but not every time—ask: "How's that feel?" Help him label the feeling so he can identify his joy/exhilaration/relief/fun.

As a matter of good manners, though, an overly effusive, "We kicked their butts!" may require some direction against taunting or some guidance to not boast in front of players from the other team. Teaching your son some "class" while helping him enjoy every second of a "sweet win" is important, too.

Losses and Resilience

Losing sucks.

Yep, son, it does. At this point in any conversation after a tough loss, your son and you can hopefully just sit quietly and move on past the initial disappointment in a few minutes. The sting will last for a bit, but the wave of sadness will travel past.

The risk, though, is that a parent will not show, by his conduct, how to *deal* with a loss. A particularly tough loss may compel a mental grand jury to immediately indict the usual suspects:

◆ **The ref.** While fans have a God-given right to complain about bad officiating at a paid and adult event, teaching your son that a single bad call is what kept his team from winning will do more damage than good. You can tell him that "Yes, the ref blew the call, and that really is unfair because the ref is supposed to do a better job."

Toy Box

On why the New York Yankees lost the 1960 World Series to the Pittsburgh Pirates, Yogi Berra, catcher for the Yankees, said "We made too many wrong mistakes."

At some point, perhaps not at the exact moment your son is complaining, you can point out to him that a game is nine innings/two halves/four quarters long and bad calls usually even out by the end of the season. At his next practice, encourage your son to concentrate on how he can improve during the other 99.9 percent of the time when the ref is calling the game correctly.

◆ **His lousy teammates.** This indictment is a boyhood favorite. "If we didn't have Joey, we could win." Well, it may very well be true that Joey needs help, but you are trying to raise a boy into a man and not a half-man who learns to complain every time something goes wrong. Your boy needs to learn compassion, forgiveness, and especially in sports, the value of a teammate.

If your son insults in a hateful way or looks at a teammate with hatred, he is helping guarantee failure by the same teammate. If the teammate fails, your son's team fails, too. The "failure" is your son's "failure."

Now is the time to show your child that he can be part of the solution and that he does not have to be a passive recipient of what he sees as impending doom. As a teammate, your son can *encourage;* he can stand next to and with a weaker teammate; he can lead his team by example. Teach him to try to smile through the tears so that he can enjoy playing a *team* game, because every team he is on for the rest of his life will have a player who does not perform well—and he could be *that player.* In the end, this lesson, that he can survive and find joy in times of trouble, will be one of the most valuable lessons you can teach your son.

♦ **The coach.** Coaches make mistakes, and your son may tell you he would have done something different. Usually this involves your son going in at the critical time in the game to provide what surely would have been the winning basket. Instead, the coach blah, blah, blah. Yes, son, coaches make mistakes, but that is not your job. And you can be pretty sure the coach knows which mistakes he made.

Some boys do have excellent ideas, and you can encourage your son to discuss his thoughts in private with the coach. For example, maybe he really thinks his basketball team would do better switching defenses. You want him to feel comfortable respectfully approaching adults. He needs to communicate with his coach without recrimination, though, in a spirit of enthusiasm for the game. If he does this, the coach will likely smile and respond in kind.

The Success of Joy

Good and bad seasons come and go. The years roll on. In the end, your son will have a difficult time remembering all his teammates or his win-and-loss records. What he will retain is what you teach him about persistence, discipline, forgiveness of self and others, and a love of playing "the game."

If you want your son to see a grown man play a professional sport with the spirit of a ten-year-old, find a video clip of Brett Favre, the successful quarterback of the Green Bay Packers. When Brett Favre is playing, he is smiling, laughing, executing, running, passing, getting crushed, getting back up, and often winning. He embodies the pure joy of playing sports and is a delight to watch on television. He wants to win, and win badly, but he *does not wait to feel good at the end of a winning game.*

Sports scientists correlate one consistent factor with long-term success in athletes. The most successful athletes in the long run are those who have the most fun! Athletes who take joy in their sport will tend to stay committed, stay disciplined, and care about their performance. Why wouldn't they? They get to do something they enjoy.

The Overvaluing of Sports

It would be hard for society to place any more emphasis on sports. College coaches earn multimillion-dollar salaries; ESPN is a mainstay of entertainment; and parents of boys easily ask, "What sport do you want to play?" not "Do you want to play a sport?" On the flip side, there is an *epidemic* of childhood obesity, a worrying medical condition. Combined with the rise of video games and the Internet as primary sources of boyhood leisure time, signing your son up for soccer or swimming may be just what he needs to stay physically fit.

Toolbox

According to the NCAA, the NBA will eventually draft only 3 high school basketball players out of every 10,000.

To keep your son's focus on *fitness* for sport while enjoying the ups and downs of his favorite team, parents themselves need to value fitness. Observing a pot-bellied father work himself into a rage Sunday after Sunday while watching the NFL is a sure signal to any boy that sports are important and fitness is meaningless.

Of course, it's wonderful to share a loathing for a *rival* to your favorite team. I (Barron) have instilled in our two sons a "must hate" relationship with the New York Mets baseball team. But our boys know that this a playful side of their father bred from the Chicago Cubs' defeat at the hands of the dreaded Miracle Mets of 1969. It's not a real hatred, of course, but a staged distaste, one that makes professional sports entertaining, something akin to booing the bad guy in professional wrestling.

Fitness and fun keep sports in focus.

When the Coach Needs Medication

I (Barron) recall assisting as a coach with a third-grade football team. The head coach was a former junior college coach who apparently believed that the louder you scream the easier it is for boys to hear. Even after a quiet word with the coach that he might want to tone it down, the coach ended the season reducing the running back's mother to tears when she showed up late with her son to the playoff game.

If you think your coach is going overboard, ask some other parents their opinion as well. Take time to observe the coach, and make sure you are not overreacting. If you feel the coach is acting abusively toward your son or other players, take along another person and talk to the coach privately. Speak plainly and talk about what you are experiencing. The coach will hopefully be willing to listen and modify his conduct. If not, talk to the commissioner or a leader of the organization sponsoring the sport, and ask for their help in tempering or replacing the coach.

Coaches are taught the power of positive coaching at the beginning of the season because it produces healthy boys who enjoy playing. And fun has been found to be an important factor in winning. A little yelling will always come with coaching; emotions can run high, and parents need to be understanding—just not so understanding that their son believes leaders can scream to get their way.

Boy Wisdom

Scream at him and you will raise a screamer.

—Harry H. Harrison Jr.,
Father to Son: Life Lessons on Raising a Boy

When It's Dad's Dream

Sons are perceptive and know when dads are interested in what they are accomplishing. They also know when dads are so wrapped up in their success that a good relationship with Dad appears to depend on whether they score or block or win. Emotions in fathers are magnified to boys, or at least, do not appear to fathers as they appear to sons. A dad who thinks he is just "making a point" may appear in a near murderous rage to a boy.

Fathers who display frequent intense emotions and spend time managing their son's sports for their own pleasure—while minimizing the impact of such an intense and overbearing focus—crush the joy out of playing for their son. We cannot overstate the potential for abuse in this area.

If you think your son isn't trying "hard enough," instead of jumping down his throat, see if you can actually talk about this issue without raising your voice or staring at him with hatred in your eyes. If not, you need to calm way, way down, and consider whether you are overinvested in his success and effort. It's his team, his sport, his failure and success, not yours. How's he going to have any fun with you screaming?

Even if your son is a real prospect with an entry on the professional scouting lists published by Scouts.com, all you'll do is take away the one thing proven to help athletes achieve a long term professional career: a love of preparing for and playing the game.

When Mom's Yelling Too Loud

What's true for dads is true for moms. Boys want to please their mothers, too. But Mom is more likely to yell in a way that is *protective* of her son. For example, she may cheer too wildly when he's at bat or overreact to a fair tackle just because her son is down. These understandable but "over the top" responses can embarrass him and even undermine his performance.

However, it's important to note that there are worse problems than too much enthusiasm. Being a consistent "no show" at his game can break a boy's heart.

When your son does poorly or his team loses, rubbing it in his face is cruel. Conversely, forcing a happy response to a loss or demanding that he "get over it" immediately is no help either. Usually, unhelpful responses come from trying too hard, a common trap for moms. Mirroring your son's disappointment is appropriate and healthy, and you can even try to lighten things up a bit, but balance it with common sense. If helping him feel better becomes more about *you*, he'll just feel worse. Sometimes the best response is to just walk alongside him and give him the five minutes he needs to change moods. He'll soon be telling you which fast-food place he wants to raid.

When He's Not Into It

Your boy may not want to play football, no matter how many times you regale him with stories of your high school championship victory. Certainly share your stories. They are wonderful, but they will not automatically draw out of your son a desire for playing football. Your son is unique. He likely has already surprised you with his skills.

> **Keep Out!**
>
> Do not shame your son into playing any sport. Unnecessary shame is the toxic ingredient in many father-son relationships and will push your son away from you at the very moment you are trying to get close.

If your boy does not want to play football or any sport right now, you can still help him understand the importance of fitness by exercising with him. (We discuss alternatives to sports in the next chapter.) Walking with your son is a real treat, because not only are you spending time together, but you're also giving him the space to access and share with you his innermost thoughts—something that takes time for boys.

Go Team!

The playground idea of "team" is understood because elementary-school kids pick teams for kickball or basketball. However, parents and coaches must help instill in boys the importance of "playing as a team," a concept akin to family.

Team Bonding

A teammate is loyal and helpful, works hard to please himself and his team, and lays down his personal chance for greater glory to help the team win. A teammate tries hard not to hatefully scorn an underper-forming teammate. (This "not hating" underperformers can be difficult for boys initially.) He goes out of his way to compliment a teammate. He also takes a tease from a teammate with good humor. A healthy boy can laugh at himself for screwing up, admit mistakes openly, but also forgive himself. He works hard to be ready to help his team the next time he is called on.

A boy who loves the game can, in the finest moments, express apprecia-tion for, and learn from, a particularly good play by an opponent.

Professional sports commentators discuss the importance of the *club-house atmosphere*. This is the prevailing mood of goodwill among team-mates that accompanies most championship teams. Your boy's efforts to act as a teammate and team leader will ensure that he, too, enjoys a positive clubhouse experience. You can assist by avoiding criticizing another player. Sowing discontent is destructive. You can acknowledge your son's disappointment, but do not inadvertently destroy the bond that will help his team succeed. This is particularly true if your boy is a star player.

So Many Choices

The variety of team sporting opportunities varies by location. Lacrosse is popular on the East Coast but generally unknown in the Midwest. ESPN and other cable channels expose boys to more sports than the three main activities we grew up with: football, basketball, and baseball. Ask your local YMCA coordinator and other parents for ideas.

Going Solo

Many boys would rather just run alone than depend on others to make a play. Consider the options for more singular sports before signing your hesitant son up for a team.

Solo for the Team

One option for self-starters is running. Track and field and cross-country are excellent choices, as are the winter sports of skiing, snowboarding, and cross-country skiing. Consider activities that he might want to do with you, too.

In West Virginia, kayaking and climbing schools are available, and boys participate in these mountain sports in regional and national competitions. Of course, what boy could resist at least trying surfing? (Hmmm, surfing, now if we could only move to Hawaii ....)

Competing Against Himself

One of the real benefits of a solo sport is the ability to measure improvement by keeping individual statistics. A runner who breaks his previous record by even one hundredth of a second knows the thrill that comes with reading the stopwatch. Great solo athletes learn to challenge themselves. Suggest your son chart his progress. Comment on his improvements, but avoid hovering.

Lifetime Sports

Golf, tennis, and bicycling are three sports boys can play almost their entire lives. If your son is strictly into team sports that have no commonly played adult counterpart, consider taking him out to the golf course or tennis court once in a while so that he can learn a sport, or two, that will accompany him as he ages.

Nature Sports

Sports that take boys outside are more than a pastime. Answering the call of the wild, whether you are hunting, hiking, or just enjoying the fresh air, may be just the thing to bring a lifetime of happy memories to your son.

Real Time Together

Fishing and hunting are two activities that boys and parents did together long before school athletics were organized in the early twentieth century. Surviving the harsh climate was the key. The added benefit was the chance to enjoy the outdoors together. Today, food is plentiful, but fishing and hunting draw millions of American boys and parents together in the woods and on the water. In some states, hunting (not just owning a gun) is a constitutional right. And, as many fishermen like to say, any day spent fishing is a success—even if you come home empty-handed—because it's better than a day spent behind a desk. This bumper-sticker truism is doubly true for parents who hunt or fish with their boy.

Of course, just spending active time together outdoors is a wonderful complement to life around the house. Our boys don't care for fishing (too bad for Barron), and would rather scramble up boulders, go canoeing, or just camp out and hike the mountains.

Safety First

An NRA safety course is an important first step for any boy who wants to hunt or shoot for sport. Many years ago, boys took their guns to school and had them held in the principal's office during the day. Then, the guns were retrieved after school so the boys could head out from there and go hunting. An innocent child approaching a school with a gun today would throw the school into lockdown. Teach your son responsible gun ownership, but more importantly, practice it yourself.

Your Values, His Values

Your son may enjoy hunting and fishing, or he may recoil at harvesting an animal for food. Do not insist that your son kill.

Toolbox _____

> If you want your son to join you outdoors, and he does not want to hunt or fish, consider buying him a camera so he can take pictures of (live) wildlife. Outdoor stores also sell inexpensive motion-activated cameras that affix to a tree in the forest. He can mount his "trophies" in frames. Of course, you could just take a nature walk together and both look for great camera shots to place in an outdoors photo album.

That your son would choose to disagree with hunting, knowing that you approve of it, indicates he is willing to think and act purposefully in his life. And that is what you want, a boy who does not blindly follow you but one who shows you enough respect that he will think and try to understand what you are saying and then express himself when he feels conflicted. It's a sign you are doing a good job with him.

The Least You Need to Know

◆ Research shows that boys who play sports with joy succeed.

◆ Teams succeed when boys learn that teammates support and defend rather than attack less-skilled players.

◆ Parents need to separate their own sports desires from their sons'.

◆ Individual sports are suited to boys who prefer to compete against themselves.

◆ Sharing nature-oriented activity, whether hunting, fishing, canoeing, or hiking, builds skill as it builds your relationship with your son.

Chapter 10

Skills Beyond Sports

In This Chapter

- Training for brains
- My son, the artiste
- Being prepared with martial arts
- Cool and confident with others

Boys' Life is a magazine for Boy Scouts. The publication included in earlier years real life adventures, told in comic book format, about boys who risked their lives to save others. For me (Barron), it was a great read sitting around doing nothing on a boring afternoon.

In 2002, the Centers for Disease Control and Prevention conducted a national survey of organized physical activity among youth aged 9 to 11. Only 38.3 percent of boys in the week prior to the survey had participated in organized activity, while 80.5 percent had enjoyed free-time physical activity. This is surprising, given the year-round emphasis on organized sports. It also means plenty of boys are looking for something to do that does not involve being driven to a game.

In Chapter 9, we discussed how sports can build skills and confidence; in this chapter, we address what boys can do other than sports. We take a look at the arts, scholastic competitions, Boy Scouts, and other worthwhile pastimes. We also discuss social and emotional skills that help boys thrive.

Brain Competition

Of course, all competitions require brains. A gymnast uses a highly refined kinesthetic intelligence, or body knowledge, to achieve success on the high bar. Here, however, we look elsewhere and discuss traditional "brainiac" activities where strategic high wires require much less movement but very sharp thinking.

Chess

One of the more successful inner-city programs is chess for boys. The same skills boys use to survive on the streets apparently translate well to the chessboard as they use logic and pattern analysis to win a model-size war. The goal, of course, is to checkmate your opponent, pinning his king and causing his flag to fall. Chess is very popular with boys, as boys outnumber girls 9 to 1 in chess tournaments.

Chess is initially taught in a club format, with unskilled players being coached on the moves for each piece. Unrated players spar in after-school sessions that usually last an hour or so. Often, the chess coach is a parent.

> **Toy Box**
>
> Chessmaster 10th edition is essential software for boys learning to play chess. Josh Waitzkin, the subject of the excellent 1993 film *Searching for Bobby Fischer*, guides your son through this classic game.

Statewide and regional competitions are held on long days spent at a local venue, such as a gymnasium. The events are coed, though you'll see few girls. Tournaments are often divided into skill or age levels to give everyone a chance to compete.

The games from these competitions are rated. A tournament is a series of three to four head-to-head matchups. The kid who wins the most games wins the tournament, but if there is a tie, and often there is, the rating computer decides the winner based on some huge algorithm that no one understands or can explain.

A boy in elementary grades will most likely rate below 1,000, and better high school players rate below 2,000. The best players in the world rate around 2,400 and above. A grandmaster generally requires a rating of 2,500. The great Russian player Gary Kasparov achieved a rating of 2,851.

Homeschooled boys are often required to forego competing in sports at schools. They are not, however, excluded from chess tournaments. Chess events are an excellent opportunity for homeschooled boys and their parents to enjoy a day or weekend trip away from home.

Academic Competition

There are several academic competitions around North America. Not all competitions are national; some are just statewide or local. Check with the school, and ask other parents to recommend a competition. Then pick one that is suited to your boy and have him try it out.

The Scripps National Spelling Bee is national entertainment and the granddaddy of competitions. Started in 1927, it has been held every year except for a brief interruption during World War II. Kids from all over the country participate in local spelling competitions and work their way up to the national level. Any child can compete up through the eight grade or under 16 years of age. A newspaper sponsors each speller.

The final rounds are held in Washington, D.C., and are broadcast on ESPN and ABC. This competition was the focus of the compelling documentary *Spellbound*, which was nominated for an Academy Award in 2003. Of the 82 winners, 39 have been boys.

Odyssey of the Mind is an international academic competition that focuses on the creative process. Teams of five to seven students plan over weeks and months to solve problems. They compete at organized events. One original problem proposed by the founder Dr. Sam Micklus was for students to create a mechanical pie thrower. The program has grown beyond its roots in American industrial design, and now reaches children in some 24 countries.

Keep Out! _____

> Academic competitions are not a required activity, so parents need to be more careful with their approach. Your boy does not need yet another demand pressing down on him. If he does not take to the academic contest idea, find something else. Also, academic competitions often require extensive parental volunteer involvement. While volunteering, parents can easily slip from assisting, to helping, to managing, and finally to assuming control of what was supposed to be a boy-centered activity.

In 2008, children in kindergarten through second grade may choose to solve a challenge known as "Rude Awakenings" which requires teams to "create and present a humorous performance that includes a character that keeps waking up in a different time and/or place from where it fell asleep. This will happen at least three times before the character returns to where it started and something or someone stops the character from 'traveling' in its sleep. The performance will also include a pet, a helpful character, and narration."

Some real favorites for boys are the competitions offered by FIRST (For Inspiration and Recognition of Science and Technology). This nonprofit was founded by Dean Kamen, a brilliant and prolific American inventor who created the Segway Human Transporter and a portable dialysis machine.

In the FIRST LEGO League (FLL), the competition uses a product known as LEGO *Mindstorms*. This toyset is actually a sophisticated combination of LEGO building blocks, computer chips, software, motors, and sensors. Boys (and girls) generally build robots in teams to accomplish a set series of tasks on a tabletop landscape. This program has excellent trophies, too, which are made of LEGOs, of course.

The FLL is for 9- to 14-year-olds. The Junior FLL is for 6- to 9-year-olds, the FIRST Robotics Competition (FRC) is for high schoolers, and the FIRST Vex Challenge (FVC) is for high schoolers. Vex uses less-expensive equipment. Check out USFIRST.org for more info.

Toy Box _____

Some boys never stop playing with LEGOs. An entire subculture of child and adult robotics enthusiasts eagerly awaits any addition to LEGO *Mindstorms*. These folks trade programs and ideas over the Internet and develop increasingly sophisticated robots with parts anyone can buy at Toys 'R' Us. One can even solve a Rubik's Cube!

Speech and Debate

What is the number-one fear for Americans? Death? Disease? No, it's public speaking. And it's a safe bet your son does not want to get up in front of his class and give a presentation, either. For adults, the classic organization dedicated to developing public-speaking ability, an instrumental skill in a democratic society, is Toastmasters. For boys, speech and debate teams often serve this important function.

High schools usually offer speech and debate teams. In addition to statewide leagues, the National Forensic League hosts the National Speech and Debate Tournament. Events are varied and include dramatic interpretation, policy debate, humorous interpretation, and many others.

Your son does not need to aspire to discuss foreign policy behind a podium to enjoy speech or debate. He can take on a character, as in a solo play, and explore an alter ego. The opportunities are mindboggling.

An introverted boy may find speech and debate a great outlet. Having the podium and a receptive audience may actually make it easier for him to express himself than in less-structured social situations. Your quiet son just may surprise you when he has the floor.

Skills in the Arts

The disgraced and friendless Shakespeare desired "this man's art and that man's scope" in Sonnet 29. Art survives collapsed civilizations and is one measure of how societies are judged. The artist in society is paradoxically held in both low and very high esteem. A boy who is exposed to art, and educated about art, will be one who learns to richly appreciate beauty as well as subtlety, nuance, abstraction, and paradox. He may even find in himself a desire and talent to become an artist.

Musician

Music is the primary art form people buy. Boys respond to music at a very young age; some parents even play music to their baby in the womb. If you want your son to be a musician, piano is an early choice for instrument because of its broad use and ability to sound good on its own. Future Beethovens often begin music lessons in second grade. Why? Second-grade fingers are wide and long enough to reach the keys.

If you want to start your son earlier, the Suzuki violin method is famous for teaching very young boys. Boys as young as four years old learn to play "building blocks" of music with much repetition. His teacher may offer a variation on this idea.

Marching bands, jazz bands, chamber music groups, orchestras, and other music groups are offered after school. Encourage boys who are on the fence about what if anything to do in band to play percussion. Who doesn't like pounding on drums? (Earplugs, anyone?)

Voice is probably the easiest musical option for boys, as houses of worship often have a children's choir that helps kids get used to singing in a group and in front of an audience. Sometimes the choirs include hand bells, a very easy instrument to play in a group setting as each boy only has a few notes to play when starting out.

School choirs are very popular, with the midwestern states leading choir development in the United States. The school's winter concert (formerly Christmas concert) is often a highlight for choirs and real delight for parents. *Is that really my son up there, singing in harmony, on key, dressed in a white shirt and tie, with his hair combed? Where's the camera?*

Actor

For us, watching our younger son intone his two lines in *A Christmas Story* after taking him to play practice for weeks was really a treat.

The nature of child acting is that everyone pretty much starts as a spear-carrier until he learns the ins and outs. A spear-carrier learns staging, props, timing, and a host of other important elements of live theater. There is no chance the company's production flops because your newbie can't remember a 20-line soliloquy. Boys who "act" may also learn by being exposed to costume and set design, lighting, audio, playwriting, directing, singing, production management, marketing, and so on.

Initial auditions for productions can be a test of nerves, as only a few spots are often open in each play. Try to be realistic in your assessment of your son's talents and ask questions of the director and other parents before taking your son to a first audition. But be persistent: eventually the boys who have a strong desire to act find a way to contribute.

Actors, surprisingly, are often introverts. Boys who prefer one-on-one time with friends, and who like solitude, frequently enjoy acting. Though this sounds counterintuitive, acting allows introverts to inhabit a personality different from their more protected inner selves. Just ask Clint Eastwood, an icon of American male identity. He describes himself as an introvert.

Professional actors often say they act because they cannot think of doing anything else. It is a calling of sorts. Perhaps your boy is hearing an important call too faint for your ears.

Boy Wisdom

Tom Felton plays Draco Malfoy, the evil boy every one loves to hate in the *Harry Potter* movies. In a 2002 interview with the BBC, Tom explained how he becomes so despicable on camera: "I used to think about things to get me angry. I have three older brothers so I did a lot of thinking back to when I was younger. Also, I just think of Draco and he gets me in the right mood. He just keeps getting worse and worse."

Artist

Toddler boys play with an infinity of objects as they explore their environment. Moms and dads can help develop these tactile and visual senses by engaging youngsters in water painting, clay making, and seasonal decorating. Modern craft stores launch a thousand Picassos a day with their cascade of craft supplies.

Truly exceptional artists often display talent at a young age. Boys who are given the opportunity to create depend on a stream of supplies, even if it is the unprinted backs of paper from your printer. Nurturing an early or developing gift will be a source of great joy.

At the age of three, our older son once confronted his father tossing out a few masterpieces. Indignant at the affront to his art, the boy demanded that we keep all future artwork at hand. Dad agreed to keep the inventory until the boy started school and dutifully stored it in several bags in the garage rafters. One of his pieces, an impressionistic painting of sunflowers in a vase, has earned a place on our dining room wall. When an artist friend stopped by one day, we asked her if she could guess the name of the painter. She studied it and asked, "Cezanne?" Good thing we saved his rejects.

What your boy saves is a clue to what he values. Writers save journals from childhood; nature lovers save unusual leaves and rocks; artists save their art.

In later years, boys can attend art camps or summer school programs and even work as volunteers at the local museum. Some schools have little arts curriculum. Check with your school to see what art education your son is receiving, if any at all.

Writer

Stereotypes of writers often include images of darkness and despair: the recluse, driven to a typewriter (now computer) by an uncaring society, condemned to spend days pickling his liver and staining his hands with tobacco, while desperately trying to capture on paper how hopeless the world has become. This image is complete bunk; there are just as many healthy writers as unhealthy ones. Writers tend to be imaginative, self-directed, and observant—seeing their lives through the lens of story. They are often introverted, which means they need time alone to recharge and are likely to be thoughtful about their communications. This does not preclude them from having close friends, broad interests, or a joyful life.

The satirist David Sedaris once became so frustrated with trying to teach students how to write that he made them all bring cigarettes and a glass of liquor to class. While he wanted those props, your son will not require them (hopefully!).

Your boy writer does need a place to write, such as a desk in a quiet place in the house. He will want a journal to write in. Early journals are, for aged writers, a profound source of material. Encourage your son to discuss the books he reads. A library card will be the golden ticket to a lifetime of literature. Encourage him to explore poetry, write for the school newspaper, and write for the stage. I (Barron) still enjoy the memory of writing a fourth-grade, one-page, three-act play about elves on strike at the North Pole.

Discipline and Survival

One of the hardest skills to pick for boys is the ability to delay gratification. Whether it is waiting to sit down to eat at the dinner table, taping *Lost* so they can get their homework done, or accepting that six-pack abs require an ounce-by-ounce approach to building muscles, boys must acquire these skills to manage their lives as adults. Here are some thoughts on how you can instill all-important discipline in your son's life.

Keep Out!

I (Barron) have represented hundreds of men accused of crimes. Repeat offenders, and there are many, evince a profound unwillingness to delay gratification. Thus clients appear in court in their twenties and thirties with several children, often by different mothers. One notorious case in 2007, not my own, involved a defendant who at sentencing admitted to expecting the imminent arrival of six children by six different mothers. The damage to society caused by boys who grow up without boundaries to keep them safe, or demands that make them work to succeed, is immeasurable.

Boy Scouts

In 1976, when I (Barron) was 14, I traveled on a train to the Philmont Scout Ranch in New Mexico. I learned to shoot a black powder rifle, helped keep the group from missing a trail, and missed a mountain music show because it was my turn to wash the dishes, which I did, in the rain. I also earned the right to wear a special belt buckle for climbing Tooth of Time Mountain. All these memories flood back after thirty-some years.

Your son can enjoy similar lessons and memories with a scout troop near you. Scouts still earn merit badges and can start as Cub Scouts as early as the age of seven.

Boy Scouts can be overwhelming. The Handbook details so much that it's easy for a boy to become immobilized by the sheer magnitude of what he can do in Boy Scouts. Who wouldn't want to go to an ocean-sailing camp, climb mountains, or go to an international jamboree? They all beat going to Target again with your parents.

> **Toolbox**
>
> The Scout Law: a Scout is trustworthy, loyal, helpful, friendly, courteous, kind, obedient, cheerful, thrifty, brave, clean, and reverent.

Help your son take the experience piece by piece. Find him a uniform. Help him set up a timeline to complete his merit badges. Put the troop meetings and camping trips on the calendar. Once he gets going, he'll become less dependent on you. He'll "Be Prepared" to take on the next challenge.

Martial Arts

Boys come with an extra gear. And parents of boys and girls will easily attest to the near constant physical motion of young boys in particular. Boys, who seem to run in fifth gear nearly all the time, drive their parents to distraction, while the parents drive their sons to the emergency room over and over! What to do! What to do?

For those of you who grew up in the 1970s, you may remember the song "Kung Fu Fighting" on the radio, *Kung Fu* with David Carradine on TV, and the homage paid to the late Bruce Lee through the infusion of even more martial arts movies after Lee's death in 1973 at the age of 32.

Parents of rambunctious boys in the Disco Days found that martial arts provided excellent activity for their sons. That choice is still valid today. The ratio of boys to girls in martial arts is 3 to 1. Martial arts teach boys to control when and how to expend energy. The discipline of the training, controlled movement, chosen defensive and/or offensive aggression, and respect for teachers, are invaluable skills for boys to learn.

Martial arts training helps boys gain confidence and discipline—plus less fear when confronted on the playground by older and bigger boys. Boys who are trained are able to take a tease and give one out in a confident, strong, playful spirit. (See Chapter 11 for more on teasing.) Martial arts training instills mettle into boys that others perceive. A trained boy can more easily engage in horseplay and banter without letting the teasing escalate into mean-spirited punching. This is even more important for boys who are overly timid or slight in build who become inviting targets for bullies.

Oriental in origin, forms of martial arts come from Okinawa, Japan, Korea, China, and other countries: karate, jujitsu, tai kwon do, and so on. It is important to look for a good teacher who has a comprehensive understanding of one form of martial arts and an appreciation for the others, too.

Before investing time and money into any class, consult other parents and visit the facility, the "dojo." For a quality experience look for these signs: classes observable by parents; classes driven by adults, not too-young instructors; CPR/first aid certifications posted; good hygiene of participants and at the facility; regularly scheduled and completed classes; and an emphasis on the track record of teachers, not free uniforms.

If you feel pressured to pay extra fees and "test" your son frequently, go somewhere else. Also, quick promotion to high rank is a sign that cash is the emphasis and not character development.

Soon young "Grasshopper" will be snatching quarters from your hand.

Toolbox

Check out the United States National Karate Foundation at usankf.org to learn how to choose a good martial arts school. This organization is a member of the United States Olympic Committee.

Social and Emotional Skills

Parents often feel at a loss as to what to do with a boy who seems lost. A friendless boy, the new kid in town, the odd duck, all can be helped with some modeling by parents. Social and emotional skills can be taught. Here are some ideas.

Conversation

Boys commonly have no interest in striking up conversation with relatives or new people. "Don't talk to strangers" can be misinterpreted, though, as "don't talk at all." While children need to be respectful of adults and not interrupt, too often boys feel uncomfortable engaging adults in what adults perceive as "normal" conversation.

The most successful pick-up line is "hi." While you don't want to teach your five-year-old how to hit on the IHOP waitress, he can learn simple greetings and social graces.

Waitress: "Hi."

Boy: silence

Waitress: "Cat got your tongue?"

Boy: (Thinking: Cat? I don't see a cat) Silence

Waitress: "Don't you worry, darling, we'll fix you up with some nice pancakes with a smiley face."

Boy: looks at Mother uncomfortably, more silence

A boy who can simply say "hi" or "I'm well, how are you?" will be miles ahead when it comes to navigating in the large, adult spaces of stores, restaurants, and theme parks.

If you want, role-play with your son: pretend you are going to a restaurant or visiting the dentist. This is a form of systematic desensitization to a common social fear. A polite and engaging boy can enjoy his interactions with adults and his peers, and the world can become more of an adventure and less a test of survival. Lessening common social fears will reduce the risk of social phobia, life-altering behavior that impacts his ability to function.

Being a Friend

While we discuss stage-specific development in other chapters, your son can make friends more easily with a few helpful suggestions from you.

Friends forgive. Boys can be mean to each other, say stupid things, and stomp off in a big huff. Boys are pretty capable of surviving these episodes on their own, and letting your son "sort it out" himself usually works the best.

There are "friends," though, that parents have a sixth sense about; sometimes a boy does not seem in tune with your son's group of friends or seems overly cruel. This surly kid may keep bugging your son to play, and your son won't know what to do. Most importantly, your son needs the skills to say to an unfriendly friend: "I don't want to play with you because you aren't very nice. You (complain a lot, hit too much, always try to get your way)."

Once your son realizes that he does not have to pretend "to be nice" all the time and that he can actually be honest with his feelings and fairly polite in delivering the news, he'll gain a much greater strength in his friendships. He'll also gain an important leadership skill. The surly kid may come around quickly, as well, after he is done pouting, and realize that acting like a jerk is a fast track to boredom and loneliness.

Hmmm. Just like adults.

At the Dance

Dancing. Yikes! "No, thanks; don't want to feel that vulnerable." While a boy won't say it in such a manner, that's what he means. He also means "I have no idea how to dance."

The only sure way to encourage a boy to dance is to make it fun. How to do that will depend on the boy. It may take Mom cranking the music and dancing with him—young boys welcome the opportunity to be active and silly with Mom. It may take some coaching from an older sister who's willing to hold back on the brutal teasing. It may take friends learning a line dance they can all do together on a Friday night. It may take classes.

A natural way to initiate boys into the culture of dance is through large multigenerational events such as wedding dances. Adults love to get kids in the mix at these events, so he'll have plenty of dance partners. And there are few experiences that top the opportunity to dance with the bride. It's also great for him to see older males having fun on the dance floor. Street dances and community festivals also provide opportunities for low-pressure dancing. In south-central Minnesota, polka radio stations play all day, and kids and adults dance polkas at big gatherings.

In most cases, boys do just fine by attending the dance with friends. They'll help him feel less alone with his fear of making a complete fool of himself, or they might all become dancing fools. Much will depend on how the dance is handled. Our oldest boy loved his first school dances because the DJ got everyone out on the floor and led them through the moves. Because nobody was singled out and there was no pressure to pair up, the boys could do what they were there to do: dance!

The Least You Need to Know

- ◆ Boys enjoy and dominate at brainy competitions such as robotics and chess.

- ◆ Art, music, writing, and acting are excellent nonsports activities for boys.

- ◆ Boys learn discipline and survival skills while having a blast in Boy Scouts and martial arts.

- ◆ Social skills such as conversation and dance, and the emotional strength to confront difficult friends, allow boys to thrive.

Chapter 11

Boys and the Art of Teasing

In This Chapter

◆ Why boys tease each other

◆ Teasing—or bullying?

◆ A class in giving and taking a tease

◆ Past tease

"Boys will be boys."

Such goes the classic line dismissing all mischief and minor trouble boys get into. For boys, boundary testing, games of king of the hill, shoulder slugging matches, and ferocious screaming all testify to a fundamental character element of aggression.

Boys are and will be aggressive. Aggression manifests itself in teasing. As parents, it is very important that we do not underestimate the profound impact teasing has on boys.

What academics call "pro-social teasing" is playful and welcomed by boys. Antisocial teasing is intended to be hurtful and is the kind parents and teachers try to squelch.

Why Do Boys Tease?

Boys who play well together find some equilibrium in their actions and words. A natural economy develops, and boys find comfort just being together. Before the ease with each other settles in, though, boys naturally want to get comfortable with their new companions. Teasing is the crucible from which boys' comfort with each other is forged whether it is comfort in use of language, choice of activity, or distribution of power.

Toy Box _____

Teasing was alive and well in the ancient Norse culture. In one old poem, a mortal, Loki, insults a god, Bragi:

> "In thy seat art thou bold, not so are thy deeds,
> Bragi, adorner of benches!
> Go out and fight / if angered thou feelest,
> No hero such forethought has."

Teasing a guy for "riding the pine" in the middle of a game is apparently one of the oldest teases in history.

Friend or Foe?

Men still shake hands as a form of greeting and to indicate they mean no harm. What do boys do? When you observe boys, you'll notice they'll check each other out first. "Weird clothes? No. Check. Weird expression? No. Check. (Note: covered in dirt does not qualify as weird.) Mean eyes? No. Check. Whew. Okay. Not a complete dork, weirdo, or bully."

Now it's on to some very small conversation.

Boy #1: "Hey."

Boy #2: "Hey."

Ahh. From such little acorns do friendships grow.

Once the threat level drops, boys will then relax to the point of being willing to tolerate each other's presence or, at least, won't pointedly ignore each other. There will be a rhythm that allows them to enjoy a mutually observed activity together.

Dominance

No parent wants his or her son to be *dominated*. The word is sooo ominous. It conjures images of the Eye of Mordor looking down over Frodo in *The Lord of the Rings*. Yet the concept is less foreboding in real life. Your son's group of friends will naturally identify the skills each member possesses. Some boys are faster, others better planners, and still others are the "brains." How well he can "roughhouse" will also determine your son's role in his social group. This playful wrestling is generally preceded by a generally playful battle of wits in the form of teasing.

Imagine several ten-year-olds playing a video game. Mike handles the controls, and Chris and several other friends are watching the action when Mike makes a mistake in the game.

Chris says to Mike, "You suck."

Mike is either going to admit his weakness, tease back, or attack. Very confident boys who are comfortable with each other already will admit they are weak at things without fearing a loss of status. Boys who are getting to know each other will generally tease back to retain some status: "You could never beat this level."

If Mike cannot come up with any comment, he may just attack, in a semi-playful way, pushing or faking a punch, to show he can defend himself.

This back-and-forth half-playing allows each boy to establish how far he can go with making demands on his friends. Boys usually know when they are pushing too much and taking advantage of a weaker boy. The parenting challenge is instilling in a boy a willingness to playfully avoid being dominated while teaching the same boy not to act overly selfish or, worse, cruel.

Unfortunately, if Mike runs away or acts too timid, he will invite further teasing, and the compound effect of Mike's timidity might ostracize him from the group. The other boys may choose not to be around him simply for the fact that he is not following the social rules.

Boys just want to have fun and get along, if they can. Failing to teach your "Mike" how to take and give a tease in a situation like this would be akin to withholding from him the very food he needs to thrive.

Boy Wisdom

Men ... form groups for purposes of defense, aggression, and war ... [they] tend toward larger social groups than is true of women ... and these groups are often organized around well defined purposes or tasks.

... Cooperation is needed to maintain the coalition, and competition emerges from attempts to increase individual status within the dominance hierarchy of the coalition. Once established, the dominance hierarchy facilitates the social cooperation needed for coalitional competition.

—David Geary and Mark Flinn, "Sex Differences in Behavioral and Hormonal Response to Social Threat: Commentary on Taylor et al.," 109 *Psychology Review* No. 4 (2002)

Humor

Playing the dozens is an African-American tradition of competitive insulting, and Caribbean and Arab cultures have other similar traditions. The American version centers around better and better insults about another boy's mother:

> "Your mother is so dumb, she sits on the TV and watches the couch."

Some day-to-day counter-teases are simply and elegantly shortened to "your mother."

Humor is grease for social wheels. When interaction among men in a group becomes tense, humor allows the tension to deescalate while permitting those involved to save face. Insults may lead to real fighting, but more often they lead to playful wrestling around boys, or among men, to a quick laugh that lets everyone get back to enjoying themselves.

> **Toy Box** _____
>
> Comedians need to shut down hecklers and are masters at quick insults. At a Rodney Dangerfield concert, a heckler asked Rodney if he was still a virgin. Rodney's reply was immediate, and in the grand tradition of casting aspersions on the sexual proclivities of the target's female relatives:
>
> "Ask your sister."

Boredom

Boys know that a quick way to entertain themselves is to challenge another boy to a teasing match. Also, how many times do boys go provoke a sister for the sheer pleasure of it? "He's picking on me!" is the lament of all siblings, but the shrill cry of the long-suffering sister is as well known to parents as the mewling of a hungry infant.

Boys can be redirected or simply disciplined for these attacks. Usually, the sister has developed a defense system (closed door), and if that fails, a punch to the boy's arm by the sister tends to set things right. Beyond redirection and discipline, parents can also simply assert that the insult was not a very good one and go into critique mode. That will often shock a boy into finding another activity.

Who Teases?

Not every boy teases, but in general most boys develop a sense of what teasing is from watching others and from observing popular culture. What would Hollywood write for many sitcoms if male-dominated insult-centered banter were banned?

Part of the Language

North Americans, for better or worse, appreciate the ability to tease and tease well. Conversely, the ability to take a tease imports a well-rounded character, a boy who is ready for the rough-and-tumble world outside the home.

Boys raised in a "cloistered" setting, such as boys reared in a home-school environment, those isolated from other children, or those raised with parents unwilling to tolerate teasing in any form, may act awkwardly around and appear odd to other children. Boys whose lives lack the language of teasing are at greater risk for bullying and social isolation.

Teasing vs. Bullying

Teasing is, at heart, a playful form of mocking. A boy may tease for domination, as well, acting out some deeper social instinct, or a boy may tease because he is bored out of his mind and wants to entertain himself. What better way than to pester a friend until he attacks, and the two can roll around on the ground in mock battle? The fact that aggression underlies teasing does not require parents to suppress teasing. To do so would be to inhibit the normal social development of a boy.

Parents who want to allow their boy to playfully tease also do not want to create a bully. What makes a bully? Parents tend to have a sixth sense about when teasing turns to bullying. In general, the body language of the boys in the encounter changes markedly. Eyes turn dark; punches start landing like it's an Ali-Foreman rematch; and the voice of each boy displays marked distress. The bullying has begun.

Toolbox

Pro-social teasing is more common than anti-social teasing; boys give out more anti-social teases than girls; and girls find teasing to be more aversive.

Worse are those instances when one boy is a certifiable bully as he appears calm and methodical in the way he brutalizes another boy either with words or conduct. These coldly dispassionate bullies are the worst; they belie a personality disorder that enjoys cruelty—perhaps not sociopaths, but genuine safety threats that need to be separated from your son immediately.

Boy Bullies vs. Girl Bullies?

Boys and girls bully in different ways. Boys tend to use physical aggression more than girls, while girls tend to use psychological torment, such as spreading rumors and making sexual comments. Bullying tends to be more verbal than physical for both genders. And contrary to popular belief, bullies are not particularly low in self-esteem or loners.

Adapting: Teaching Teasing

John Lennon sang "All we are saying, is give peace a chance." That's a nice sentiment, but it's not very useful to a boy who wants to avoid having his nipples twisted off in the locker room.

Boys need the skills to survive and thrive in an environment that values wit (comebacks), aggression, and rough play. Boys do not need to be our social experiments in passive resistance. After all, we're not the ones who risk getting the crap beat out of us because he can't figure out how to respond in a semi-normal fashion around his peers.

Teasers expect to be teased back. This is the social contract, like it or not. It is a norm of behavior for boys that allows other social interaction and trust relationships to build. Teasing is, essentially, a custom.

You teach your boy to chew with his mouth closed, cover his mouth when he coughs, shake a hand offered to him, and say "hello" when answering the phone. How strange would it be if your son picked up the phone and said nothing? Teasing is simply something parents need to teach.

Having said all this, there are many books decrying a "culture of cruelty" among boys. This book, however, is not a digression on gender politics. Boys can be very cruel to each other. Thankfully, trained teachers are confronting bullying on the playgrounds; parents are educating themselves about bullying; and resources are being directed to reduce the profound levels of violence in our culture.

Taking a Tease

So what should you teach about teasing?

First, help your son develop a sense of humor about himself. When your two- or three-year-old makes a mistake, the "oops, that's silly" or "are you being silly?" line will quickly teach your son that there is humor in error. A child who begins life with the understanding that the joke is sometimes on him will be in a better position to receive barbs later when other boys aim jokes at him directly.

Second, show your son that you can take a joke yourself. A parent who can handle a mild fat joke, take a shot about a bad dinner, or laugh when a boy points out he's been walking around with his fly open displays an attitude of self-assuredness and good humor.

Third, as a boy gets older, don't withhold your teases, but be mindful that you need to deliver teases playfully. A humorless tone from a parent may be interpreted simply as cruel humiliation.

If a boy resents a tease, back off. If you're hitting a nerve, get off it. Then talk about what your son is feeling. The teasing may help him access some genuine feelings of inadequacy or concerns that demand the teasing stop and the conversation begin.

Giving a Tease

A boy who appreciates humor about himself will no doubt start delivering the teases right back. If you want to teach a boy how to tease, pick on a "bad guy" action figure or save a good insult for a referee who misses a call in an NFL game. Everyone gets to insult the ref; it's a group activity!

Our second boy was learning the language of teasing and decided to write out an insult and give it to his father. He wrote: "Your domb." d-o-m-b. "You're *dome*" or "That's *dome*" has become a favorite family tease.

If your son comes up with a really good tease for you, acknowledge his wit. As the saying goes, the difference between the perfect word and a good word is the difference between lightning and a lightning bug.

> **NO GIRLZ ALOWD! Keep Out!**
> If a particular tease is worn out, make it off limits and tease the boy for being boring. No boy wants to be boring!

Just the Right Amount

When your son overdoes it (10 fat jokes in a row), you can playfully wrestle him down or just tell him "that's enough." He'll learn where your line is and then know when he's crossed it. He'll also recognize your body language and learn when to shut up. Of course, he'll also want to cross the line, and that will require patience as a parent. Provoking a parent can be fun.

Transcending Teasing

Teasing is a social custom that permits boys to relate well, while giving an outlet to natural aggression and a desire for dominance. Your son can learn when to tease and when not to tease. Teasing for boys, like a handshake for men, opens the door to meaningful communication.

Teasing, and Then What?

The skill of taking a tease and giving one will enable your son to engage with the other boys in an atmosphere of mutual comfort. Your son will then need to employ his other skills of sharing, listening, and cooperation to establish good friendships. Boys who tease can choose to bully as well. Parents need to intervene when a boy turns from playful to cruel. A boy needs to be able to recognize the boundaries, and parents must establish the boundaries, both for their boys and in their adult relationships.

The Value of Desire

"Concrete dense guys." That is one phrase that identifies men with a limited emotional range. With such lack of subtlety comes a lack of awareness of desire. Boys will often not articulate what they want but will act out in frustration. They just know they are mad.

A boy who teases about the same thing over and over may be expressing a desire that he has not fully identified. If a boy is stuck on an idea, sit down with him and talk about what he thinks of the person he is teasing. What does the other person think of your son? This conversation may uncover some desires your son cares about or real or imagined fears he is worried about.

Tease This Way

According to a study at the Stanford University School of Medicine in 2005, men differ from women in the way their brains experience humor. Women analyze and think more about cartoons and are surprised to find cartoons funny. Men don't analyze as much when they view cartoons and already expect them to be funny. This may explain the great mystery about why boys get Monty Python's absurd humor and girls think it's stupid. You can't think about it too much.

Teasing creates laughter, and laughter reduces stress; less stress, more fun is just the right prescription for boyhood.

The Least You Need to Know

- Teasing is a custom for boys.
- Being able to take and give a tease is an essential social skill for boys.
- Parents can teach a boy how to tease well.
- Playful teasing is not bullying.
- Boys don't exhaust time analyzing humor as girls do.

Chapter 12

Boys in the Middle

In This Chapter

- ◆ Pack of plenty
- ◆ Just saying no to girls
- ◆ Not quite grown
- ◆ The joyful goof

Middle school boys are an odd mix. They are full of energy and goofiness. One moment they shine; the next they seem to be possessed. Middle school teachers deserve combat pay.

Although sixth, seventh, and eighth grade are the grades most identified with middle school, some school districts keep kids in middle school or junior high on a seventh-, eighth-, and ninth-grade plan instead.

Boys aged 11 to 14 are still boys, big boys, but not quite young men. A parent of a boy in the middle begins to glimpse the young man inside.

The Boys' Club

Middle school boys have a distinctly male aroma as few girls are around to perfume the air. Boys in the middle definitely like their male companions, and the early middle school years are pretty much an all-boys event. Let's point some binoculars at these packs.

Running in Packs

One of the great joys of parenting is watching your son wander down the street in the company of a band of like-minded mischief-makers. An adventure of epic proportions takes hold in the minds of boys as they gather to scale a construction site dirt pile. Who can climb to the top and claim to be king of the world? That is, until the younger brother tackles him from behind and off they tumble. This play is vital to the development of a socially aware and competent man-to-be. But why do middle school boys run in packs?

There are several reasons, but the first is that it's fun! Boys this age tend to have a highly developed social life. Of course, for "social life," you must count a plan that requires all the boys to "meet at butt-cheek rock." A social group exemplified by the phrase "butt-cheek" is very much about fun.

Packs of boys in the 11-to-14 age group are more than happy to be left alone to pursue hours and days of uninterrupted leisure. A typical day for a boy this age would include a variety of video games, Ping-Pong challenges, and various attempts to hit another boy over the head with a pillow as hard as humanly possible.

Toolbox _____

At a recent funeral, three men eulogized their 74-year-old friend. They all remembered their days of running in a pack—a pack that started in grade school and lasted almost seven decades. Those men were eulogizing Barron's father. What we see when our sons run in a pack may very well be the start of a lifetime of love, caring, and friendships that will endure beyond our days.

Another reason is safety. The world is still a daunting place to be, especially when you've stepped away from the help of your superheroes. School playgrounds can not only be an immense source of fun but also a terrifying place to feel vulnerable. British school children in particular seem to report being terrorized on the playground. Here in North America, the bully lurks in the minds of children. Schools have done an admirable job in breaking the hold of elementary school bullies because principals and teachers educate and intervene more quickly than in years past. Thus, your child's playground experience is likely less frightening than yours was. This is, of course, completely dependent on your local school. Yet your son will choose to run with friends when he can because he knows he will feel much safer. Boys in the middle are also physically stronger and are more capable of hurting each other, while at the same time, are more likely to withhold expressing any hurt.

Boys need to learn to relate. Even homeschooled and protected children are exposed to group dynamics in larger families or at church. Humans are social creatures, some more than others, but boys tend to want to *do things* and want to do things together. Less emphasis is placed on talking and more on action. Active boys want to do active things, and the most active thing to do is often a group activity.

Groups demand some modest order, and those who choose to lead often impose order. When no adults are around, boys will sort themselves and generally seek some dominance order but still maintain an egalitarian flavor. Like-age boys will often let one boy lead, but only to a point. Most groups are not dominated in a bad way but simply led in a prosocial manner. Boys learn this socialization *without adults:* how to get along with each other, how to let others in the group have their way, how to assert their individual desires, and how to protect each other from threats outside the group.

It is very important to allow boys to run in groups without adults structuring the time. Nowadays, parents often spend way too much time organizing their child's life. Do you want him to get into Harvard? Then leave him *alone* so he can be *bored*. Your son's bored mind will soon turn creative, assuming *you* can stand the wait.

We all remember having to wait out the crying when our boys were infants. Now is not the time to answer the cry of the bored. Stand firm!

At most, suggest he go down the street or call a friend. Likely he will soon find a child who is equally bored, and they'll find two friends, and so on, and so on. Your son is now not bored but running in a crowd that has potential for greatness. That mountain will soon loom for all of them. A large pile of dirt must be climbed, and all the better when conquered by the local regiment.

Most parents don't have to worry about gangs, as in, my-son-needs-to-brush-up-on-the-federal-sentencing-guidelines-gangs. Certainly groups can promote mischief, but some mischief is normal and desirable. Children learn from mistakes. An old teacher of Tony Blair, England's former Prime Minister, once remarked something to the effect that the minister as a student was "averagely naughty, but not particularly wicked." Packs of boys playing together are a very good thing, a necessary, essential thing.

As parents, you need to monitor packs, preferably by talking with your son at snack time, during walks together, or during conversation at bedtime. These conversations will reveal the facts or hints that lead to the facts of group play that may be hazardous. A firm and gentle "you guys were lucky you didn't get hurt; you need to stay off the bulldozer/suspension bridge/_____, okay (boy nods)?" will usually do the trick—at least for a while.

We need to be vigilant about the real and common risks to boys (unsupervised water, traffic) as well as the real but more remote risks (perverts, kidnappers). Packs of boys may sometimes lead to trouble, but they will certainly lead to more confident, fun-loving, happy boys who value each other as well as their families.

Aversion to Girls

Because many early middle school–age boys display a profound dislike of girls, a "Girls Keep Out" sign is often affixed to the central theater of boyhood operations, the tree fort. Girls are *weird*. This is true to some extent—to your son. Girls are certainly different, and therefore weird to many young boys. Girls talk to each other—*a lot*. Girls look different: longer hair, weird jewelry, and, ooh, the smells, who needs that? Also, most boys on a playground reject any human who cannot throw a baseball: thus the cutting elementary school insult, you "throw like a girl."

Toolbox

Teach your son to throw like a boy. Have him grasp the ball in his dominant hand, and stretch out his ball hand even with his shoulder. Position his feet shoulder width apart, and point his opposite shoulder and foot at the target. He should look at you, his target, and throw—*not push*—the ball toward the target. Have him throw with force, snapping the wrist through. Demonstrate first and then have him try it, and remember to make it fun.

Many men admit later in life that girls were often better students and better athletes even in elementary school. But they also remember smarting at losing the girls vs. boys dodgeball game or getting beaten by a girl. In a perfect world, there is no shame in this. But boys want to feel they are different from girls, and doing well in sports is a prime source of distinction for many young boys. We, of course, want our young sons to respect these alien girls and accept them readily. This, however, is much easier said than done.

Don't push time with girls on your son. He most likely will spend plenty of time with them at school, church, and other co-ed activities. Sports teams at this age can also be coed. Modeling respectful behavior is the best method of teaching respect for girls.

But parents should still teach boys manners. Boys at this age can easily learn and remember to hold the door open for a woman, wait until a woman enters or leaves an elevator, help a woman who has dropped an item, and say "yes, ma'am." These simple courtesies are not an attempt to subjugate women to a subclass of society. They do not teach men that women are unequal to men. At the same time, parents need to emphasize the skills of women as athletes, business leaders, politicians, and so on.

Fathers and sons, though, still enjoy sharing an inside joke about girls now and then. Ask nearly any boy if he has had to wait forever for his mother to get ready before the family could head out to do something fun, and he'll emit a huge groan and roll his eyes. Groucho Marx once started a book with the foreword: "I wrote this book in the long hours while waiting for my wife to get ready to go out." This is humor all men understand.

There is nothing particular to be done about your son's aversion to girls. The rise in his testosterone level at the start of puberty will displace the displeasure of being with girls with a curious desire to know more. The rise in testosterone will fuel new impulses toward a physical connection with girls.

Taking His Time

Boys in the middle linger between clear childlike behavior and full-blown adolescence. Parents may see body changes that appear dramatic but not as much maturity to match the growing body. For boys in these years time speeds by and slows down, all at the same time.

Short Boys, Tall Girls

Perhaps you remember your eighth-grade dance. In the 1970s, boys danced in their shiny print shirts with collars the size of quesadillas and their shoes stacked three inches high. In the '80s it was punk to Miami Vice cool, while the '90s offered the opportunity to wear grunge. At all these events, the boys tried to dance slowly with their heads nestled firmly in the nape of their partner's neck.

Toy Box

Boys in the middle can be tactless, even cruel, but wily educators find teachable moments for insensitive boys. For example: a veteran female middle school teacher in New York City, when called *fat*, writes *voluptuous* on the chalkboard and goes on to explain how to use this better choice of words.

Nothing says eighth grade more than tall girls swooning over boys who look like their little brothers. While size gives physically maturing boys in seventh and eighth grades a physical advantage, early maturity also brings an elevated mood and a more positive self-image. The opposite is true for girls. These mood and self-image differences are not apparent in sixth-grade boys.

Keep Out!

A boy in middle school can provoke feelings of dislike in his parents who, before this stage, had not felt so unkindly toward their son. For example, he may act like a know-it-all or display terrible social manners. These negative feelings about boys in the middle are very common but can arouse immense guilt in the parent. Take comfort in knowing that other parents of middle school boys are struggling with the same reactions. Acknowledge the feelings as they arise—they're real, but temporary. Avoid hateful words or actions that may spring from such sentiments. Just admitting the feelings to yourself usually reduces their hold on you.

Soon Enough Is Soon Enough

Boys in the middle need permission to *not* grow up too fast. Parents who pester their sons about girlfriends or note body changes frequently may find that their son is indifferent or hostile to discussing these subjects. Parents do their son a disservice in rushing him into an image of a young man, when all the boy wants to do is hang on to boyhood a little bit longer.

For boys in the middle, parents help their son when they adopt an attitude that recognizes that "soon enough" is right on time. Each stage in a boy's life brings its challenges and rewards, and parents recognize this as soon as their baby starts to move around the room crawling. Nothing is quite so shocking as realizing that your baby boy is mobile and that the alert level needs to jump way up.

Just as your son decided when to crawl for the first time, he will also decide to confront the fears and possible rewards that lie beyond the familiar horizon of his boyhood. Hormones will eventually help fuel this drive to the frontier, but while we wait for nature to take its course, it is important that your son experience a loving relationship in the home that says, "No need to rush, we love you just the way you are right now."

The Joy of Not Caring

One of the joys of boys in the middle is watching them enjoy play just as they did when they were in second grade. In one summer day, these boys seem to eat everything on the shelves while downing a pallet of soft drinks. A pack of dirty, sweat-soaked adventurers will pile into the kitchen, dig into several hundred calories, and be off to play in room-size forts that take several hours to construct.

In these moments you realize that boys can find plenty of joy in the middle years without having to think too much about girls, or image, or, God forbid, what they are going to do with their lives. Parents look wistfully at the play surrounding them, and, in these respites, reconnect with the child within. This is his gift to us: to show us that we also can refuse the demands of time and revel in the *now* with our closest friends.

Get Goofy!

Goofy is the word that best describes boys in the middle when they get together to play. They put each other up to enormously stupid challenges. Above all, they have fun—goofy, hilarious fun.

Enjoying Silly Boys

One favorite challenge of boys in the middle is to see who can eat the hottest food imaginable. At a place called Quaker Steak & Lube, our youngest and his friends passed one evening upping the ante of who could eat the hottest chicken wings. The hottest sauce was *astronomically* hot and required the person ordering to sign a waiver. Good marketing! Each boy got a chance to be heroic and take home a bumper sticker attesting to his bravery.

For boys in the middle, there is a fine line or, perhaps, no line between bravery and stupidity. These silly

> **Toy Box**
>
> A classic dare among middle school boys is to challenge each other to see who can taste the grossest combination of substances. One deadly mixed drink known to have been consumed in our house contained ketchup, mayonnaise, milk, Coke, hot sauce, and several random spices. Yuck!

boys continue to peal with laughter at fart jokes and open zippers. They make vigorous attempts at lunchtime to compel a classmate to laugh so hard milk shoots out of his nose. As they become a bit more world-wise, these boys also enjoy parody because they recognize the inside part of the joke.

Perhaps boys never grow out of this love for goofiness. In *Scrubs*, one of our favorite TV shows, the two male lead characters, J.D. and Turk, are doctors and best friends. In one episode, a female doctor named Elliot is speaking with a patient on the phone. The patient is in the room with J.D. and Turk. Elliot is able to identify that the patient is being treated by J.D. and Turk because the doctors can't stop from laughing when the patient uses the word "duty" in a sentence.

Playing Along

While boys in the middle are on the cusp of losing pure boyhood, parents can share this stage with their sons. Dad or Mom can accept a challenge to try the hottest wing on the plate. They can also listen to their children and really try to understand their sons' desires, even if these wishes appear silly.

In the film *A Christmas Story*, young Ralphie wants only one thing: "An official Red Ryder carbine action two-hundred shot range model air rifle with a compass in the stock and this thing that tells time." Ralphie obsesses and plots for this gift. All the while, his mother and teachers dismiss this request, because, they tell him: "you'll shoot your eye out." On Christmas morning, Ralphie finally gets his BB gun. Ralphie's parents had been listening even as they scolded and punished him for his other misdeeds.

Absurdity reigns, and the sillier the better. Parents of boys in the middle can play along and refresh their own sense of humor.

The Least You Need to Know

◆ Boys in middle school enjoy running in packs.

◆ An aversion to girls for early middle school boys is normal and not a reason for concern.

◆ Boys who mature early physically enjoy elevated moods and an enhanced self-image; boys who mature later struggle more.

◆ Boys need to mature at their own pace.

◆ Boys in the middle are goofy, love absurd humor, and benefit from parents who find joy in this silliness.

Boy Gets Hormones

At around the age of eleven, your son's body will begin to flood with sex and growth hormones. He will grow taller, faster, and stronger. If you're at a restaurant, his gaze will linger on the waitress even as he is describing the fun he is still having with his pack of friends.

Part 3 explains in straightforward language how your son is maturing and how you can ready yourself for this major developmental phase. We help you understand his desire for a stronger identity, ever-present friends, and relationships that involve much more than teasing and arm punching.

Chapter 13

Puberty in Perspective

In This Chapter

- The puberty process
- These sheets are private
- Changes you can see, hear, and smell
- What he worries about
- His self-image

Ah, puberty. As an adult it is hard not to look back on puberty with a mix of fascination and horror.

Howard Stern's autobiographical movie *Private Parts* includes a hilarious scene where he is sitting dejectedly in the high school locker room watching a long parade of fully mature boys walk by. Men can relate.

This chapter discusses a wide range of puberty issues, which will help you arm yourself with courage to converse with your son on this important and bewildering phase of his life.

A Process, Not an Event

Puberty is a phased process of development that occurs over a wider range of ages for boys than most parents realize. Fortunately, early sexual and physical development for boys is generally welcomed where early maturity for girls brings a host of negative thoughts. Your son will advance through this process that may start as early as 10 years old. Some days it will appear as if by magic that he is growing from a child to a sexually mature male. Undoubtedly, he will be taller than Mom. Here's how he gets there.

At around the age of 11, your son's body will begin the process of changing from a boy to a man. Observing your son for this anticipated stage in his life will be easy. For a quick gauge, listen to your relatives at the holidays. The "I can't believe how tall you've gotten" remarks directed at your son will come fast and furious once puberty arrives.

At this stage a boy's body is producing several hormones that drive male development. The easiest to remember is simply known as the growth hormone, which is produced by the pituitary gland. Every vertebrate species has a pituitary gland, a highly complex and important pea-size gland found at the base of the brain behind the bridge of the nose.

Growth hormone, thyroxin, insulin, and other hormones affect growth rate. The parathyroid, a group of usually four glands in the neck, pump out a hormone, PTH, that along with vitamin D and other compounds, regulates bone growth. Leptin, produced in adipose tissue, which is located mostly under the skin, is a hormone that alters body composition.

Toy Box

Actor Alex Baldwin's vicious motivational speech in the movie *GlenGarry GlenRoss* helped make his career. At one point in his diatribe to a group of despondent aging real estate salesmen, he places a set of decorative brass knockers over his crotch to make his point about what it takes to be successful.

And then, of course, there is the all-important hormone for boys, testosterone. Testosterone, not surprisingly, is produced in the testes, the plural form of the word testicle. Popular culture celebrates and parodies testosterone and testicles. A man who takes on a challenge that other men shrink from has "brass balls" or a "big set."

Your son's body will mature in fairly predictable stages. The first visible sign of puberty will probably occur in a place parents don't see, the testicles. They will begin to grow. He'll be about 11½ years old at this stage. As his testicles grow, the outer sack, called the *scrotum*, which holds the two testicles, will redden, thin out, and enlarge.

Only after the testicles and scrotum have grown significantly will the penis start to mature. This will begin to happen when he is just shy of age 13. His penis will lengthen and grow in circumference. His genitals will not reach adult size until he is over 15 years old.

Until he is about 13½ your son will likely not display pubic hair. The first hair he gets will be long and downy and grow at the base of his scrotum and penis. His pubic hair coverage will expand along with everything else. The hair will become curly, pigmented, and more coarse until it reaches the adult stage of development. This will occur a few months after his penis, scrotum, and testicles have matured.

Under the Sheets

The arrival of sexual desire may come slowly, or it may arrive with a crash. I (Barron) remember one summer evening when as a 13-year-old, I viewed a woman in shorts, very *tight* shorts on an extremely well-shaped backside. You get the point. My pituitary gland, which had been storing up hormones like the Hoover Dam, took this as a sign to open every floodgate. I distinctly recall being *seized* with wonder at this beautiful woman's body and thinking *this* is what they've been talking about all these years!

Wet Dreams

Nocturnal emission is the polite term for what happens when a boy spontaneously ejaculates semen while sleeping. This occurs through no effort at all and is a function of his developing body and his evolving psyche. Boys involve a larger portion of their brain when thinking about sex than girls do.

Wet dreams can occur during a sexually stimulating dream or may happen simply because the genitals are stimulated by rubbing against a sheet. Wet dreams decline once a boy begins to masturbate.

If your son is confused or embarrassed after experiencing a wet dream, explain in simple language what is happening. To help him maintain some privacy, encourage him to take the sheets off his bed after he has a wet dream and put them in the laundry. This will avoid the inconvenient discovery of the event by Mom or someone else.

Masturbation

Masturbation means that a boy is manually manipulating his penis to the point of orgasm. An old saying states that 9 out of 10 men admit to masturbating and the other guy is a liar. Perhaps the last man lied because society has cloaked this ancient form of self-satisfaction in taboo. In the nineteenth century, some idiotic parents prevented their boys from masturbating by making them wear a painful erection-stopping chastity belt.

Masturbating does not cause blindness, madness, or illness. While a boy may fear he will run out of sperm, he can rest assured that he will not. Masturbating will also not prevent him from fathering a child later in life. It is not for losers, either, but is done by nearly everyone in every station in life.

Masturbating is a basic, universal, natural, and normal way of satisfying the sexual urge and exploring sexuality. It also has the side benefit of not risking pregnancy.

Some boys take it too far, of course. A boy who, new to the game, is pleasuring himself to the point it is interfering with his homework, chores, or relationships needs to slow down or stop for a while. "Jacking off" too much can cause skin problems if he does not use some form of water-soluble lubricant. Lubricants for sex, by the way, are one of the top sellers at national mainstream retailers.

The Importance of Privacy

For boys, waiting and watching for changes during puberty is a source of intense interest. Privacy will be an immediate concern at home, and something denied at school locker rooms.

If he's nervous, don't force your son to change in front of other men at the local swimming pool locker room. Modeling a lack of concern is more important. Modesty is fine, but a boy will become comfortable changing at the pool if his dad doesn't make a big deal of it either way.

At home, a boy can have a lock on his room, provided there is a quick way—key/pick above trim on door—to open it and he understands you will have complete discretion to look in his room at will. A lock will at least help prevent your son from being walked in on.

The sly parent also notices but reveals nothing when a boy walks away with a Wal-Mart bra sale advertisement. Most parents will knowingly overlook a *Playboy* stored in a secret place, too. Violence-laden pornography, on the other hand, is not acceptable and will require intervention.

Given the cascade of explicit images on the Internet, you will want to review the Internet pages your son has been visiting. Tracking software programs will allow you to track and sometimes block pornography on a computer. Keeping the computer where an adult can see it, such as the family room, is the best defense against online porn along with clear rules on what is viewable and what is not.

> **Toolbox**
>
> Net Nanny is a very popular Internet tracking program that's also used to block websites as the parents see fit. Instant message tracking, though, was not included in the mid-2007 version of the software. The Internet is a fast-evolving medium that even keeps the heads of leading software manufacturers spinning.

Physical Changes

A whiff of your boy, redolent of eau de longshoreman, will easily clarify that body changes are underway. Your son's hormones are now coursing though his body, making everything bigger, stronger, and, well, stronger smelling. And there are other more emblematic changes associated with puberty in boys.

So Long, Soprano

As your son's body grows, so grows the larynx or voice box in the front middle of his neck. This change will start between the ages of 13 and 14. As puberty advances, his vocal cords will lengthen and thicken.

The easily distinguishable portion of the larynx is generally known as the *Adam's apple*, as in Adam ate the forbidden fruit and it got stuck in his throat. Physicians know the Adam's apple as the laryngeal prominence which is more prominent in boys than in girls.

The pitch of his voice will lower as the vocal cords mature. This does not happen overnight, and the advancing vocal cords will jump to a new pitch, or crack, once in a while when he speaks. The crack people notice is the voice that suddenly sounds very high. Voice cracking, also called breaking, appears to concentrate for boys around age 14½. These occasions will, unfortunately, probably take place at the most embarrassing times, such as during a class presentation or when he is trying to speak to a girl he likes or when he says the Christmas dinner prayer. Help him anticipate and understand the change in his voice, and encourage him to find humor in this unique time in his life.

The Skinny on Skin

A boy in puberty will generate additional oil in his sebaceous skin glands. This excess oil and dead skin will block pores in the skin which will cause the skin to become inflamed and erupt in a disorder known as *acne*. In boys, acne is often an irregular response to increased testosterone. If left untreated, acne can leave significant scars. Moreover, acne can leave a boy feeling unattractive at the very point in his life where attracting people to him becomes more important.

The good news is that acne is much more treatable today, and far fewer boys are being left scarred for life by this bane of puberty. Visit a dermatologist as soon as you suspect your son's skin is at risk. An occasional pimple or blackhead is not much to worry about; daily showering and a regular face-washing routine will take care of that. For boys who are at risk, a dermatologist will likely prescribe some combination of isotretinoin and an antibiotic. Hormones, exposure to special intense lights, and other treatments are available as well. A pharmacist can recommend over-the-counter medication.

P-U-berty

Your son will also start to stink, well, more so than he usually does. But this time it's not just because he raced his friends by rolling down a construction mound of dirt. During hormone-infused puberty, the sweat glands and associated bacteria will be combining to generate a more aromatic and memorable odor.

Buy him a roll-on deodorant, and insist that he use it. Old Spice has made a comeback among boys, so you may find that standing in his wake dredges up childhood memories of hugging male relatives. Check to make sure he is showering frequently, too.

Coordination

Coordination changes in boys during puberty. Boys achieve, on average, the most rapid height gains in the middle of their thirteenth year. Their body fat content decreases while, for girls, it increases.

Competitive athletes may find their games falling off as their bodies alter the angles of attack. Legs and arms lengthen too rapidly for some boys to adjust easily, and their games temporarily go in the tank.

On the other hand, for boys who were not already very athletic, parents may be very pleased to see their son who had two left feet in elementary school blossom into a more coordinated and graceful player.

Boys often ask their parents at this age, "How tall am I going to be?" To give him a ballpark figure, try using the following formula:

(father's height + 5.12 inches or 13 cm) + mother's height ÷ 2

Kids often wear braces on their teeth at this age, and orthodontists will x-ray a boy's wrist to estimate how tall a patient will grow. So if your son won't believe you when you tell him how tall he'll grow, run the query past the orthodontist.

My Boy Is Shaving!

Slowly but surely, your son's facial hair will start to creep out. At first, softer, shorter ones will grow above his upper lip; then a few will grow on his chin. Later the hairs will thicken and darken. You might initially catch yourself thinking your son needs to wash his mouth off. That's one of those "Aha!" moments.

A full beard—where he looks like Fred Flintstone at five o'clock after a hard day at the quarry—will not mature for several years. He will also be growing thicker, darker hair on his legs, arms, and armpits during this time.

Buy your son a good razor. He can watch and learn as Dad lathers up and explains the strokes. Some men feel that the best shave still comes with a razor handle that takes a single disposable blade and expensive English glycerin-based shaving cream that is applied with a badger-hair brush to skin that is warm and wet. African American young men who suffer from more skin bumps from shaving may want to try this high-end approach to shaving.

Toolbox

Health24.com and other sites offer step-by-step tutorials on how to get a good, close shave if Dad is not available.

Some boys have skin that is sensitive to shaving, so if your son develops a rash, switch shaving creams. Consult a dermatologist if that does not work, because some men are allergic to the lanolin found in many shaving creams.

By the way, it is very hard to find an old-school barber who will shave a man's face with a straight razor. One good reason for this is the availability of relatively close-shaving modern razors, which you can find for a few dollars at any store, like Target, that sells shaving supplies.

His Secret Worries

Puberty brings not only physical changes but also a time of worry for many boys. In addition to the challenge of managing the testosterone-fueled fury, many boys confront fears, such as "not measuring up" or being hated by parents or so-called friends, so let's shine some light on these darker shadows of puberty.

Locker-Room Fears

Penis size is a concern for boys and men. Like most boys, he's probably more concerned with the size of his penis when it is not in an aroused or erect state. A penis in this flaccid state is sometimes referred to as *soft*. Boys are never really observed outside of sexual activity in an aroused state, and while curious about their erect size, they are more concerned about being seen as normal in the locker room.

However, most men who consult a physician regarding penis size—probably a very large group—have normal-size equipment. If your doctor is performing a sports physical on your son, you might want to suggest that the pediatrician ask your son if he has any questions. A wise doctor will hopefully throw in a comment that everything is normal.

Author and humorist Garrison Keillor tells a story about his teenage concern that his penis was curved. His doctor told him he was normal, but the ecstatic young Garrison, who wanted to scream to the world this result, was dumb-founded as to whom exactly he could share the information with.

As for safe and effective means of *looking* bigger, doctors recommend trimming public hair and getting in shape. As for changing the physical appearance of the penis, there are no meaningfully safe and effective methods short of the kind of massive surgical recon-struction that might happen after a tragic accident.

> **Toolbox**
>
> The question boys wish to ask but don't is: Is my penis normal size? According to the Mayo Clinic, 3–4 inches flaccid and 5–7 inches erect are the aver-ages. The penis is measured from where it emerges from the body to the tip. Only an *erect* penis *less than 3 inches long* is considered abnormal for size purposes.

The ridiculous vacuum pump machines men read about are considered completely ineffective and potentially harmful. Creams do not work. One method of cutting the suspending ligament to drop a penis down to appear bigger deprives a man of the local strength needed to main-tain position during sexual activity. A penis that looks longer but won't follow directions is pretty much useless.

Your son will likely be normal in size. Address any real concerns with a visit to a pediatrician or urologist.

I'll Never Be Good at Anything

Crisis in self-confidence is common during puberty. Boys who observe better athletes, better students, and more popular boys can spiral downward to feelings of inadequacy and despair. On top of this, recall from Chapter 1 that boys do not have the same brain connections with regard to feelings as girls do. Their feelings are not as hardwired from the amygdalae, the primitive brain center, into the cerebral cortex, the more analytical part of the brain. Thus boys, while feeling low, may be unable to express the same level of understanding of their feelings as girls can.

Mothers can be frustrated by the lack of insight by boys. They drill and drill for some expression of feeling from their son and come away disconnected. Moms and dads need to realize that their son's brain is still developing and comes with more limited access to the type of emotional insight that comes to women. Men are still capable of a wide range of emotion, but boys are not as attuned to analyzing these feelings.

Build confidence though genuine and kind positive feedback. Encouraging a son to participate in activities that he both enjoys and for which he shows some natural proclivity will help him find value in himself. Of course, we want our sons to feel inherently valuable. At this age, though, belonging and being valued by people outside of himself will be very important to your son.

Think outside the box when it comes to finding a confidence-building activity. You might explore volunteering, taking karate, participating in a club sport such as lacrosse or riflery, taking an art class at a local college, becoming politically active, attending a cool snowboarding camp, and so on. While being on the football team is a healthy choice, many boys do not wish to play.

Boys need a steady stream of positive comments. Share your stories of how you felt when you were his age and overcame an obstacle. Remind him that you failed, too. Family stories are important legacies, both the victories and the losses. Keeping alive an oral tradition of sharing the highs and lows of life will help your son find confidence that he can persevere in challenges and find value in day-to-day living.

I'll Never Have a Real Friend

Isolation can be very difficult for boys growing into men. They want to have bodies that they and others accept, and they want to have friends who accept them. Boys can lose social status for stupid reasons or for no reason at all. Real friends can be hard to find.

Loneliness in a crowd is a common malady for boys. Parents can help by first recognizing that their son is not making connections. Does he make an attempt to plan time with classmates? He may prefer one or two close friends to a pack, but if he doesn't have anyone, it is time to take some action. If he has moved, plan time with his old friends, even if this requires some driving and a couple weeks' notice. Look for connections at your mosque, temple, or church. Encourage participation in the activities noted previously. Friendless boys lack confidence.

Discuss with your son that you've noticed he is spending lots of time at home. Be honest as you tell him you want to see him out and about more, and then ask him for some solutions. Problem solving will likely be much more productive than focusing on how sad he must feel. Help him identify his feelings, of course, but also engage him in a process whereby he takes active control of his life. Friendless boys may not only be sad and perhaps even clinically depressed, but they are also likely *immobilized* by the lack of social interaction.

Keep a weather eye out for older boys who want to connect with your son. Boys can be victimized by older bullies who delight in falsely befriending boys and then humiliating them or roping them into an unhealthy relationship.

> **NO GIRLZ ALOWD!!** **Keep Out!**
>
> The risk of clinical depression in boys is significant. Parents need to be aware that suicide is a leading cause of death for teenage boys. Seek evaluation and treatment by a therapist and physician if you have any concerns about your son's mental health. (See Chapter 18 for more on this topic.)

Again, share stories of how you made friends and lost friends. Hearing, briefly, about how a friend betrayed you and how you made new friends may give your son the charge he needs to seek out his own stories of friendship.

My Dad/Mom/Parents Hate Me

When your son says "Dad hates me," this is a clear demand for more attention from his father. The same is true for Mom. Few moms and dads hate their children, thank God. But plenty of boys feel hated when their parents spend little time with them. The demands of work and mere survival may take priority at times, and boys are resilient. However, a boy who takes the time to express such a deep sense of detachment needs immediate attention.

Make special plans to attend to your son to alleviate the suffering he is feeling. Express your love for him openly and without reservation. Make sure he understands that your displeasure with his conduct is not an indication of hate for him or even a lack of love for him.

Moms and dads need to make each other the central part of their lives, and single parents need to attend to their adult relationships as well. Parental authority resides at all times with the parent. But while we are disciplining our boys and prioritizing our adult relationships to maintain our own emotional health, it is important to embrace our children frequently, be generous with our praise, and look for opportunities to connect each day—even if that means talking while doing the dishes together. If Dad wants to read the paper, he can hand his boy the comics, and they can read together. A simple action like this says "I see you, son. You might like this; now, let me read."

Self-Image and Puberty

Who am I? For boys reaching the end stages of puberty, self-identity becomes a source of joy and anxiety. Some boys take a "throw it on the wall and see if it sticks" approach, and freely change clothes, hair, and friends. Other boys keep the same hairstyle they've always had and try *not* to be noticed. Follow some of these ideas to help your son foster a healthy and fun exploration of self.

Complimenting His Image

A parent can do worse things than overpraising a child. While we do not want our boys to think they've "hung the moon," as parenting columnist John Rosemond writes, we do want them to have a healthy self-image. This starts with good modeling by parents.

Parents who praise each other and go out of their way to compliment, sincerely teach boys that compliments are more than courtesies but are rather a vehicle for expressions of fondness and love. Praise your son's image. Find a thing you like: his smile, his eyes, his cool Jimi Hendrix shirt. In doing so, you'll help him realize that he's got plenty to like about himself.

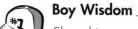

Boy Wisdom

Show him your high school yearbook so that both of you will know how goofy you once looked.
—Harry H. Harrison Jr.
Father to Son: Life Lessons on Raising a Boy

The Stealth Approach to Cool

While boys appreciate a sincere compliment given in private, they easily shrink from attention and praise in front of anyone who is unfamiliar with their parents. To "assist" your son in his improving his image, start with the compliments and keep them going as you drive to the mall.

Give your son a limited budget, and let him pick out his own clothes. Plan for an extended visit. You can nix the overtly sexual shirts or the clothes that invite gang retribution, but wide latitude is called for here.

A wild suggestion may come up now and then. One of our sons hinted obliquely that black dreadlocks were cool. And this remark came from a blond Norwegian. The reply: "Okay, provided you've got good grades."

Pick your battles wisely. Fads come and go, and every boy wants to be somewhere close to the fashion of the times. Can you imagine how ridiculous your son would look in your gym shorts from high school, or, more importantly, how he would feel wearing them? His future therapy bill would be enormous.

Pay attention when your son is shopping. If you can't afford an item now, keep it in mind for a special gift. Consider talking Grandma into buying your son a pair of Vans instead of loafers.

The Joy of Manhood

There's an old saying that people should spread the Gospel, and, if necessary, use words. Boys need to see their fathers partaking of life fully. Dads need to share the joys and the sorrows, but especially the joys. Smile when you see your son. You haven't been together for hours. He needs to see men who love life, and he especially needs to see a man who loves him.

Remember, boys at puberty are especially attuned to storytelling. Boy Scouts have a great tradition of storytelling, and there are too few opportunities for men to pass on the accumulated wisdom of the generations in this form. Tell your son about the first time you got dumped by a girl you liked, about how you met your partner for life, or how you fumbled the ball at the goal line—and survived.

Pass on the joy of being a man to your son. The world is plenty full of misanthropes, sad middle-age cynics who seek company for their misery. Your son needs a man who finds joy in living.

Seek it for yourself and pass it on.

The Least You Need to Know

- Sexual maturation, puberty, is a years-long process for boys.
- Privacy is important for boys in puberty.
- Puberty heralds many physical changes, including a rapidly growing body, oily skin, a lower voice, and facial hair.
- During puberty, boys confront significant fears relating to self-image.
- Parents, especially fathers, can raise boys to be healthy men by sharing the joys they find in life with their sons.

Chapter 14

Finding His Identity

In This Chapter

- ◆ The dawn of self-consciousness
- ◆ The meaning of "popular"
- ◆ Dancing to his identity
- ◆ Challenging Mom and Dad

From his toddler years, your son has been exploring his world and discovering his place in it. But until now, that world has not extended much beyond your front yard. His hungry toddler mind—with its questions, "What's dat?" and "Why?"—has grown into a hungry adolescent mind, with questions like, "Do I really believe this?" "Are adults really right about everything?"

And he's questioning *himself.* His increased capacity for abstract thought allows him to imagine how others see him and to consider new possibilities for who he can be. He is like a scientist, researching the world and inventing himself.

In this chapter, we'll focus on your son's lively laboratory and how you can help him discover who he is—without too many explosions.

Fears in the Mirror

In Part 1, we talked about parental mirroring as an important way to help your baby boy learn about who he is. As a teen, the mirror in the bathroom becomes his new consultant. If you think your son is unique in his ability to stare blankly into the mirror for the good part of a morning, think again. He may look like he has no concern about his image, but, chances are, he's *worked at* that "didn't try" look. Let's explore the kinds of questions he may be asking his personal "mirror, mirror on the wall."

Am I Weird?

"Do I fit in?"

"Are people secretly laughing at me?"

"Does anyone notice me?"

Teenage boys walk a tightrope between conformity and individuality. He wants to stand out as an individual but does not want to stand alone. He wants to make his friends laugh but is terrified of being laughed at. He may brutally criticize adults for their lack of originality, while taking care to wear the peer-sanctioned "uniform" of baggy pants and layered shirts.

Toolbox

According to David Elkind's theory of adolescent egocentrism, teenagers tend to make two common errors in their perceptions. *Imaginary audience* refers to the belief that people are watching and evaluating everything he does. *Personal fable* is the belief that he is unique (and therefore often misunderstood), all-knowing, and invulnerable. Though the scientific basis of these classic concepts has been challenged, they tend to ring true to anyone who spends a lot of time with teenagers!

Concerns about being weird among peers are common for teens. Brain imaging studies are providing some clues to why this may be. It seems that, in adolescence, the control centers for thinking, planning, and behaving are being reassigned from the "primitive" structures deep in the brain to the more sophisticated prefrontal cortex—a process called *frontalization*. With frontalization comes the ability to think more abstractly, to see things from multiple points of view. A team of Harvard brain researchers, led by neuropsychologist Deborah Todd-Yurgelun, suggests that this newfound ability makes teens more vulnerable to feeling watched and judged. Their studies showed that, as teens' abstract reasoning skills improved, their level of social anxiety increased. The longstanding observation that teenagers carry around an imaginary audience may actually be a sign of their improved brain function!

It is helpful to remind your son that, though he is legitimately concerned about how others see him, his "audience" is also very busy being concerned about how they are coming off.

Am I Attractive?

Much attention has been given to the pressures on girls to be thin and beautiful. The playing field on appearance seems to be evening out, but not in the direction of self-acceptance. Boys are catching up with girls in their concerns about appearance. Girls want to be thin, and boys want to be toned. Though your son may seem obnoxious as he walks through the house with no shirt, patting his toned "abs," he's as hungry for affirmation as a girl with carefully applied makeup.

Instead of dismissing your son's concern about his image, help him bridge the gap between ideal and real. Teens tend to fixate on their flaws, so help him take reasonable action instead. If he has a husky frame, help him find clothes that complement him. If he's got acne, help him deal with it. Set him up with a dermatologist; get either a prescription or over-the-counter medicated concealer; and keep him accountable for good skin care. Recent studies show that boys are much less likely than girls to wear sunblock but are no less prone to skin cancer. Though our son is not likely to be motivated by fears of cancer, his concern about peeling and disrupting his tan does get him to put on the sunblock. Your son's interest in looking good can be a great incentive for a healthier lifestyle.

One of the best ways you can help your son feel better about his image is to get him moving. A 2007 Harvard study, which included data on 3,410 boys, revealed that boys who increased activity by 10 or more hours per week were 45 percent more likely to have "increased social self-perception"—to feel better about how they were viewed socially. The reverse was also true: lowered physical activity was associated with a lowered sense of social regard. Note that the study did not look at athletic ability or weight loss—just increased physical activity. Mowing the lawn counts! In addition to boosting his sense of self, physical activity is also known to be a natural antidepressant and a great way to reenergize.

Am I Smart?

Though the image of the "slacker" has been popularized in movies like *Ferris Bueller's Day Off* and *Office Space*, the guys who slack are usually portrayed as extremely resourceful and intelligent. They have the charm and social intelligence to attract love and friendship despite their lazy ways, and the "slacking" itself is often the result of careful planning and advanced technical knowledge.

These slackers are cool because we know they *could* excel if they wanted to. A boy who feels completely lost in algebra while his friends are nodding their heads in understanding is not likely to feel cool. He is more likely to worry that he's missing the brainpower "everyone else" seems to have.

The problem for boys is that they often use the slacker image to cover over insecurities about their intelligence. The thinking is, "If I didn't try, that means I *could* do better." When people comment, "You can do better than *that*," they only reinforce his cover. In his imagination, he can do anything, and he may start to channel his ambition into fantasy rather than action. Meanwhile, he is dropping behind in school and beginning to limit the very options he may hold on to in fantasy.

To draw on another movie, the intellectually challenged *Forrest Gump* lived an exciting and successful life through the strength of his character and work ethic. When someone accused him of being stupid, he would simply quote his mother: "Stupid is as stupid does." We would all do well to share that wisdom with our sons, adding that "smart is as smart does." Fantasy is great for inspiration, but real success has more to do with what we do than how we're wired. If your son is struggling in school, help him figure out how to *get* smart. Often the answer is as simple as asking for help.

Boy Wisdom

Success is 10 percent inspiration and 90 percent perspiration.

—Thomas Alva Edison, American inventor

Though it's simple in theory, boys will often do everything in their power to *avoid* asking for help. Boys are prone to the thinking that they should *know*—even before learning or experience teaches them. This thinking is a major set-up for boys and men and often explains the anger and frustration they so often express.

If your son is struggling, don't let him off the hook! Explore with him what he needs, and don't give up until you hit on what works. Sometimes what works is taking him out of an honors class that is above his head and placing him in a class where he can experience mastery and restore his confidence. Sometimes a tutor bridges the gap by providing help in a more private setting. Sometimes your son just needs to work through a problem rather than escaping it because he doesn't immediately *know*.

Another way we can help our sons is to look at intelligence more broadly. As we discussed in Chapter 8, new models of intelligence take into account more than the old "Rs" of "readin', 'ritin', and 'rithmatic." Daniel Goleman's research, outlined in his popular books, *Emotional Intelligence* and *Social Intelligence* (see the Resources appendix), draws attention to the importance of these overlooked competencies in achieving success.

Growing up means accepting our limitations as well as our strengths, and doing this can be hard for an idealistic teen. Letting him know that he's terrific *because of*, not in spite of, how he's uniquely constructed will help pave the way for a strong identity.

What Makes a Boy Popular?

We asked our teenage son this question, and he replied, "Fun, funny, outgoing, crazy—in a way that's funny, you know a lot of people." As we talked, he identified appearance, social skills, and "not being weird" as key factors in popularity. When I asked him what "weird" meant, he talked about kids who make comments that are "out of place."

Our son's distinction between "crazy" and "weird" provides insight into the importance of social intelligence in a teen culture. Crazy attracts; weird alienates. When I (Laurie) traveled to the Amazon with a group of mostly eleventh-grade boys, I observed crazy in full color. One boy was particularly gifted in this regard; he was able to be childlike and free with his humor, but he was also tuned in to whether others were having fun. He got a group of boys, including our younger son, involved in making videos in which one of them—the "robot"—would appear to knock down all of the others by blinking his eyes. Crazy. When I had a chance to talk to the instigator more seriously, he shared a simple but profound philosophy of life: "I like to be nice to everyone; life's too short to be stuck-up."

Fun and friendly, not smug and stuck-up, were the key ingredients to his success. This boy was clearly having fun, and people—including us adults—liked being around him. While few boys exhibit his kind of social power, boys do know how to have fun, and most of them know how to be friendly.

If a boy in middle or high school is feeling anxious about his popularity, he's probably not having fun. The lack of inhibition that comes with "crazy" is anchored in a sense of social safety. While he may not be able to work a crowd, your son can probably entertain a small group of intimate friends. When "popular" is seen as relative to the group he identifies with, it's much easier to pull off.

To the extent that school is a group activity, extroverts tend to have the advantage. But then, popularity is more valued by extroverts. Introverts prefer to have a few really good friends than to be known by everybody. In fact, an introvert would probably find it annoying to have kids in his space all the time. He may prefer to keep a "low profile" and make his way without the confinement of a social group.

But what about "weird"? The word can refer to behavior that is out of place, obnoxious, or bizarre, as our son's comment suggested. But let's face it, what's cool at school can be pretty narrowly defined, which leaves a lot of room for weird. Most of us know what it's like to feel unpopular, even if the experience is confined to a certain life phase or social setting.

Keep Out!

If your son is getting feedback that he's weird, he could be part of the problem. Is he intentionally annoying other kids to get a response? Does he see others as below him and flaunt his superiority? It's tempting for a parent to assume that others are the problem and react in a protective way. But get the facts. Even when others *are* unfairly judging him, you help him more when you empower him to manage the situation.

We may take some consolation in the knowledge that boys tend to be less concerned about popularity than girls. And some boys who used to be shunned are finding a place in popular culture. The real *Revenge of the Nerds* is seen every day as we hear about Bill Gates's fortune or we see how girls swoon over the openly weird character of "J.D." in the comedy *Scrubs*. And in the popular thriller *Live Free or Die Hard*, the brainpower of the jittery computer hacker gave him as much charisma as the hard-bodied detective he was assisting.

Some very famous "weird boys" have turned ridicule into motivation to make it big. Walt Disney, who was off in la-la land (or Disneyland!) during his early years in school, dreaming and doodling, didn't let criticism get in his way. Though his family had little money, he found a way to take night classes at Chicago's Academy of Fine Arts, and the rest is an amazing history. And if Disney's legacy isn't cool enough, your son may be interested to know that actor Leonardo DiCaprio was nicknamed "Leonardo Retardo" in school.

Trying On His Identity

As your son sorts out his identity, you may see him morph from one character to another without notice. Teens literally "try on" different identities through changes in hairstyle, clothing, and musical choices. But if you know what's going on, you can keep up.

Music Is Key

As your son experiences the drama of his teen years, his music captures something that words alone cannot. The soundtrack of his life helps him narrate the story of his emotions and experiences. Music is an accepted way for boys to amplify, rather than close down, their feelings. Hearing an angry rapper or a "chill" alternative artist may help him feel understood and less alienated. This may be why he reacts so strongly if you abruptly turn off a song he's enjoying. The small gesture of asking *him* to turn down or shut off his music (usually so you can *speak)* shows more respect.

But when our 16-year-old son plays music, we sometimes ask him to turn it up! That's because he's often playing *our* music. And he's not the only one. On July 2, 2007, a *USA Today* news article reported that more and more kids are looking to the past for their "new" music. Classic rock artists, from the Beatles to Steve Miller, are idols to boys young enough to be their grandsons! In fact, you may hear your son express nostalgic sentiments similar to yours: "Why can't anybody make music like *Bohemian Rhapsody* anymore?"

Shared musical preferences can be a wonderful way to connect with your son. He may even want to pick your brain about concerts you attended or music trivia from "back in the day." And when he's listening to the new stuff, he can return the favor—you'll probably be amazed at how much he knows about the artists he likes. Even when you hate what he's playing, finding out what *he* likes about the music will help you understand him better.

With the advent of MP3 players such as iPods, listening to music is becoming a more private experience for teens. Though the new technology may keep your house quieter, it's also easier to miss out on a chunk of his experience. When he's rocking to the silence, ask him what he's listening to. Our son is usually happy to hand over the ear buds and let one of us have a listen. Your son's musical preferences will probably shift frequently, and asking him "What are you listening to these days?" will help you keep up.

A CBS story in June 2006 noted that the vast reach of the Internet and the ability to purchase individual songs are together allowing teens to create mixes of songs that better reflect their individuality. The report noted today's youth are less likely to be defined by a particular musical genre, such as the Deadheads or "punks" of earlier generations. Your son is no longer limited to what's on the radio—finding music he likes may feel more like a treasure hunt, and the prize is self-discovery.

Toy Box

Teen lingo is another way our sons distinguish themselves from us. We were cool, but they're *chill*. While we may be familiar with chill as a verb, as in "chill out," the word has been upgraded to an adjective as well. A person who is chill is relaxed and low-key and is unlikely to get upset or react to things. Music is chill when it's easy to listen to and helps you relax. Sounds a lot more hip than "easy listening"!

The Rap on Lyrics

In 2006, viewers of the 78th Annual Academy Awards may have been shocked to see the hip hop song "It's Hard Out Here for a Pimp" receive the award for Best Original Song. But shock about music lyrics is nothing new. Back in 1956, ABC Radio refused to play "Love for Sale" by Billie Holiday because the lyrics were about prostitution. Do songs such as these inspire consciousness about subjects we'd rather avoid, or do they inspire *behaviors* that really should be avoided? Can music hurt our boys?

In August 2006, the journal *Pediatrics* reported that listening to music with sexually degrading lyrics was associated with earlier sexual activity for adolescents. The finding came from a survey of 1,242 adolescents aged 12 to 17, who were interviewed at three points: baseline and one and three years later. The study took into account 18 predictors of sexual behavior, such as previous sexual experience and religiosity. What is interesting is that sexual lyrics *without* degrading messages did *not* influence early sexual activity.

In the study, songs were coded as sexually degrading when they "depicted sexually insatiable men pursuing women valued only as sex objects." Though such lyrics are clearly degrading to girls, they reduce boys as well, "depicting them as sex-driven studs whose individual desires are subsumed in their gender role." If this is the kind of mirroring boys receive, they may begin to see themselves in a stereotyped way. I (Laurie) recall having a discussion with a group of adult mentors at a youth retreat on love, sex, and marriage. The men in the group opened up about the pressures they had experienced as teens to always "want it" and to be responsible for initiating sexual activity.

Though the study used sexual lyrics from various musical genres, rap and "rap metal" were the most abundant sources. So should you ban your son from listening to rap?

If history tells us anything, it's that hysterical reactions to teen culture can actually *undermine* parental influence—think "reefer madness." As soon as kids realized that marijuana did not make them insane, everything parents said about it became suspect.

Rap is simply the art of saying rhymes to the beat of music. According to the online Rap News Network (www.rapnews.net), rap belongs under the broader category of *hip hop*, "an American cultural movement composed of four main parts: breakdancing and graffiti art along with two more well-known aspects known as hip-hop music; they are rapping (emceeing) and DJ-ing." A type of rap sure to alarm a parent, *gangsta rap*, is defined as "An edgy and often profane hip-hop style where the common element is the content: gritty street tales that portray a dim reality where the artist can be the subject or the observer."

But you don't have to know the difference between "old school" and hardcore rap to have a discussion with your son. Ask him to show you his playlist, and look up some lyrics online. I was humbled when our older son showed me the lyrics of "Dear Mama" by gangsta rapper Tupac Shakur. The song is an expression of love and appreciation to his mother, who struggled to raise him in a culture of poverty and violence. The son depicted in the lyrics is no angel: he admits dealing drugs to buy his mom a diamond necklace.

As our son showed me these lyrics, he said, "I thought you'd like this one." His offering of this song draws attention to the complexity of "dangerous lyrics." One boy may be drawn to the image of a tough thug; another may be moved by the song's social commentary; and a third may identify with some of the lyrics—or just the musical quality of the song—and ignore the rest. Through my son's ears, I could hear a heartfelt tribute to a courageous mother. And he was right—I *did* like it.

Before you ban, listen. And find out what *he's* hearing and what the song means to him. You may be amazed at, and inspired by, the philosophical depth of some of his music. Even controversial lyrics can open up a valuable dialogue between you and your son. If you're appalled by certain lyrics, let him know and tell him why. You can always have him delete a song or hand over a CD—and you may need to do just that. But when you use his music to help him sort out his values, the songs—and his life—will take on more depth.

By the way, don't let your focus on lyrics distract you from a rising health concern relating to boys and music: hearing loss. According to the Mayo Clinic, any sound over 90 decibels can cause hearing loss. Rock concerts come in at about 110 decibels. *Men's Health* recommends ER-20 High Fidelity earplugs as a cheap solution that won't distort the music. Another rock concert danger is the dense "mosh pit" of fans in front of the stage. Trampling is a regular occurrence and can result in serious injuries. Consider your son's size and physicality if he wants to experience the pit, or have him attend with an experienced "mosher." If you're concerned he'll get swallowed, advise your son to enjoy the concert from the stands instead; the music will no doubt be loud enough!

Though rock concerts use massive speakers, a little device in your son's ears may be even louder: his iPod earbuds. These tiny speakers can produce sounds up to 120 decibels! Northwestern University audiologist Dean Garstecki, in a *Science Daily* news report, indicated that this popular "rock concert" volume "is enough to cause hearing loss after only about an hour and 15 minutes." And he's seeing the damage. He and his colleagues are detecting hearing loss in young people that they usually see in older adults. Garstecki recommends a 60 percent/60 minute rule: limit use of these devices to an hour a day and keep the volume below 60 percent of maximum. Though your son may laugh at the 60-minute part, he'll probably have less trouble complying with the lower volume. Our son took the warning quite seriously, however, as he has already been diagnosed with a hearing limitation. He alternates the iPod ear buds with music from his computer speakers—a kinder, more distant option.

Hair, Clothes, and Identity

What happened? The son who was content to wear the same shirt for days suddenly cares about how he looks! What's even more amazing is that he carefully selects the items to wear and painstakingly gets ready, only to produce a look that says, "I picked this off the floor and threw it on." Ah, the secret vanity of the teen boy!

His concern about his appearance is often a relief to parents, even with the increased water bill from his marathon showers. But what happens when he comes home from his friend's house with his hair shaved and eyebrows cut into a tiger pattern?

You may want to count to 10 before you react. It is certainly appropriate for you to set limits on his experimentation, especially when health issues are involved, but it helps us to remember that it's *fashion* he's experimenting with—not drugs or the law. Clothing can be changed; hair will grow back. And for a teen, "taking your word for it" is hard. He wants to experience life more directly. And fashion is a pretty harmless form of experimentation.

Toolbox _____

Fashion does not have to be expensive. Discount stores increasingly offer designer brands for a fraction of what the boutique stores ask. In order to avoid power struggles on cost, agree to pay the discount store price, and if your son wants the high-end option, let him pay the difference. Another great option for today's boys is the thrift store. Rather than paying $20 for a vintage-look T-shirt, he can get *real* vintage for cheap. Our older son enjoys the local thrift store's "$3 a bag" sale!

Find out what the school's dress code is; decide where your outer limits are—how do you feel about piercings and tattoos?—and communicate these boundaries. Beyond that, replace criticism with curiosity: learn about the trends; ask him what he likes; help him shop. And what will be your reward? Beyond understanding him better, a teenage boy can be an honest and valuable fashion consultant, especially when your wardrobe is getting a bit *too* "vintage."

Big Thoughts

When you tap into his world, you may be surprised to learn that he's not only into girls and video games. His mind and his culture are rich with intellectual curiosity, passion, idealism, and activism. While he may have little to say about his feelings, if you can get him talking about a cause or opinion he cares about, you'll start to see his passion. He may even get you excited about concerns you've forgotten. Teenagers are the ones who often "shake up" an overly comfortable society and inspire change. As he takes things apart and asks the tough questions, his energy can be contagious.

Challenging Authority

His energy may also be exhausting. After all, he's often questioning *you!* His voice is getting deeper and louder; he's taller; and he's got that *attitude*. When he expresses his opinions, he seems so sure of himself. He suddenly appears to have it all figured out, trashing the last decade of your instruction. You may wonder what has happened to your son.

As self-assured as he appears, we know that looks can be deceiving, especially with teenage boys. In a *USA Weekend* survey of 272,400 teenagers, the two top influences in the respondents' lives were parents and religion. But don't expect your son to broadcast this reality. He wants and needs to become *more than* your son, and he's busy sorting out how to do this.

When he disagrees with you, ask him about his point of view. By sharing his thinking—out loud—he is exercising his capacity for independence and self-expression. This does not mean you have to agree with him or indulge a request even after he delivers an award-winning argument. But allowing him to disagree with you shows him that he can have his own mind and your respect, too.

Here are some ways to help him develop his mind without driving you out of yours:

◆ Tell him when you are *not* in a place to discuss something. When he's on his way out for the evening is not the time to open up a debate about his curfew. Table it until you both have time.

◆ Help him tolerate the frustration of feeling "right" and being denied. You can applaud his reasoning and acknowledge his feelings, but you are the parent and the answer may still be "no."

◆ Sometimes his "Why?" is not a question but an attempt to wear you down. When he keeps harping on the same thing, trying to get you to move a boundary, it's time to end the conversation.

◆ Teach him to argue in a calm voice. Boys often think that the louder the volume, the better the argument. Tell him you will wait until he lowers his voice or until later when he's calmer, before you will give him the floor. And watch *your* volume, too.

◆ Create opportunities to debate *issues*, not just his rights and freedoms. A healthy political debate around the dinner table is a great way to be together and separate at the same time. Asking *him* questions requires him to think about and clarify his point of view. Know yourself: if your emotional convictions make it hard to be open, acknowledge this and move on to a less heated topic.

The Parental Fall from Grace

It's not easy to see your son's adoring smile replaced by a smug, judgmental sneer. One conversation or look can bring home that dreaded feeling: "I'm no longer cool (in his eyes)." Ouch!

While you remain extremely important to him, his peers are his new frame of reference, and they're simply more interesting to him right now.

Don't take it personally, and don't stop being the parent. Trying to stay cool is a big trap, and it often backfires anyway. He's all over the map these days, and he needs you to stay constant. You'll actually come off better to him if you stand strong. Build up your parenting muscles and your confidence. Work out, talk to friends, reinforce what you like about yourself, and see his growing independence as a tribute, not an insult. His adoring eyes are not gone; they're just averted for now.

The Least You Need to Know

◆ A teen boy wants to look good without appearing to try, to be unique but not weird, and to be smart enough to slack off.

◆ Being popular among a small group of friends is easier than taking on the whole school.

◆ Listening to his music together is a great way to help him sort out his values.

◆ Debating issues helps him develop his thinking and his identity.

◆ As he challenges you, he needs you to remain strong and confident.

Chapter 15

Loving Him, Loving His Friends

In This Chapter

- ◆ Friends on the go
- ◆ She's a "girl friend"
- ◆ Putting out the welcome mat
- ◆ His cyber-network
- ◆ Playing the world: online games
- ◆ When a friend is not a friend

Though you're not likely to see your son and his friends walking arm-in-arm or intimately discussing feelings, his buddies are central for him right now, and how you treat them counts. That is, if you can catch them.

Girls and their friends talk; boys run. In his younger years, his pack ran from house to house in search of adventure. Now they're running out the door, heading to the basketball court, movie theater, or some other version of "out."

Until he gets his license, he'll need you or another parent to drive. Picking up boys who live across town from each other can be a hassle, but the opportunity to connect with his friends is well worth it. In this chapter, we look at how we, as parents, can widen our embrace to include his larger, quieter, and increasingly mobile group of friends— including the ones that he hangs out with in cyberspace.

At His Best

He's been sullen and lifeless all day. His friends come over, and the color returns to his face. He's suddenly animated and engaged. What happened?

It is hard to define the pleasure of friendship, but we can certainly see it in his face. These are "his people," a friend or group of friends who chose each other. They are together purely because they want to be— not because they grew up in the same house or share a class. The acceptance he feels with friends helps him relax and let down his defenses. He is then at his best and most real. We want to be around him, too!

His Friends Matter

From the outside, it's easy to assume that boys move between relationships without much thought. We see them hanging out and joking around, but we're less likely to see the hurt a boy feels when a friend leaves him out or the pain he suffers when separating from a buddy who's moving away. We associate these "traumas" with girls, along with images of their slumber parties and shared secrets.

But girls do not have the corner on any of these experiences. Boys, even in their teens, have slumber parties; they just call them "sleepovers" or "staying over," and they are just as likely to talk well into the night. Boys get close to their friends and share their ups and downs—they are just more likely to do so while involved in a shared activity.

And boys can be fiercely loyal to each other. Male friendship models— think of "buddy cop" movies—teach the importance of being able to rely on each other, to provide "backup." Any parent trying to get information from a teen boy will see his reluctance to "rat out" a friend.

Gossip is expected among girls—it's part of the fun and the drama—but boys are more likely to keep quiet when asked about a friend. It's not that boys don't gossip; recent studies suggest that boys gossip as much as girls. But there are differences. A study of preteen gossip at The University of Michigan reported that, the closer boys get, the less they gossip. The closer girls become, the more they gossip. And a 2007 study of undergraduates from the University of Leicester, England, indicated that girls talk about girls more than boys talk about boys.

Intimacy among boys is much more subtle than what we observe among girls. If your son is hurting, a friend may say "I care" by inviting him out to shoot hoops. Boys connect through action rather than words. The two of them may never directly refer to your son's feelings, but they may not need to. Girls, by contrast, tend to "narrate" relationships by directly acknowledging feelings, intentions, and outcomes.

The ease of interactions between boys can be refreshing. Instead of having a big discussion, supplemented by consultations with other friends, they just throw a ball or say "nice shirt" and move on. In their side-by-side activities, feelings are often shared but without a sense of demand or expectation.

The downside of this indirect communication is that boys may overlook how relational they actually are. Add to this society's emphasis on boys' independent and competitive nature, and boys may indeed devalue the importance of friends. This oversight is evident in the number of married men who lose contact with male friends.

> **Toolbox**
>
> Teach your son to have respect for his friendships. Encourage him to return calls in a timely manner, to be there when he says he will, and to expect good treatment from his friends as well.

Girl Friend, Not Girlfriend

Boys may seek out female friends for their skills in narrating relationships. Guys often feel more comfortable opening up to a girl, knowing that she is less likely to judge or tease him. Girls seek out male friends as confidants as well, feeling safer talking to someone outside of her group and, perhaps, away from the gossip.

More and more, friend groups include a mix of boys and girls. So when a girl shows up at your door, don't assume. Our older son *hates* when we jump to the conclusion that a girl friend is a girlfriend.

Friendships with girls are extremely valuable for boys, establishing a basis for respect and mutual understanding that will carry into his future relationships with women. Treat these girls as his friends, not as girlfriends. Whether she hangs out with him in a group or alone, acknowledge their friendship and take an interest in her—in other words, be friendly!

Opening Your Home

Boys tend to see their own homes as boring; so don't be surprised if he pushes to meet up somewhere else. And where they end up seems to have little to do with luxury; we have friends with a fully appointed recreation center and in-home movie theater who lament that their son usually wants to go somewhere more "fun." A good game system may be essential, but usually "not my house" is preferred.

As your son grows, the preferred place to hang out may be the home with the most liberal policies or the least supervision. Some parents, out of concern that their child will drink and drive, will voluntarily become the "party house," seeing to it that underage kids drink alcohol "*responsibly.*" This, of course, is an oxymoron, since underage drinking is illegal and condoning it is anything but responsible. And parents who enable underage drinking can end up in jail, especially if a teenager they have served gets hurt.

But don't become his buddy in order to embrace his buddies. Your son will likely resent your efforts to join in. Here are some tips for engaging your son's friends:

◆ Ask your son to introduce you to his new friends. If your son brings someone new by and forgets to introduce you, introduce yourself—and give your son a refresher course on introductions later.

◆ When you meet the friend, memorize his name as well as one interest, such as the sport he is involved in. When you later greet the friend by name and ask about his interest—i.e., "how's the team doing?"—he'll be impressed.

◆ Program his friends' phone numbers into your cell phone. If your son forgets his cell phone or doesn't answer, you'll be able to reach him through his friends.

◆ Meet the parents of his close friends, and work together to establish a helpful network to keep your kids safe. You may not have time to have them over for dinner, but you can at least make a friendly phone call, and it's *so* much better to do this when there's no crisis prompting it.

◆ When friends stop by, show them you're glad to see them, and make them feel welcome in your home. Smile and greet them by name; invite them in; ask how they're doing. If your son gets to them first, make a point to stop what you're doing and say hi.

◆ Have food. Growing boys can't get enough of it, and food still says "love" to them. Feed them.

◆ Take them places. While you're driving, you get to overhear their entertaining antics while getting to know them better. It's worth the high cost of the gas.

Everyone wins when friends share their homes as well as their parents. Both of our boys have had friends stay with us while their parents were away, and we have enjoyed the same favor. When the parents are also friends, shared vacations allow friends to taste new experiences together, under the safety net of family. And parents are often relieved to have on-site entertainment for their sons.

Toolbox

To have a separate space in your home where your son and his friends can hang out is ideal—as much for your own sanity as theirs! A basement with some recycled furniture may actually be more comfortable than a highly decorated great room, so don't sweat the details.

Teach your son to use good manners with parents of his friends. While some parents encourage a first-name relationship, have him use the more respectful "Mr.," "Mrs.," or "Dr." and surname unless directed otherwise.

It is gratifying to see a son bond with other parents. The world becomes a friendlier place when "home" isn't limited to where he lives, and loving adults are an abundant resource.

His Web of Friends

If you think it's tough to catch your son and his friends before they bolt out of the house, try keeping up with his contacts online! Our older son types at the speed of light and can as quickly stop the action when we enter the room. His active online social life would be very easy for us to miss. Catching these friends requires more than a greeting at the door—we need to *catch up*.

IM Talking

He and teens and preteens everywhere are "talking" online. Instant messaging, or IM, allows kids to send messages back and forth in real time. The computer screen is today's telephone, with IM providing numerous "lines" simultaneously, including free "long distance" connections to friends far away. If your son and a friend are both on a computer, they can talk. The often-cryptic conversation types out on the screen in one box, while another exchange may be going on in a box on another part of the screen, and so on.

For boys who enjoy punching video controls, the physical challenge of fingertip talking may be part of the draw. But, for whatever reason, boys are hanging on this "phone" for long stretches. According to a 2007 press release by Pew Internet, 87 percent of boys ages 15–17 have used IM, compared to 97 percent of girls in the same age range.

So how in the world do you say "hi" to these friends? While you may not get to have a direct relationship with all of these friends (some you already know), you can get to know the makeup of your son's online social club and see to it that his "web" is not drawing in bad news.

The good news is that IM is generally safer than chat rooms because your son sets up his own contact list and can block people he doesn't want on the list. Still, when fingers are doing the talking, teens can be more "out there" than they might be otherwise. Talk to your son about what boundaries he employs when he sends and receives messages. The written word is a powerful tool, and one that can do damage.

Teach your son that just because someone sends a message, he is not compelled to read it or to respond. Some messages are annoying and intrusive—help him exercise his right to delete and block! Other messages may intend harm; he should block the sender of these messages but also print the message and give it to you as evidence.

Online bullying, or *cyberbullying*, happens when one minor targets another minor in a deliberately hurtful way. When an adult pursues a minor online, it's *cyber-harassment* or *cyberstalking*. If an adult tries to lure a minor into a meeting offline, this is sexual exploitation by a pedophile. If your son is being targeted online, visit wiredsafety. org, where you can report the abuse and get help. If there is an offline threat, contact the police.

Just as adults can easily become consumed with managing e-mails, your son may have a hard time limiting his online conversations, which can start up anytime he's using the computer. You can purchase software, such as *I.M. Control*, that limits his IM time. Programs like *Enuff PC* can time overall use, as well as specific computer activities. These programs let the user know how much time remains, helping him budget his use.

> **Keep Out!**
>
> With the increasing use of acronyms and codes for sending quick messages, your son can type along right in front of you and still keep you in the dark. POS is code for Parent Over Shoulder, and 9 is code for Parent is Watching. For a dictionary of online shorthand, check out netlingo.com.

Talk with your son about his IM life; go over his contact list with him, and "meet" his friends by having him tell you about them. Commend him on his ability to maintain connections with his friends. He'll probably find you annoying, but that comes with the turf. If you're lucky, he'll appreciate your interest in knowing him more fully.

My Space, My Face, My Group

Social networking sites such as *MySpace* and *Facebook* allow subscribers to construct a personal site with photos, personal profile, and blog entries. The blog is the diary of today, except it's meant to be shared.

These sites offer a boy the opportunity to play with his identity in a tangible, visible way. Though girls are the top users of these networks, boys are catching on, perhaps *because* they're so popular with girls. Members can exchange messages and photos, and, together with IM, get to practice communication skills and strengthen friendship networks. Unfortunately, the network with Mom and Dad can be weakened in the process. Here are some ways to connect with your connected son:

◆ Assume he's got an online profile, and tell him you'd like to see it. Parry Aftad, Internet lawyer and creator of wiredsafety.org, suggests giving your teen a day to "clean up" his profile before you view it for the first time. Tell him you want to visit the site with him tomorrow. This empowers him to make needed changes and avoids the trauma or embarrassment of a "break in."

◆ Create your own directory of his Internet access points, including any e-mail addresses, social networking sites, and online memberships, including interactive gaming sites. Everything he joins comes with a username and password. Get all the codes.

◆ Be sure your son knows to *never* give out a password to anyone but you.

◆ Don't use your access to keep constant surveillance; remember what it was like to be a teen. On the other hand, if you are concerned about him or his activities, you have a right to check in without his permission.

◆ Know who has access to his site. Private sites are protected by a password and can only be accessed by specified friends or networks. Facebook is restricted to real-life networks, such as his school, along with selected friends, while other sites may provide the option of being open or private. Keep it private.

◆ Make sure he's not providing any identifying information beyond his first name: no address, phone numbers, or specifics on his parents, school, or workplace. You may feel comfortable allowing more information for a school-only network, where the service acts as a school directory.

◆ See wiredsafety.org for help in keeping up with the rapidly expanding Internet options for your son, and help in keeping him safe.

Getting involved is not only about keeping him safe, it's also about *knowing* him. Sit down with him and look at the photos on his site; ask who's who and how he knows the people on his friends list. If someone seems particularly important to him, but you haven't yet met that person, tell your son you'd like to meet him or her.

When safe boundaries are in place and online interactions enhance, rather than replace, "live" relationships, cyber-connections can help boys get closer to friends and stay in touch. You and your son can benefit as well; many parents use IM to talk to a son who is away at college, for example.

Let's Play Video!

While girls dominate the IM world, boys hold the controllers on video games. According to *HarrisInteractive*, a market research firm, almost all boys (94 percent) report they are playing some kind of video game. In 2007, the firm surveyed 1,178 kids between the ages of 8 and 18. They found that 8- to 12-year-old boys were spending an average of 16 hours a week playing video games, compared to 10 hours for girls. Teen boys were playing even more—18 hours a week, while teen girls' play declined to 8 hours a week.

Multiple-player and interactive online gaming have transformed video play into a social activity. Boys may get together and play a game with the use of extra controllers, or they may meet online, as characters in a video adventure or war—along with a few million other friends. In 2007, Blizzard Entertainment announced that its popular interactive game, *World of Warcraft*, had 8.5 million players worldwide. To add to the excitement, your son may gear up with a headset and microphone

Toy Box

If you thought it was weird when spelling bees and poker competitions showed up on sports channels, hold on. The World Series of Video Games has arrived! The annual competition, which began in 2006 and secured TV coverage in 2007, brings in top performers from around the globe to compete for titles and monetary prizes.

and talk with the players. With the introduction of live chat features, the game becomes more like a stadium event, with people yelling out their allegiances. So much for quiet computer time! Add the guitar controller for Playstation's popular *Guitar Hero* games, and you'll see how animated your basement can become.

Is it safe for him to be talking to players from around the world? As with any online activity, he shouldn't disclose identifying information. And in this case, he's not playing anyway—his *character* is. If you are concerned about voice identification, some systems offer a *voice mask* to disguise the player's gender and age. Though most gamers want to *play*, a disruptive player can be blocked, muted, or, in some systems, reported.

Be sure to balance his online time with family time, friend time, and alone time. When he treats the computer like a life-support system, it's time to shut it down and give him time to breathe on his own.

Is This the Wrong Crowd?

Because his friends hold so much influence right now, the wrong friends can pull him in the wrong direction. So what do you do when you're getting a bad feeling about his buddies?

Why Does He Like These Kids?

It's easy to see our sons as innocents who can get tainted by bad seeds, but it's not that simple. Find out what attracts your son to these friends and what kinds of activities they share. Is your son drawn to the excitement of the risks these boys take, or does he care about someone who happens to be a troublemaker?

Though your son may be up to no good, he may also be trying to help a friend out of a bad situation or just be drawn to a new way of thinking. We may talk about diversity all day long, but when your son reaches out to someone outside of his group, do you get nervous?

Talk to your son. As we discussed in Chapter 14, he's trying on different identities and may be sampling new friendships as well. He'll tell you the good stuff about these friends, so listen. Make a clear distinction between the person and the behavior; regardless of who the person is, if his behavior is harmful to your son, set limits on the relationship.

Separating Gossip from Truth

We have had the experience of being "warned" by another parent about a boy, only to develop great respect for him through our direct experience. Put gossip to the test. First, question whether the "reporters" are talking about the boy's behavior or referring to his parents, social status, or race. Unorthodox parenting practices can be fuel for gossip but may have little relevance to your son's relationship with a friend. If the report *is* relevant and troubles you, talk to your son. He may be able to shed light on a one-time incident, but an evasive or defensive response might suggest a coverup.

Secondly, does the gossip match up with your direct experience of the friend? If you don't know him and your son isn't talking, consult with parents you trust who have had more experience with the boy. Finally, look for changes in your son. Is he more defiant and angry? Does he seem "out of it"? Has he become more secretive?

Gossip, by its very nature, is dramatic. Real life is often much less interesting. Prematurely judging someone your son cares about will only alienate him. Checking out the facts and making your own judgment is good modeling for your son. He's learning to think independently; be a good teacher.

Barbarians at the Gates

If your son's friend is caught selling drugs behind the school, you probably won't care how nice he is. A buddy who expresses anger with his fists is not good company. A friend caught up in his own self-destruction is not in a position to be a friend.

Draw a line. Make it clear to your son that he is not allowed to go out with or bring home that individual. And then find out if your son is involved with similar activities, and, if so, get him help. Even if your son is the good guy trying to rehabilitate the friend, he needs to know that you won't allow the association. If the friend wants help, you can provide a referral, but your son deserves to be a kid, not a social worker.

Your son may kick and scream about your decision, or he may surprise you and breathe easier. It's hard for boys to set limits on an out-of-control friend, and when you do it for him, he may be grateful. Whatever his response, you'll breathe easier, and your son will be safer. Good job!

The Least You Need to Know

- ◆ Boys bond in the context of shared activity.
- ◆ Acknowledge and support his friendships with girls.
- ◆ Know his friends by name, and welcome them into your home.
- ◆ Don't let intimidating technology keep you from parenting his online activity. Catch up and check up.
- ◆ When friends put your son in danger, it's time to put an end to the association.

Chapter 16

Girl and Gay Smarts

In This Chapter

- ◆ From Mars to Venus: understanding girls
- ◆ Those awkward first moves
- ◆ Finding out what girls want
- ◆ What he learns from the media
- ◆ Sex, love … and rejection
- ◆ Building gay character

Girls. The creatures he used to think were carriers of cooties are now looking pretty good. In fact, they seem to be all he thinks about. They're in his music, his fantasy life, and now he has the chance to get close to them for real. Help!

For your son, the prospect of getting close to a girl is probably both thrilling and terrifying. To some degree, girls remain a mystery to him. As he's trying to figure out how to start a conversation, his hormones are yelling, "I want—now!" His response may closely resemble that of a deer caught in the headlights of an approaching semi.

Though you may be the last person he'll come to with his anxieties and desires, you can help by knowing what it's like to be in his sneakers and teaching him the skills he needs for the journey. And if his path reveals that girls don't do it for him, he'll need your understanding all the more. Grab your backpack—we've got some ground to cover!

How Do I Talk to Her?

If your son likes a girl, he may feel overwhelmed at the prospect of having an entire conversation with her. Though he may be comfortable with "small talk" and exchanges about school, he wants more. But as he sees her chatting with her friends, he may wonder how he could possibly hold her interest the way her friends do. He knows how to talk with his buddies and even girls who are his friends, but can he meet the standards of a *girlfriend?* He's probably picked up on the fact that "talk" is important to her, and he doesn't want to screw up.

John Gray's book *Men Are from Mars, Women Are from Venus* (see the Resources appendix) started a revolution in our thinking about male-female communication. By looking at men and women as creatures from separate planets, each with its own language, Gray could help the male "Martians" learn the language of Venus, and vice versa. Couples could then work to *translate* their communications rather than continuing the age-old complaints, "He never tells me what he's feeling, or "She always want to talk!"

> **Boy Wisdom** _____
>
> Without knowing about life on Venus, Tom didn't understand how important it was just to listen without offering solutions ... You see, Venusians never offer solutions when someone is talking. A way of honoring another Venusian is to listen patiently with empathy, seeking truly to understand the other's feelings.
>
> —John Gray, *Men Are from Mars, Women Are from Venus*

These very complaints are familiar to mothers and their sons. While it's crucial for us to learn the language of our sons, he also needs to know how girls relate. And, perhaps for the first time, he has an incentive to know.

Mothers, seize the opportunity! Helping him understand *you* may be a first step to helping him understand girls. I (Laurie) recently used a simple exchange with my boys as a "teachable moment." I was suffering from a nasty cold and shared how crummy I felt. Both of our boys started giving me suggestions: "Why don't you take some ibuprofen?" "Maybe you need a nap." I told them I could see they wanted to help, but a lot of times a girl just wants someone to be sympathetic. The boys were baffled by the idea that a girl would want them to *do nothing* and just talk with her about her misery. They teased me about how stupid that was, but I could tell they were "taking notes" inside their heads.

Knowing how to talk to a girl means knowing how to *listen*. This information may be a relief to your son, who may be feeling pressure to be clever and come up with fascinating topics for discussion. Tell him to be fascinated with *her*, to find out what music she likes, what she thinks about, and, for bonus points, what she is *feeling*. And if teaching your son helps him be more tuned in to you, all the better!

It is interesting to note that, in the language of teens, the two stages of a relationship are *talking*, as in "we're just talking and getting to know each other," and *going out*, which means the two have agreed to be boyfriend and girlfriend. Ironically, a boy and girl who are going out may never actually "go out" on a date!

It's His Move

Your son may be a master strategist at the chess table or on the football field but feel stumped on how to move forward with a girl. How does he direct the conversation to the subject of going to the movie on Friday? How does he draw enough information from her to know if she's even interested? How will he take her hand or put his arm around her without looking as awkward as he feels? And how in the world does any guy get a girl to kiss him?

For a boy, a "date" not only means asking her out but also deciding where to go, providing transportation, and footing the bill. It's all on him, and he hasn't attended a single class on the subject. And just when he thinks his stress level is at an all-time high, you politely ask him, "Are you going to ask that girl to the dance?" If he experiences your question as an assault, it's probably because he's been assaulting himself with the same question. Your inquiry just adds to the sense of demand he already feels.

It's time to draw on the same patience that got you through his potty training. Now, just as then, he can experience efforts to help as pressure and backfire. Just as then, as confused as he may be, he wants to figure it out by himself. And just as then, he needs your trust and affirmation that he is right where he's supposed to be. Here are some ways you can reduce the pressure and build his confidence:

- Compliment him. When he looks good, tell him. When you see a girl respond to him, tell him what you observed. He'll see through exaggerated or patronizing comments, so keep it real. Notice what he does well, and tell him why he's fun to be around.

- If he doesn't want to talk about it, just move on. This is easier said than done, especially for Mom, who learned on "Venus" to dig deeper when someone is not talking.

- Tell him what it was like for you. Sharing funny stories about your early dating life can lighten the mood and help him feel less alone.

- When he shares his interest in someone or his success in asking a girl out, celebrate with him. It is easy for a boy to dismiss the courage *he has already demonstrated* when he's worried about the next two steps.

- Tell him what information is mandatory. You are the parent, so you need to know where he is and who he is with, and he must abide curfew. Both sets of parents need to approve dates. When you establish and enforce safe boundaries, you don't have to "pry" to find out what's going on.

- Do the parenting part, and let the rest go. Accept that he'll strike out sometimes. Girls will challenge him, thrill him, hurt him, love him tenderly, and endlessly confuse him. But, through it all, they will be teaching him. And, for better and for worse, *that's* the education he's interested in.

If he does ask the "how to" questions, and some boys are eager for information, you can draw on your own experience to let him know what worked for you. Help him shift his focus from "doing it right" to following her cues, which we look at next.

Keep Out!

When you peek into the excitement of your son's world, you may want "in." You are understandably curious about his love life, in part because it brings you back to a time that was very alive for you. If your son says, "Get a life!" take his advice. Don't look to him to fill in what you missed or are missing. Instead, let his aliveness inspire you to find your own passion.

What Do Girls Want?

Girls love compliments. Girls love attention. A girl wants to be pursued—*if* she likes the boy, that is. When she likes a boy, she might act aloof while throwing him a coy smile or a teasing comment. If a girl playfully hits a boy on the shoulder, that's a good sign. If she laughs when she's around him, that's a good sign. If she touches her hair, she's unconsciously signaling her attraction.

If she's not interested, she will avoid the boy—especially if she knows *he's* interested. Avoiding is different than playing "hard to get." If she's playing hard to get, she may flirt with someone else or act indifferent, but she'll do it *in his view*. If she's avoiding the boy, she does *not* want him to see her—she avoids eye contact and plans her path so she doesn't meet him.

When she's dating, a girl loves little touches, like a flower in her locker or a card on their one-month anniversary. She likes little touches physically, too—a brush against her cheek or a touch to her hair. Guys who worry that they have to make a grand gesture can relax; she savors the small stuff. She also likes taking walks together, going out for ice cream, and watching "chick flicks" that make her cry. Romance still wins, and chocolate is always good.

Girls fantasize about boys in the context of a story. They enjoy the suspense of an unfolding romantic drama and linger in the stages of talking and kissing. Yes, *talking* is part of the fantasy, with his confessing desire for her. Girls love to be desired, wanted, and loved. They have surging hormones, too, feel "turned on" and think about boys constantly. But while visual stimuli, like a glimpse of a girl's cleavage, will arouse a boy, a girl is more likely to be aroused by eye contact, a smile, the sound of a boy's voice and his words.

Remember the research on girl babies in Chapter 2? They like looking at faces; they hear better; and as they grow, they think in story. Boys want to get in and handle things—then and now. A boy's body is also set up to "get in" without much thought. A girl not only enjoys sexual suspense, her body *needs* it. And for her body to feel sexual pleasure, she needs a boy with skills. Surveys indicate that girls today are more sexually assertive, setting boundaries, communicating what they like and don't like, and feeling more pride in their sexuality. This trend is good for boys, relieving them of the burden of mind reading and always being in charge.

Learning from the Media

Your son receives a great deal of free sex education from the media. In the movies, boy meets girl, boy dates girl, then boy beds girl—and the sequence may be repeated with another girl—all in the space of a couple of hours. If the drama is on TV, things move even faster. How do you give your son a model of a fulfilling, *safe*, and mutually satisfying relationship, when what he sees is so stripped down (perhaps literally)?

Of course you'll want to watch the ratings, but even PG-13 movies show the "early to bed" sequence. And couples aren't just having premarital sex; they're having pre-*relationship* sex!

> **Boy Wisdom**
>
> I'm not saying that women don't think about sex also. I'm saying that women are capable, for at least brief periods of time, of *not* thinking about sex.
>
> —Dave Barry, *Dave Barry's Complete Guide to Guys*

Before you panic, keep in mind that the media can and does depict positive aspects of relationships—true love is often at the center of good drama. The key is in knowing—and seeing—what he sees and talking about it with him.

Reality Check

It's helpful to remind your son that what's on the screen is very different from reality. A compact drama needs to capture the whole life cycle of a relationship, and sex is a big seller. Things progress rapidly because producers want to fit it all in. A logical explanation like this is much easier for a boy to accept than a lecture on the evils of the media.

Both positive and negative depictions of relationships can provide teaching opportunities, so supplement your viewing with discussion. It's good for his mental and moral development, and friendly debate on a movie's worth can be fun.

Morality Check

What kind of model of sexuality do you want your son to adopt? If you aren't setting the "marriage first" boundary, what kind of boundaries are you offering, and why? Do your religious practices offer guidelines? Do you agree with them? What boundaries were helpful to you growing up? How would you do it again if given the chance?

With couples getting married later, the rise of divorce, and the diversification of lifestyle choices, the place of sex in it all can feel very murky. How do we guide our sons when *we* feel so confused?

Many parents choose to look the other way, especially with boys. The confusion doesn't go away; we just pass it over to our sons. As parents, it's our job to *get* clear, as best we can, on what we believe is right and wrong when it comes to sex—and to tell our sons, explicitly.

A Real Conversation About Sex

You talked with him about sex back when he was more interested in trucks than girls. Now the topic is relevant to him and, while he'll probably feel extremely uncomfortable having a "sex talk" now, he will also be listening in a new way.

A report from the National Campaign to Prevent Teen Pregnancy revealed an interesting finding: parents said that *friends* had the most

Toolbox

Be prepared for your teenager to ask when you first had sex. He's old enough to hear a straight answer and will benefit from your current perspective on how your choice worked out for you.

influence on their teen's decisions about sex. The teens said that *parents* influence their decisions about sex more than anyone else. The report referred to the tendency of parents to underestimate their influence as a "crisis of confidence."

As much as your son may try to convince you otherwise, what you say does matter. A study by the Center for Disease Control and Prevention found that teens who discuss sex with a parent tend to wait to have sex, have fewer sexual partners, and are more likely to name a parent, rather than a peer, as a good source of information about sex. The study also found that, when parents did not talk with teens about sex, they were more likely to go to peers for information.

Talk. He'll listen.

Getting a Clue

When you sit down with your son, you need to have a sense of what's going on in his world. Here's an update. A report on the sexual behaviors of teen boys and young men, compiled by the National Campaign to Prevent Teen Pregnancy, indicated the following trends:

◆ Between the years 1988 and 2002, there has been a steady decline in the number of teenage boys (ages 15–17) who were having sexual intercourse.

◆ Between 1991 and 2003, a steady decline was also found in the number of high school boys having multiple sexual partners.

◆ More boys are using condoms.

◆ Teenage boys and girls are more likely to participate in oral sex or mutual masturbation. Oral sex is more often performed to the benefit of the boy and is not generally considered "sex" by teenagers.

◆ Parents continue to be clueless, and underestimate the frequency of sex among teenagers.

Another emerging trend in teen culture is the "hook up." When two people agree to "hook up," they consent to sex—minus the relationship. They may go to a room at a party, have sex, then separate. Kissing may be avoided because it implies intimacy. Partners are likely to be drunk when they hook up.

Limits and Values

Find a time to talk to your son when you're both relaxed, ideally when you're already discussing his life. You can start by asking him about his views on sex, what he thinks is important, and when he imagines becoming sexually active. Depending on when you have the conversation, a more relevant question may be, "Are you sexually active?" or "How long have you been sexually active?"

By inviting him to share his beliefs, you get a read on where his thinking is, that is, if he's honest. By talking with you, he also gets a chance to become more conscious of his own values regarding sex. You may be surprised at his thoughtfulness on the matter. Or not. He may just shrug uncomfortably, grunt and say, "I don't know." If so, you can respond, "That's okay, but we want to go over some things with you."

He's probably learned the basics in health class, but he needs to hear you say that, until he's ready to start a family, there is *never* a good reason to have sex without protection. A girl telling him she's on the pill is not enough—he needs a condom. A pill will not protect him or her from STDs, and the risk is too high—unwanted pregnancy, AIDs—for him to rely on anyone else's word. It's also important that he sees himself as accountable for using protection rather than leaving it up to her.

He needs to be absolutely clear that "no means no." Girls can certainly give mixed messages, but if he's not clear what she wants, it's time to slow down. Before he can truly be responsive to her, and she to him, they need to develop a foundation of trust and honest communication. That won't happen if your son participates in a hook up.

Keep Out!

While we have long been aware of the downside of early sexual activity for girls, we are learning that boys suffer, too. A longitudinal survey of 6,500 teenagers from across the United States revealed that sexually active girls *and* boys are significantly more likely to feel depressed and are also more likely to attempt suicide. And, contrary to the image of the conquest-happy male, over half of the sexually active boys said they wished they had waited longer before initiating sex.

Falling in Love

He's with her all the time, and when he's not, he's with her on the phone or at the keyboard. At the dinner table, he's off with her in his mind. He seems softer and happier. He's "in love."

If your teenage son falls in love, do your best not to minimize or bad talk his relationship. For him, this is as real as it gets. Invite the girl to dinner. Spend some time with her. Be kind. Chapter 21 discusses the experience of meeting his future bride, but his love interest at this stage will most likely drift away. It may take a few years. He needs to see more of the world. A boy who goes to college is unlikely to maintain a relationship with his hometown girl.

Ask him about his girlfriend, but help him stay on track with school and work. His love need not lead to bad grades or a bad work ethic. If he falls in love before you talk to him about sex and relationships, don't delay. Speak right up and mention contraception.

Rejection Boot Camp

When an unexpected "Dear John" instant message arrives, your son will naturally be down for a few days. A simple, "that sucks" or "I'm sorry" may be all he needs to verify for him that you understand he is hurting. Attempts to cheer him up may leave him feeling more alone. Give him room to grieve, but don't let him check out of his life. He needs the structure of daily activity—school, chores, sports—to keep him grounded.

If your son stays down for what seems too long a period (weeks), and his normal functioning (school, work) is being negatively affected, he may be experiencing depression and may benefit greatly from seeing a therapist or a psychiatrist. Clinical depression is dangerous in teens. After the age of nine, boys commit suicide at an increasing higher rate than girls. Older teen boys kill themselves at approximately *four times* the rate of girls.

Encourage your son to go out with his friends as soon as possible. Once he starts to circulate and touches base with his buddies, he'll feel more attractive.

As soon as possible, help him recognize that weathering rejection is a crucial life skill. Commend his ability to pick up and move on. Share stories of rejections that you endured, and explain how failed relationships helped you get to better things. Every actor and writer has a story of the numerous rejections they had to endure before they made it big. The logic is the same for really great relationships; you keep at it until you find the role of a lifetime.

Sometimes he'll be the one ending a relationship, which is hard in a different way. While he should be kind, he does not have to be pulled back in by guilt or her distress. Again, "it sucks" sums it up. Losing a relationship is a hard passage for him, and it's hard for you to witness, but he needs to know that he can handle it. He'll be okay.

From Girl Smarts to Gay Smarts

How do you respond if you discover that what looks good to him is not a "she" at all, but a "he"? Maybe you notice a book he's checked out on the topic, or perhaps he tells you directly. At some point, the pieces fit together, and you realize that he is gay. When this happens, and it can take a while, your assumptions about his future suddenly fall away. Feelings of shock and loss are normal. When what you think to be true changes, it's scary. How do you get your head around this new reality?

When parents discover that a child is gay, they go through a series of emotions similar to that of a grieving process: shock, denial, guilt, emotional expression, personal decision-making, and finally, acceptance. If he comes out to you, he has probably already received support and may be prepared for your emotions—at least on paper. Gay support organizations, which he has probably accessed online, advise against coming out to parents until the individual is strong enough to deal with—and even *help* with—his parent's reactions.

As ready as he may feel, he's probably terrified that he'll lose your love. You'll need time to catch up, but hold tight to the reality that he is still the same boy you have loved from the start. Hug him. Tell him you still love him. You can tell him that you're confused and scared, but that you are with him. He'll be all right, and so will you.

Keep Out!

Studies have found gay boys to be *up to seven times* more likely to have attempted suicide than straight boys. Critics challenge the legitimacy of these studies and caution against assuming that gay equals unhappy. As with any boy, investigate signs of depression or suicidal thinking. Gay males who are more effeminate seem to be at higher risk, as are boys who have not yet come to terms with being gay.

Thankfully, he is not alone and neither are you. A strong community of people have been through exactly what you're experiencing. And if he's coming out to you, he'll probably have resources to offer you as well.

In his book *The New Gay Teenager* (see the Resources appendix), Ritch Savin-Williams comments on the new social landscape that gays inhabit. "Their world is permeated as never before by tolerance, if not by outright acceptance." In addition, closeted gay teenagers who used to be completely isolated can now obtain information and support via the Internet.

Am I Gay?

Perhaps your son feels attracted to guys but is still questioning his sexual orientation. *OutProud*, the National Coalition for Gay, Lesbian, Bisexual and Transgender Youth, offers the following questions to help him find clarity:

◆ When I dream or fantasize sexually, is it about boys or girls?

◆ Have I ever had a crush or been in love with a boy or a man?

◆ Do I feel different than other guys?

◆ Are my feelings for boys and men true and clear?

If he is truly attracted to boys, it may take him a while to accept this reality. Many gay boys *try* to like girls, and some may even have sex with a girl to prove that they are straight. Some boys find they are attracted to boys *and* girls and come to identify themselves as bisexual, although this is more rare. On the average, a boy who identifies himself as gay recognizes this reality around age 12, accepts his orientation between the ages of 15 and 16, and finally tells someone when he's 16. Coming out in a more public way may take much longer.

What Gay Is, and What It's Not

The term "gay" may refer to any person who is sexually oriented to persons of the same gender or only to *men* whose sexual orientation is to men (as in "gay and lesbian"). Beyond that, the word gay tells us very little about who a boy is.

Gay is *not* a personality style. The assumption that gay men are effeminate is widely promoted in the media, and flamboyant gay men tend to be more visible than the doctors, lawyers, and accountants who live quietly, perhaps with a male life partner, in Anywhere, U.S.A.

People sometimes confuse being gay with dressing like or wanting to be a woman. Men who like to cross the gender line, usually by dressing as a woman (or in *drag*), are considered *transgender*. A *transsexual* male feels like a woman trapped in a man's body and seeks to correct the discrepancy through a sex-change operation. It is helpful to remember that "trans" refers to crossing gender lines.

The issue of whether gay men are more like women is a complex one. A large-scale study conducted at California State University in 2005 found support for the *gender inversion hypothesis*—the idea that gay males are more feminine and lesbian females are more masculine. However, the same study noted that homosexual participants were "more variable" on gender-related traits than the straight participants, suggesting that gay individuals may feel less constrained by gender roles than heterosexuals.

Leonard Sax, author of *Why Gender Matters* (see the Resources appendix), draws attention to research that challenges the stereotype of the effeminate male: in certain physical manifestations, including penis size, gay men tend to be "hypermasculine." Your son may be gratified to hear this bit of information!

Toolbox

Resources for gay youth and their families are abundant. OutProud, The National Coalition for Gay, Lesbian, Bisexual & Transgender Youth, offers extensive information through their website (outproud.org). Most high schools have a Gay-Straight Alliance (GSA), which allows gay teens and their straight friends to share support (gsanetwork.org). And the support and advocacy group, PFLAG, Parents, Families and Friends of Lesbians and Gays, has chapters throughout the country (pflag.org).

The fact that it is so hard to pin down "what is gay" brings home the reality that a gay man is, first and foremost, an individual. We are finding that both sexuality and gender are more fluid than society would like to think. While categories can aid understanding, they can also reduce and dehumanize the people they seek to define. One of the gifts of parenting a gay child—and there are many—is learning to see *and love* beyond categories.

Confidently Gay

While adults may worry and debate about the topic of homosexuality, our children are growing up in a whole new world. Teens today don't carry the weight of our fears and prejudices. They are growing up with openly gay schoolmates; they know that being gay is not a disorder; and they look at us and don't seem to get what all the fuss is about.

However, this kind of acceptance is not universal, and gay boys are still vulnerable to teasing, judgment, and homophobic hostility. But gay boys are also getting thicker skin and taking on the challenge of deciding for themselves who they are and what they value.

Boys who accept themselves as gay are real warriors, breaking through limitations and prejudices, internally and externally. To use an old-fashioned term, they *build character*. Savin-Williams' research emphasizes the pride and resilience gay teens develop, as well as their giftedness in embracing diversity. But he also challenges us to take our understanding to the next level: to acknowledge that gay kids, just like straight kids, are neither heroes nor villains—they're just kids. As he puts it, "they are ordinary."

The Least You Need to Know

- By explaining their own feelings, moms help their boys understand girls.

- Boys can relax and slow down. Girls like the suspense of a slowly unfolding romance.

- When characters in a movie go from first date to bed, remind your son that the actors need to cover (and uncover) everything in about 90 minutes. That's not life.

- Teen boys who talk with their parents about sex wait longer to have sex, have fewer sexual partners, and regard their parents as helpful consultants.

- Gay boys are growing up in a new age, with peers who understand, schools that teach tolerance, and private avenues for support via the Internet.

Boy Gets a Life

He is taller than you now.

Your son is in high school and, while he won't easily admit it, family and you are still important. From avoiding unhelpful interrogations at home to helping your son survive being stopped by the police, this section guides parents in how to deal with the particular challenges of raising a son who eats much and talks little.

This final section also prepares you and your son for his launch from the nest. Whether it is off to college or the workplace, Part 4 helps parents let go with more confidence and less fear.

You've prepared him well. Your good boy is going to make a great man.

Celebrate your success!

Chapter 17

He's in High School!

In This Chapter

- High anxiety
- Schwing set
- Role on
- Making the grade

Your son is now entering high school.

What?

Nothing alerts a parent to aging—for the son or the parent—like the realization that: "This is it! My son only has a few more years at home."

Your son will face many challenges as he moves into high school. And the text in this chapter will help you *help him* confront his fears about his safety, his identity, and his academic ability. You'll be straining to keep him safe at the very time he is stretching to break free. Your efforts are not going to be easy, but they will be worthwhile. He may be six feet tall, but you're still in charge.

His Brave New World

I (Barron) still remember entering high school and just marveling at the new world surrounding me. Two upperclassmen basketball players were known as the "twin towers" and were something like 6' 9" and 6' 10" tall. The school had almost 2,000 students, all rushing to a wide variety of classes.

Reading the high school curriculum was like reading a menu. Some classes I wanted to taste (biology); other subjects I did not want to go near (trigonometry). Of course, every student had preferences. As an emerging math hater, I struggled in math classes while other students appeared to enjoy playing "seek and destroy" games on their Texas Instruments calculators. Still other students excelled at sports, while another group perfected standing across the street smoking cigarettes.

As I walked among giants, I knew I needed to learn much about and from high school.

Will I Have to Fight?

Attending a large school with hundreds more students raises the potential for your son to be bullied. If your son has managed to avoid bullying so far, he will likely do well. If your son has suffered from bullying in the past, you will need to watch for any behavioral changes once he enters high school.

High school students can be menacing, as upperclassmen often possess the strength and speed of an adult, but their decision-making ability is that of a teenager. Violence, usually fighting, occurs, and for the same stupid reasons that adults fight: a perceived slight, a stolen heart, and so on.

Unfortunately, some schools suffer from more profound threats. Active gangs, weapons, and poor security combine in an undercurrent of threatened violence. These undercurrents distract from the day-to-day learning, and freshmen need to learn quickly how to stay away from such threats.

Your son will likely never have to fight. He will, however, need some street smarts to pick up on when his actions invite abuse. Have some common sense, and allow your child to dress in a way that protects him. Fashionwise, clothes help. If he does not have a senior classmate he can confide in, have him talk in private to a veteran male counselor, administrator, or teacher about how to avoid trouble, and more importantly, who to avoid.

Keep Out!

If gangs are a real (not imagined) danger at your son's school, learn what he needs to wear to avoid offending the idiotic sensibilities of these violent thugs. Usually this means simply avoiding wearing an offending sports team logo or jersey or a particular color of clothing. If the administrators won't talk about the "dress code" issue, talk to the senior police officers assigned to the school. They will know.

Will I Fail?

High school brings new challenges to the former "brains" of the class. Your son will no longer stand out immediately because of his intellect as much stiffer competition will surround him in classes designed (hopefully) to challenge him. He may be very aware of this risk initially, or it may dawn on him quickly once he attends his first set of classes.

In any event, you will need to be prepared to help sustain him through this struggle and fear. It is very easy to denigrate your son's efforts if he does not immediately do as well in high school as he did in the early years of schooling. Parents easily chalk it up to ennui or teenage laziness. More likely it is a product of not comprehending the material combined with an attitude that says: "If I don't try 100 percent, I really can't say I failed."

He may very well fail at something in high school. If he masters all his classes, he may fail at sports. If he runs for class president, he may lose the election. Or he may simply not be as popular or well liked as he was in middle school. Failure can be academic, athletic, or social. The potential for humiliation in high school is bottomless.

Your constant support is essential. Your willingness to observe, identify, and, perhaps, intervene will be crucial to your son's thriving through the inevitable failures. You won't be able to help him pick a girl (really, don't try), but you can help him buy some clothes that fit and are fashionable. You can feed him healthy food and encourage/require him to exercise. You can hire a tutor when you see he is struggling in a subject. You can send him to sports camp or take him to the batting cage to work on hitting the 80-mile-an-hour fastball. What you must try to avoid—and this is difficult—is falling into a default mode of criticizing your son. Even though he looks like he is taking it, hearing your humiliating words wounds him.

When you confront a behavioral failure, an appropriate, well-thought-out consequence and a fairly calm voice will do more to correct the problem than screaming insults. When you stay tuned in to his fear of wider failures and offer encouragement and some of your own stories, he'll realize he is not alone and his fears will diminish.

You cannot, nor should you attempt to, shield him from all failure. You, of course, would not want to set him up for obvious failure either. Successful people have another word for failure: experience.

Boys Are Hormonal, Too

Boys in high school will have ridden the rising tide of puberty to the schoolhouse doors and will arrive with a burgeoning interest in girls. A few boys will have no reaction to girls and will develop an interest in other boys (see Chapter 16).

An old saying states that boys reach their sexual peak at seventeen and women at thirty. Not surprisingly, there is also a well-known— no doubt from the sunrise of human existence—desire flowing in 17-year-old boys to take a sexy 30-year-old woman to bed.

Here are some thoughts on hormones and high school boys.

Testosterone and Emotion

Testosterone is a hormone produced in the testicles. As your son's muscles fill out, you will witness his emotions and desires magnify in intensity. Aggression and libido (sex drive) are amplified by this principal hormone.

Testosterone basically turns up the volume, way up that is, on the adolescent demand of "I want it." The flaring look in your son's eyes, the intensity you may never have seen before, can be a bit off-putting. For some parents whose sons tower over them, it can be downright scary.

As a parent, it is important to recognize the fuel source for this intensity. Resist the impulse to give in to unreasonable demands simply to avoid what are now more aggressive confrontations. Your son needs you now more than ever. His body is driving him at a level he does not fully comprehend, not only toward sexual desire but also impulsive, poorly thought-out behavior. It is also helping drive his positive ambitions as well.

If you begin talking to your son, and he becomes intensely angry and will not listen to reason at that very second, avoid responding in kind. Indicate that you will not engage in a shouting match, and delay the conversation until later. Not too much later; wait until he calms down in a few hours or the next morning. As boys love to eat, try to talk over a meal. Or go for a walk together. Your boy will likely be ready to listen to you, even if you need to dish out a consequence to him.

Testosterone is the E ticket to life as a teenage boy. Even if your son develops later than his peers, his brain will begin to ready him for life as a man. His body will prepare him to reproduce. While your son is physically capable of fathering a child, hopefully he will have no desire to become a father.

By being aware of his hormone-driven emotional intensity and setting limits on how you will interact with him, you will let him know that you are present for him. When the storms of adolescence try to drive him off course, he will know—even if he won't admit it—that you are the safest harbor in his life.

Lust 24/7

Ah, lust—one of the seven deadly sins. A high school boy whose mind does not consider lust at some point is likely suffering some detachment from reality. I (Barron) distinctly remember the perfume worn by a girl, Donna, in my geometry class sophomore year. I remember her hair, her face, the back of her head, and …. For several minutes each day, geometry was the furthest thing from my mind. I never talked to Donna other than to say "hi." I suppose the looming threat of her football player boyfriend's fist hitting my face was a strong disincentive to pursuing her; that, and the fact that at the time I weighed about 120 pounds. In any event, I remember her name and the intoxication I felt being next to her. Should Donna have agreed to kiss me, I would have gladly accepted the wages of sin because my head was so out of kilter.

If your son appears in a fog, he may be lost in a fantasy with a girl who has captured his imagination. While girls in general may be a distraction, some special girls can prompt a state of mental fixation. These infatuations will come and go. The rare boy will enter a long-term relationship at this stage.

Boy Wisdom

Teaching these three elements [love, sex, commitment] simultaneously but with respect for the separate power and magic of each gives boys a great deal of insight into what is otherwise an undistinguishable, muddy mass of feelings and urges. It gives them a language. [It] is more essential to do the separation with boys if we want them to focus on the third, commitment.

—Michael Gurian, *The Wonder of Boys*

Talk to your son about lust, sex, love, and the eventual joy of committing his heart and his life to one special partner. Boys may hear about cheap experiences with girls around school, but what they need to hear is that loving a woman—body and soul—brings much greater rewards. The more he treasures his sexuality as a gift to give to a true love, the more likely he will be to wait for the right person. Masturbation ("taking care of it yourself") can be discussed as a natural, shame-free way of satisfying the sex drive.

Will he wait until marriage to have sex? The statistics say no. According to a 2007 report by the Centers for Disease Control, 25 percent of 15-year-old boys have had vaginal intercourse. That figure rises to 89 percent for men ages 22–24. But he may not have as many partners as popular culture implies. According to the same report, men ages 30–44 had an average of six to eight different female sexual partners, while women in the same age group had an average of four male sexual partners.

Having a Role

We discussed identity experimentation in Chapter 14. Let's now take a look at some of the particular roles you may find your son playing once he starts high school. Depending on the identity he attaches to, you'll play a vital role in helping him find his place. You are not lost or forgotten. You're just not going to get much recognition as a parent for a while.

Leader

Your son's leadership skill may be apparent early in life or may emerge as his confidence grows. Success breeds success.

Boys like to risk, and risking can be an important part of being an effective leader. Bold thinking and a willingness to take a chance combine to create dramatically improved results for all kinds of groups. If your son enjoys high risk and high reward, he may want to try his hand at running for student government or taking charge of a club activity.

Leadership opportunities in high school also translate well to a college application. Encourage your son to participate at school or church, but do not push him to assume a role he expresses no interest in. You want him to develop his own leadership skills, not simply be an instrument for your well-meaning but unhelpful ambitions for him.

> **Boy Wisdom**
>
> When I was a boy of 14, my father was so ignorant I could hardly stand to have the old man around. But when I got to be 21, I was astonished at how much the old man had learned in seven years.
>
> —Mark Twain, American writer and humorist

Loner

If your son enjoys time to himself, he may simply be introverted and so gains power and strength in solitude. He needs to be away from the crowd. He will likely have a few friends, but these friendships will be very important to him.

A loner is not necessarily lonely. Many introverts cringe at the thought of too many large group activities. They just are not that enjoyable after a while. They are not energizing.

Make every attempt to discern what it is your son enjoys about being alone, and listen to him. He needs to know you love him for who he is, especially if he's a journal-writing book lover—in other words, a boy who does not gather much applause from high school culture.

Keep Out! _____

If your son is withdrawn, emotionally unavailable, and appears detached from reality, his behavior deserves scrutiny and action. Discuss your concerns with him and with others, including parents, teachers, and your physician. Teachers who see your son interact with others can provide great insight into what he's like outside the home. It is one thing to enjoy solitude, but a predominately hostile and paranoid worldview is not normal and may even be dangerous. Get him help.

Rebel

"You're tearing me apart!"

This was the famous line from the 1955 film *Rebel Without a Cause*. James Dean played Jim Stark, a teenage terror, a middle-class new kid in town who felt little love from his family and engaged in knife fights and car races to prove himself to others.

A rebellious child needs many things. The main thing he needs is consistent firm rules from parents who provide a stable home. He must know his parents aren't going to cave when he throws a tantrum. Family therapy may be very helpful to break the power struggle and give your son a chance to reconnect with you.

A rebel may also just be a child who thinks differently. He may love to wear his hair in dreads, read radical philosophy, or if his parents are old hippies, crank up Rush Limbaugh. That your child is not like anyone else may be a cause to celebrate, not to cringe. And if he is inspired to change things, help him channel his rebellion into activism. The concern comes when your son constantly rebels against your authority on the one thing he must abide by: your rules about his safety.

A rebel who does not do what his parents tell him to do, to the point of exhaustion, is an incorrigible. That is, the boy is unwilling to adhere to parental authority. Teenage boys who wander at will, use drugs, steal, and refuse to obey can be put into state custody on a petition from the parents. This is the very last resort, but may be necessary to prevent a boy being sent to a detention center for delinquent conduct.

Give your son credit, and ask him why he acts, thinks, dresses in that way he does. He may surprise you by providing a well-thought-out, original answer that reflects his genuine personality.

Entertainer

A boy who likes to entertain is fun to be around. He likes attention and works for it. He may be introverted, entertaining to experience a personality that protects his inner life, or he may simply love to be around as many people as he can be, an A-list extrovert.

Consider encouraging your entertainer to improve his skills in theater and other performing arts. He may have a real talent. If the jokes are getting old, tell him that, too. He needs to know when the audience is tired.

Also, check in with your son to see if he is being bullied. Many professional entertainers have said they became the class clown to protect themselves from abuse. If your son has significant fears about attending school, you'll want to know about them. A son who is trying to be funny all the time to avoid being attacked is under an unhealthy amount of stress.

Hero

In small towns across the country, the high school hero is alive and well. *Friday Night Lights* was a 2006 television series that spotlighted the intense high school football culture of a Texas town. Some football and hockey players have commented that a Super Bowl or Stanley Cup championship in no way equals the pressure and thrill of a high school state title.

Watching your son play on a team, especially a team that is winning, can be very exciting. He's pumped, and you're along for the ride. If he gets hit, you cringe. When he gets up, you breathe a sigh of relief as he moves on to the next play. Sports can be exhilarating. As a parent, the challenge is to keep the focus on your son and stay in tune with his moods. He may decide that he does not care for the role of hero and would just as soon spend time learning the guitar instead of how to get free in the secondary.

If he does stay in and enjoy sports, help him see beyond his time as the weekend hero in waiting. High school is the end game for the vast majority (some 97 percent) of boys, at least as far as public sports acclaim.

Heroic efforts can be made in all activities, of course. Hopefully your son will enjoy success in whatever he does and have a chance to accept congratulations from his peers and teachers. Band, art, theater, debate, robotics, chess, dance, cheerleading, rodeo, high school bowl, and a host of other high school competitions elevate the best teams or individuals.

Make every effort to appreciate your son's chosen activity. Even if you're tone deaf, attend his concerts. He wants to be a hero in your eyes. He is your hero when he tries his best. So make sure he knows it!

Regular Guy

Boys want to stand out, but not too much. Crazy fun is cool. But odd man out is bad.

The regular guy is likely going to be your son. If he plays sports, he may be fighting valiantly on the defensive line. If he is in the orchestra, he might be sawing away at third violin. Many boys fit no popular stereotype in high school. If they experiment with hair or clothes, they are just trying to get along. They are not trying to make a statement.

Sticking by your son and loving him is the mainstay that will help him handle the ups and downs of a regular guy's day at a regular high school. His role is simply to be himself. It is hard to ask for much more from a boy.

What About Academics?

High school is the time for students to build on the concrete knowledge they have acquired and turn to more abstract levels of thinking. Abstract thinking requires an appreciation for subtlety and paradox.

High school tests do not always ask for answers that are written on a page in the textbook. Students must find the answer through an analysis of the information provided. High school can be academically very challenging, even for students who have done well in the past. With the distractions of sports and other activities, boys can quickly begin to fail their studies. But these ideas can help you keep him on track.

This Is Hard!

"I have no idea."

This is a typical answer a parent of a high school boy gives when consulting on a homework problem. For most parents, trigonometry, French revolutionary politics, and the atomic weight of copper is knowledge that dissipated long ago. Adults sometimes forget how hard high school classes can be.

Most high schools offer graduated levels of difficulty: regular, honors, and Advanced Placement (AP) for college classes. Since boys tend to overestimate their ability, they get in trouble faster than girls. To avoid academic problems, parents of boys need to monitor their son's progress each week. Look at his binder. Is it neat? Has he handed in his assignments? What are his grades on the pop quizzes?

Schools often wait too long to report a problem. Especially keep a close eye on your son in the first few weeks of a new semester in high school. Ask for frequent written reports (e-mails) from the teachers in classes where he is struggling.

If your son needs to step down to a class that is not so demanding,

Toolbox

Tutor.com offers live homework assistance. Boys can even use an interactive white board to draw math equations "freehand" with a mouse on this website. This service is often free when you follow a link from your local public library.

do it. Don't let his or your pride get in the way of a successful—as opposed to failed—education. Hire a tutor to help him, or use a free online tutor like tutor.com. But don't be afraid to adjust his academic load.

Competing Priorities

"Is your homework done?"

You'll quickly tire of asking this question to a busy high school student. To avoid this annoying interrogatory, sit down with your son after school and set time deadlines for him to complete his homework. Be flexible, too, as teachers sometimes forget to coordinate with other teachers and your son may literally have six to eight hours of work to do.

If your son keeps pushing weekend homework off until Sunday evening, require that he complete two to three hours of schoolwork on Saturday. You may just have to say no to trying out for a play if he is struggling already with time commitments.

Prioritizing means just that. All time demands are not equal. If your son is doing well, though, don't say no just because you think he might struggle. He needs to learn his limits. He may also surprise you with his energy level and pull off a schedule that would leave you gasping.

Taking Himself Seriously

Teenage boys have a hard time taking a long-range perspective and sometimes tend to treat their lives flippantly. Of course the executive function area of their brain—their ability to plan and follow through—is still developing, so this is no great surprise.

Keep in mind that statistics show boys make up 55 percent of high school dropouts and get into much more disciplinary trouble than girls. Boys cannot be left to flounder, because the risk is too great.

A son who is nonchalant or appears disinterested needs some benchmarks to gauge his progress. Goals, even modest ones, that he sets will take the pressure off you as the bad guy and put the onus on him to step up. Well-thought-out goals, when met, create a foundation for a purposeful life and future success. Short-term goals (organize binder each week) to longer-term goals (graduate with honors) can be written down. Give him a chance to learn what high achievers have known forever: "setting your mind" on doing something works.

The Least You Need to Know

◆ High school boys worry about safety, acceptance, and success.

◆ Parents must educate boys about love, commitment, and safe sex.

◆ Your son's chief role in high school is to be himself.

◆ Because boys are at greater risk for failure in high school, parents need to monitor achievement in between report cards.

Chapter **18**

Beyond Rage and ESPN

In This Chapter

- ◆ What's behind dead-end conversations
- ◆ Maintaining close ties
- ◆ Understanding his posture and body language
- ◆ Building emotional strength
- ◆ Recognizing symptoms of male depression

As your teen boy flips from channel to channel, long legs sprawled across the couch and eyes fixed on the screen, "remote" may describe more than that device in his hand. But wait; when his favorite team is losing, he'll come to life—in a kind of *Incredible Hulk* way, vividly demonstrating his outrage with each bad play or call.

Teen boys are masters of contradiction: they can be passionate one minute and poker-faced the next. And unless his passion is in the "Yes!" category, it's often some variant of anger: annoyance, irritability, fury, aggravation, frustration, hostility, disgust, or full-out rage.

Whether he's closed off or going off, a teen boy's emotions can be more off-putting than inviting. So how do we connect with him beyond rage and ESPN?

Boy of Few Words

What is the biggest challenge of parenting a teenage boy? For most of us, it's *talking with him*. Soon after his voice deepens, his speaking becomes mysteriously limited to occasional grunts and one-word responses—at least with his parents. According to him, everything is either "fine" or "good." If we push, he gets mad. If we assume we know what he's feeling, he gets mad. As we search for the one perfect sentence he *might* tolerate hearing, we have to wonder: is there a better way?

There is a better way: *his* way. Rather than seeing him as resistant, rude, or remedial, let's look at what is normal for boys.

Toy Box

My 15-year-old son and I (Laurie) were enjoying a special day together. We have the tradition of back-to-school shopping, one-on-one, complete with lunch at a favorite restaurant. Sitting across the table, we had a perfect opportunity to "talk." As he dug into his spaghetti, I tried a couple of questions, which just annoyed him. Then I decided to try a casual statement about what I was observing: "So, it seems that you're enjoying group activities with guys and girls these days." His response: "Just … stop … talking."

Clearly defeated, I asked, "So how 'bout those Cubs?"

At least I got a laugh.

Interrogation Doesn't Work

He comes in the door after a long day of school, probably followed by some kind of practice. He's been gone for over eight hours, and you want to know how his day went. So you ask, "How was your day?" He replies, "Fine."

Great. His answer does nothing to paint a picture of his day and effectively closes the conversation. If you're like most parents, you don't give up. You ask more questions. But if he's like most teenage boys, he stays with the one-word responses. The more you interrogate, the more likely he is to get annoyed.

Let's look at what's going on for him. I recently asked our 16-year-old son for his take on the "how was your day?" question. He replied: "It would take forever to describe my entire day to you. You have no context for what's happening."

Our son's response shed light on a number of problems with the question. First of all, "How was your day?" is a tough question for all of us. In social exchanges, an appropriate and even *expected* response is "fine." We've all probably had the experience of considering an honest response—starting with "do you have an hour?"—but thought better of it. The cognitive task of scanning an entire day and coming up with a summary that captures it all is tough for anyone, but tougher for a boy.

A boy's brain more naturally works like a map, so scanning his day is not a problem. But you didn't ask him "What happened today?" You have asked him to draw a *subjective conclusion* about his day: "*How was your day?*" Concluding how he feels about his day is an exercise in futility—and possibly stupidity—in his mind. One, he doesn't value this type of information, and, two, he may not be that good at verbally labeling his feelings. His feelings, housed deep in his brain stem, need to make a trip to his cerebral cortex for verbal translation. In a girl's brain, feeling and talking skills have richer connections. In response to "How was your day?" her emotional memories seem right at hand, as do her words to describe them.

For our son, it would "take forever" to reconstruct his day for me. And that's the way he would approach it. He does not sort the events of his day in terms of their emotional relevance. He scans the map more impartially. Barron, who is much more eager to share his day with me, can describe so many details of a case he's into that my head hurts. My head hurts because I don't have a map for organizing all the data. If he tells me how he *feels* about the case—the information I really want—I'll have a lot to say. We each value and track different information.

Please note that there are vigorous critics of those researchers who point to wiring patterns in the brain as any proof that girls and boys process emotions differently. They await more rigorous large-scale studies before venturing any conclusions.

Under Pressure

Another problem with the "How was your day?" question, as our son alluded to, is that answering it would be *work*—he has the burden of updating me and trying to provide a context to the events of the day. But he's "off work!" He's finally home from school, where he's felt pressured all day to give the *right* answer. Boys, more than girls, tend to see the world in "right or wrong" dichotomies. So when you eagerly ask him how his day went, he is likely to feel pressure. He's wondering what you're looking for and how to respond correctly. "Fine" is a safe and noncommittal response.

Parents are often puzzled when they get a hostile response to what seems to them a friendly question. For a girl, the question may indeed feel like an invitation to *unload* and *relieve pressure*, but that's not so for a boy. He'll unload and relieve pressure by *not talking*.

As parents, though, we rely on him to fill us in, and "Fine" just doesn't do it. So thinking you're helping him, you ask another question, and then another. Now the pressure is really on for him. He senses your dissatisfaction, and his concern about doing it right is only amplified. He just wants a break, and he hates disappointing you, so his feelings come out (as they often do) as some form of anger. You wonder what his problem is, and are left feeling frustrated and snubbed. Everyone feels bad.

A Different Kind of Conversation

It's important to remember that our sons do want to be known and understood, and they do crave closeness with their parents. But *how* he experiences closeness may be different than what you expect.

A great way to look at his version of closeness is to observe him around friends. He and his friends relieve pressure through group interaction, structured activity, and side-by-side conversations.

The Round Table

Having dinner together as a family is a great way to facilitate conversation because, around the table, everyone shares the burden of communication. Boys especially enjoy hearing a parent disclose elements of his day and, if there's a sibling at the table, the competition factor can be an incentive to talk.

Boy Wisdom

At the dinner table recently, the family turned to me (Mom) and asked, "So what happened for *you* today?" I told them about a dream I had woken up with and what the dream had taught me. I added that I often find spiritual guidance through dreams. We'd had many discussions about religion, but in this dinner conversation, I shared something more intimate. Our boys were all ears.

We find that dinnertime conversation starts slow, but snowballs as one thought leads to another. Here are some tips for conversing with boys:

- **Share your day.** We notice that our boys perk up when we share elements of our day. Then they get to interrogate *us*, and their questions provide great opportunities for learning.

- **Discuss impersonal topics.** What's fun about conversing with boys is that they enjoy talking about ideas and facts. Talk about a weird bit of news or something interesting that you have learned. Once you get the ball rolling, you may be surprised to discover how much your son knows!

- **Give them time.** Our boys know to ask to be excused from the table, and they often ask as soon as they shovel the food in and take the last gulp of milk. However, we often deny their first request. Once we all sit back with satisfied stomachs, thoughts from the day are more likely to surface.

- **Ask specific questions.** Rather than asking for a global summary of his day, give him a context to work with. Ask him how his coach ran practice today, or see if he's put any new songs on his iPod.

◆ **Share humor.** If all you ask about is how his test went or what homework he has, he'll associate talking with work. Tell a joke; share an embarrassing but funny moment; or as Barron does so well, talk in a British accent. Your son may groan, but that's part of the fun!

Do Something Together

Girls experience talking as an activity; boys prefer to talk while doing something. Girls converse face-to-face; boys are more comfortable shoulder-to-shoulder—again, while doing something.

Activities, such as walking the dog together, golfing, and shopping, provide nice stretches of time for conversation. The activity takes the focus away from his disclosures, reducing pressure and awkwardness. Just being together is rewarding, so let conversations serve as the icing on the cake.

The more you involve yourself in *his* activities—i.e., volunteering at his team's fundraiser—the more context you have for the events of his life, and the easier it is to converse with him. Though we want to teach him good social skills, the burden should not always be on him to "fill us in," but on us to witness—within reason—his life. Though we often can't be there, we can get to know his friends and the parents of his friends; we can have him play his music for us; and we can take the time to learn what's going on at his school and in his community.

Involve His Friends

If you want some good—and free—entertainment, be the driver for your son and a group of his friends. To my surprise, I have found my son to be much more open *with me* when he's with his friends, and his friends enjoy the attention I provide them. In their comfort zones, they regress and indulge in an inane kind of humor. Like morning talk show hosts, they laugh freely at themselves and each other, and it's contagious.

The Posture

At some point, teen boys seem to all look alike. They have the same hair *du jour*, lanky limbs, huge feet, layers of baggy clothing, and "the posture." The purpose of the posture is to convince everyone in sight that *they don't care*. And it works!

Let's consider why boys posture and how their body language helps and hurts them.

Self-Protection

From the first time he gets called a "crybaby" or a "wimp," a boy learns to hide parts of himself that might be viewed as weakness. As your boy becomes a teen, his social world is composed of bigger kids—ones who could potentially hurt him. A posture of indifference protects him from ridicule and embarrassment. In a way, he is "off the radar screen" of anyone who might be looking for an easy target.

So your son and his buddies, who you know to be warm, friendly, and conscientious, may closely resemble a group of thugs as they walk down the street. The body language keeps them from being hassled, but there is a very real downside to this habit.

"Adults Hate Us"

The hard thing for adults to remember is that, despite the protective exterior, teen boys want to be understood and liked. The biggest problem with the posture of indifference is that people *believe* what they see.

My son once shared with me the hurtful side of this reality. He and his friends had walked into a store to buy some snacks. He felt the eyes of the adults around them suspiciously look them over, and he felt hated. As we talked, he stated matter-of-factly, "adults don't like us [teenage boys]."

His statement sadly held some truth. And it would appear that teenage boys don't think much of *adults*. But appearances often lie.

> **Keep Out!**
>
> Your son needs to know when to drop the posture. As "stupid" as his teacher may be, he's the one who will look stupid if he gets poor grades.

Yes, he is trying to establish an independent identity, and he is figuring out that adult behaviors can be hypocritical, if not just plain stupid. He may even feel temporary emotions of hatred as he tries to break loose but knows he still needs you. But he needs to know he can question and challenge you without destroying you or losing your love.

Seeing His Soft Center

It is up to us, as adults and as parents, to see beyond the posture of our boys, even when they provide us few clues to what they are really experiencing. I (Laurie) recall a male client of mine sharing, as a 30-year-old, the hurt he carried from a hateful coach. The client admitted being disrespectful to the coach and not stroking the man's ego as his teammates had. My client had maintained a posture of smugness, and the enraged coach became abusive. Though he *looked* impenetrable, the boy took to heart the coach's words about how he would not amount to anything. The man who came to my office was brilliant and college-educated but was parking cars for a living.

Teenage boys are still boys, and they still look to us to help them figure out who they are. How do we give back good stuff when they dish out their negative attitudes? It's not easy, but here are some thoughts:

- **Get your strokes from other folks.** Do not look to him to build your ego! Teenage boys need confident parents, even as they work to break us down. Get support from each other, from your friends, from other parents, or from a therapist. Take the time to engage in the activities that fill you up and give you pleasure. Take care of yourself.

- **When he's provoking you, address what he's *doing*.** Be very specific about which behaviors are unacceptable—i.e., yelling—and tell him you will only continue the conversation if and when he stops that behavior.

- **Practice wide-angle vision.** He is the same boy you held in your arms as a baby, who stuck up for his sister the other day, who still glows when you tell him you're proud of him. *All of who he is*, including his amazing potential, resides inside him *all of the time*.

◆ **Don't take it personally.** This is much easier said than done, but it is key. A boy who is uncomfortable with his emotions will try to pressure you to feel the same way. So if he's angry, he'll try to make you mad. If he feels put down, he'll put you down. But all that's really happening (as long as you've kept safe boundaries) is that your boy is *feeling*. If you don't take the bait by retaliating, you are in a much better position to see him.

Emotional Strength-Training

The stronger your boy becomes emotionally, the less often he'll need to posture. Emotional strength is not the ability to *hide* or *extinguish* emotion but, quite the opposite, it's the ability to *allow* a range of feelings without becoming intimidated or overwhelmed. If we aren't scared by feelings, we're in a much better position to deal with them.

But feelings for teenage boys are, almost by definition, overwhelming. The teenage brain is still developing, and emotional edges feel sharper. And this is not helped by his surging testosterone. Then there's the fact that he lacks the life experience to know that things usually work out. How can you help?

If you want an emotionally strong boy, it helps to build your own emotional tolerance. Observe your feelings as they change through the day. Don't judge or fix; just observe. When your son gets upset, practice not reacting. Stretch your tolerance as you calmly witness the strong emotion. Eventually, you'll be able to see beyond surface feelings (usually anger) to emotions that are harder for him to express.

One of the most difficult skills to learn is to simply sit with someone who is in emotional pain—to just *be there*. When I (Laurie) was training to become a clinical psychologist, I was corrected for handing a client a tissue because the gesture can communicate: "Get a hold of yourself" or "I'm uncomfortable with your tears." My supervisor assured me: "The tissue box is next to him; he'll take one if he needs one." What the client really needed was my presence.

Even with my training, though, to see my boys hurting can be hard for me, and I don't always do great "therapy" with them. But they are good about correcting me when I'm off. If I try to explain away their feelings, they readily protest. Boys often prefer a simple validation: "Yeah, it sucks."

Toolbox

When he's emotionally distant from you, make connections through action rather than words. Make him his favorite snack; challenge him to a game of H-O-R-S-E or chess; or ask him to play one of his new songs for you.

You *can* help him be good to himself when he's suffering. Because boys are still socialized to see feeling as weak, your son may add to his own pain by turning on himself. If you notice him criticizing himself, try saying "You've had a hard enough day, take it easy on yourself." Encourage him to take a run or have a hot bath, something that will leave him feeling cared for rather than beaten down.

His Anger Is Not in Charge

So what do you do when his anger is directed toward you? What if he's mad because you just told him he has work to do or that he can't go to the movies?

Again, the simple answer is to do nothing. When you rescue your son from his feelings by giving in, he learns that his emotions are in charge. When you stand firm and allow him his feelings, he learns that the intensity will diminish and that he'll be okay. A world controlled by his emotion would be a very scary and unstable place for him—and for you! Help him learn that he can have emotions *without his emotions having him*.

Share Your Feelings

If you want to have a dead-end conversation, ask him how he feels. As we've discussed, boys lack an easy language for emotions. They commonly respond, "I don't know." It has taken me years to take this response literally. A boy who says he doesn't know what he's feeling probably *doesn't know!* He's not just trying to keep you in the dark.

A better way to teach him to verbalize feelings is to share *your* private feelings. He's probably seen you angry—most likely at *him!*—but have you shared your sadness or embarrassment or fear? Boys are often relieved when adults—especially male adults—talk about vulnerable feelings. Talking about your emotions not only educates him on the language of feeling but also creates a context for the discussion. He may even say, "I felt like that when ..." With the focus on you instead of him, he may feel more comfortable exploring his own emotions.

Monitoring Escapism

Girls tend to move *toward* difficult feelings in an effort to find relief; boys prefer to move away from feelings. In order to move away from feelings, boys often engage in activities that provide distraction. And those activities often involve some sort of electronic screen.

Taking a break from feelings can be healthy. Girls who revel in the drama of their emotions could benefit from a break—or at least *their parents* could benefit! But seeking constant distraction from feelings is not healthy. That's why it's helpful to limit his use of television, gaming systems, and the Internet, with one exception: let him IM his friends. Interacting with close friends will build him up—and he might even get around to sharing what he feels!

Depression in Boys

Your son, who is normally ravenous, pushes the plate away. He's more irritable than usual, and he seems to snap at you at every opportunity. He's not easy to like.

When a boy becomes a "pain," he's probably *in* pain. Maybe it's a temporary bad mood, but if sulky, snappy, and self-destructive behaviors hang around for a couple of weeks, he might be depressed.

Not What You Think

In his book *I Don't Want to Talk About It* (see the Resources appendix), Terrence Real tackles the topic of male depression. He notes that, while girls internalize pain and blame themselves, boys externalize pain and see themselves as victims. Our son recently hurt his foot while playing basketball in his flimsy sandals. Instead of focusing on his carelessness, he complained, "This sucks—why does this *always* happen to me?" The injury meant he couldn't start training with his friends for cross-country track, a real loss for him. A girl in a similar situation might be in tears, focusing on her regret over her behavior and her loss.

A girl in tears looks depressed, and her behavior draws help and comfort from those around her. A boy inventing conspiracy theories to explain his bad luck is more likely to repel those who might comfort him. In response to my son, I (Laurie) blurted out, "You have to admit that wearing sandals was pretty stupid." True enough, but my comment was also stupid; he was fully aware of his mistake and didn't need a reminder. I was responding to my own discomfort with his way of expressing himself. When I realized this, I apologized and just validated what he was feeling. All of the sudden, his anger lifted, and he became more approachable.

Though my son was not suffering from depression, he was in a depressed mood, masked as anger. We need to recognize that, for boys, an "angry at the world" attitude can be a red flag for depression. Getting angry with him will only add fuel to his flame; reaching past his anger to the hurting boy is the beginning of healing.

The National Institute of Mental Health reports that, after the age of 14, males are half as likely to be depressed—meaning *diagnosed* with depression—as girls. Yet, The Boys Project reports that, for every 100 girls aged 15 to 19 who commit suicide, 549 males of the same age kill themselves.

Boy Wisdom

First, the covertly depressed man must walk through the fire from which he has run. He must allow the pain to surface. Then, he may resolve his hidden depression by learning about self-care and healthy esteem.

—Terrence Real, *I Don't Want to Talk About It*

So what are we missing? Depression in males may get missed because boys don't often seem visibly depressed. In addition to externalizing, they often self-medicate depression with addictive substances or behaviors—from alcohol to excessive television use. Alcohol is often a factor in teen suicides.

We can help our sons by being gentle in response to their anger, providing compassion rather than retaliation. We can help our sons by calling them out when they numb themselves with feel-good distractions. And we can help our sons by finding them help when they are slipping away.

When He Needs Help

First of all, if your son tells you he's having thoughts of killing himself or if he comments that life is not worth living, *take him seriously.* You need to know how far these thoughts have gone. How long has he been having them? What does he imagine doing? How often does he have the thoughts? Does he have a plan to commit suicide? If so, what is the plan? Has he already made a suicide attempt?

This is not the kind of conversation that any of us want to have with our sons, but it is crucial we follow up. In most cases, suicidal thoughts are just thoughts, but if he expresses any *intention* to hurt himself, get immediate help. You can take him to the emergency room of any hospital, or call 911 if you need police assistance. They will evaluate his risk and admit him to inpatient care if needed.

Any form of suicidal thinking is a sign of significant inner turmoil and demands a response. Set him up with a mental health professional; remove any firearms from your home; and keep any pills under lock and key.

The main indicator of serious depression is hopelessness, a sense that he's given up on life. Other signs of depression include the following:

- Changes in appetite
- Low energy
- Loss of pleasure in formerly enjoyable activities
- Sleeping more or less than usual
- Significant weight gain or loss
- Feelings of guilt or worthlessness
- Ongoing sad or irritable mood
- Difficulty concentrating

Fortunately, a depressed boy does not have to stay depressed. Psycho-therapy and antidepressant medication are both effective forms of treatment, and the two approaches can complement each other when used together. Ask his school counselor, pediatrician, or other parents for a referral—you'll want someone who is comfortable with, and experienced in, working with teen boys.

Being Me, Feeling Loved

An emotionally healthy boy feels secure in the knowledge that he is loved. That security can be particularly important in his teen years because he is coming into his own. He knows that you loved him when he saw you as his hero; will you love him as much when he needs you less, when he questions your way of thinking, and when he even tries to push you away?

It is our job as parents to stay secure enough to keep the love flowing, even when he rolls his eyes in response. Okay, you don't have to kiss him in public, but kiss him goodnight. He may not want an in-depth feeling analysis, but an arm on his shoulder can mean a lot. And when his emotions are riding on the action on ESPN, sit down and ride with him.

The Least You Need to Know

- When he says he doesn't know what he's feeling, he probably *doesn't* know.

- Use family discussions, shared activity, and impersonal topics to get him talking.

- Witnessing his feelings is more important than "saying the right thing."

- If you want him to share his vulnerable feelings, pull yours out of the closet as well.

- If you think he may be depressed or suicidal, get him professional help right away.

19

When Your Son Tastes Life

In This Chapter

◆ What driving means to boys

◆ Altered states

◆ Staying on top of things

◆ Disciplining your teenage son

For your son, "sweet 16" is indeed sah-weet! It's a magical time because he's getting his license, not just to drive, but to taste a range of exciting new experiences. His hormones are in full force, and he's hanging out with other kids whose hormones are in full force. Can this also signal trouble? Probably.

Parenting a teenage boy can feel like walking a tightrope—for you and for him. He desperately wants your trust and respect, but he also really wants to check out some forbidden fruit. You want to trust him and foster his growing independence, but you know the temptations he's getting exposed to. The easiest route for parent *and* son is to establish an elaborate system of denial.

He'll do his tasting out of our sight, and we'll stay smug when other parents talk about their teen troublemakers.

As easy as that route may be, we want to *know* our teenage boys. We want access beyond the occasional grunt or monosyllabic response. And we also want him to be safe. We can keep him safer *and* know him better by knowing his world—even the parts we don't like to see. So get ready: this chapter is here to burst your bubble of denial.

The Joy of Driving

It seems just yesterday when he was making "zoom" sounds for his Hot Wheels cars, and now he's actually *behind* the wheel. Getting a license is a major rite of passage for a boy. He, who's always enjoyed things that move, is now able to be in the driver's seat.

His ticket to drive opens up his world. He can get places without an escort from Mom or Dad, and he can take a girl on a real date. Because guys still tend to be the drivers on dates, he'll also feel social pressure to get qualified.

Beyond these practicalities, though, driving can become a significant part of a teen boy's identity, associated with power, control—even masculinity.

Power and Responsibility

Unlike his Hot Wheels, a real car can do real damage. As he's initiated into the role of driver, he takes on an immense responsibility. Like Ricky Bobby in the popular movie *Talladega Nights*, boys like the feel of being behind the wheel, and many just want to "go fast." And he's been practicing, not just with his Hot Wheels but also with his video controller. Thing is, with a real car, he won't just lose points if he crashes: he could lose everything.

So how do we, as parents, keep him safe without taking the joy out of his newfound power? It helps to know where the risks are. According to a 2003 *USA Today* report, the majority of fatal crashes involving teens occurred at nighttime or when there was at least one passenger in the car, and almost three fourths of the drivers in these crashes were male.

Car crashes are the number-one cause of death among 16-year-olds, and kids this age are the most dangerous drivers.

Toolbox _____

We had our son participate in a driver's training course. It wasn't your typical "behind-the-wheel" with a history teacher earning some extra bucks, but an intense skills training with *race car drivers*. And it was *free*. The four-hour training course was provided by *Driver's Edge* (www.driversedge.org), a nonprofit organization founded by race car driver Jeff Payne and dedicated to reducing the accident rate among young drivers. The course runs trainees through high-risk scenarios and teaches them how to respond. Our son got to purposely drive into a skid in a brand-new BMW. Now that's the kind of course a 16-year-old — *and* his parents — can appreciate!

For these reasons, it makes good sense to wait on nighttime driving and chauffeuring of friends until he's tracked some miles. States such as North Carolina that have adopted Graduated Driver Licensing (GDL) laws—laws that restrict nighttime driving and passengers for new drivers—have seen a significant drop in crashes among this high-risk group. And because teens are much less likely to wear a seatbelt when driving with friends, don't be above checking the belts before he takes off with his buddies. Do it once, and he'll do anything to avoid another inspection.

Yes, Officer

Because few things are more intimidating than being pulled over by a police officer while one is driving, it is very important that your son know what to do in this type of situation.

The first thing he needs to know is that the officer is concerned about his own safety, that is, not dying in a shootout. This is why a police officer approaches a stopped car with a hand on his gun, ready to draw. Police just don't know who they have pulled over. In Minnesota recently, one soccer mom of 20 years was arrested because she was identified as a wanted radical from the 1970s who had been on the lam for three decades after attempting to kill a police officer. So teach your son that a traffic cop is not making a judgment about him personally when the cop walks up ready to draw. The American Civil Liberties Union (www.aclu.org) publishes for free on the Internet a *Know Your Rights* pocket card for individuals stopped by the police. Among several suggestions learned from long experience: don't get into an argument; remember that your words can be used against you; keep your hands where the police can see them; don't run; and don't touch any police officer.

Next, teach your son to say "Yes, Sir" or "Yes, Ma'am" and to at all times be respectful and calm. Traffic stops take some time, and your son cannot get upset and show impatience.

Respect pays off in the long run, too. In cases too numerous to mention, Barron has seen charges eventually dismissed or open dockets arranged mainly because the young man accused of a traffic violation or crime was respectful. Cops are not prosecutors, but they do influence prosecutors. Prosecutors routinely have *80* misdemeanor cases a day. Given the crushing workload, defendants who show up dressed like they are going to church, smile, are polite, and did not give the cop any grief are going to get the best result. Your son's lawyer can become aggressive if need be, but not your son.

To impress upon your son the importance of taking responsibility for his actions, have him pay for a portion of his lawyer's fee, even if his case is ultimately dismissed. Or have him pay the fine and court costs back to you if the prosecution is successful.

If you can get a dismissal, you might also be able to seek an *expungement*, a legal ruling that wipes out an arrest record as if the arrest had never occurred.

A final note: if your son runs, he will get arrested in a rough manner. The police *hate* people who run.

Life's a Party!

Why wouldn't your son want to "party"? He's enjoyed movie scenes where everyone is drunk and free and living it up, and he wants a piece of the action. But a good reason for him *not* to go there is *you*. According to The White House Office of National Drug Control

Policy (ONDCP), "Research shows that parents are a powerful deterrent to drug or alcohol use, even when teens are far from home. The majority of teens say the greatest risk in using marijuana is upsetting their parents or losing the respect of friends and families."

Let's look beyond the glossy images of the party life to the real risks the "high life" poses to your son's future.

Drinking

After a long tradition of holding the edge on teen drinking, boys are seeing girls catch up. The fact that girls are "holding their own" is not a happy achievement, and concerned parents, educators, and policymakers are responding.

While underage drinking poses legitimate risks for boys and girls, the playing field is not as level as it might seem. Boys remain much more vulnerable to developing a lasting problem. Here's the trend, gathered from national surveys between 2002 and 2006, for boys in relation to girls:

◆ On the average, boys first try alcohol at age 11, compared to girls at age 13. Between ages 12 and 17, about 9 percent of kids of both genders abuse or are dependent on alcohol or an illicit drug. Regular drinking begins, on the average, at age 16 for both genders.

◆ Between the ages of 12 and 20, about 22 percent of boys and 17 percent of girls acknowledged *binge drinking*—defined as having five or more drinks on a single occasion at least once in the past month. About half of the binge drinkers were binging three or more days a month.

◆ By ages 18 to 20, the *majority* of boys are binge drinking. In a study where the threshold was six or more drinks on a single occasion, 73 percent of males and 48 percent of females reported binge drinking.

◆ At age 18 and up, alcohol increasingly hooks the guys, while females are more able to leave the party life behind. During ages 18 to 25, rates of substance dependence or abuse were 26 percent for males and 16 percent for girls. By age 26, men were twice as likely to be dependent on or abusing alcohol.

◆ *Harmful drinking*—defined as more than four drinks per day (more than two per day for women) over the past month—was evident in 12 percent of males and 9 percent of females aged 17 to 20. But only for the males, harmful drinking at this age predicted harmful drinking at ages 30 to 31.

So, bottom line, girls can more easily "take and leave" alcohol than boys. This may be related to the fact that girls have more acceptable outlets for emotional expression. We've probably all seen a parody of a drunk guy blubbering to his buddy, "I love you, man." Somehow this expression only becomes acceptable when he's drunk, while girls can express affection to each other without concern.

> **Keep Out!**
>
> A link has recently been identified between alcohol problems and ADHD, a disorder that affects significantly more boys than girls. In a group of 15- to 17-year-olds, teens with childhood ADHD reported being drunk 14 times in the past year, compared to only 1.8 times for their peers who did not have ADHD! (See Chapter 8 for more on ADHD.)

Boys not only get a permit to express feelings when they're drunk, but they can also use alcohol to "drown out" feelings they are not able to process. But because alcohol is a depressant, drinking can establish a vicious cycle of increasing feelings of guilt and worthlessness, while also promising to relieve these feelings. When a boy uses alcohol to medicate, he's got a problem.

Smoking, Chewing, and Inhaling

Nowadays, when we think about boys smoking, we are more likely to be thinking about marijuana than cigarettes. But cigarettes are still around. The good news is, the number of male adolescent smokers has decreased steadily over the past 40 years. The bad news is, teens still underestimate the risks of smoking, believing they can smoke for a while and then stop. This is just not so. In its addictive potential, nicotine has been compared to heroin, and the Mayo Clinic has reported that 70 percent of adolescent smokers wish they had never started.

If your son hasn't started, help him keep it that way. If he has just started, help him stop. Boys seem to take more time to get addicted—183 days versus 21 days for girls—so seize this window of opportunity. Talking to him about long-term consequences will make his eyes glaze over, but noting the immediate problems—reduced stamina, bad breath, and yellow teeth—may get his attention. Better yet, have him talk to an addicted teen who is trying to quit.

Smokeless tobacco, a popular alternative to cigarettes for boys, is used by 5.6 percent of middle-school boys and 11 percent of high-school boys. Users place the product between their gum and cheek, suck on the tobacco, and spit out the juice. Boys might associate the habit with their baseball and NASCAR heroes, forgetting that good health is the key to athleticism. Smokeless tobacco causes oral cancer and nicotine dependence, and teens who use it are more likely to become cigarette smokers.

And what about "weed"? Marijuana is the most commonly abused illicit drug in the United States, and boys smoke it more than girls. However, the popularity of the drug appears to be declining. According to the National Survey on Drug Use and Health, the rate of current marijuana use among 12- to 17-year-olds decreased significantly from 8.2 percent in 2002 to 6.8 percent in 2005.

Research reveals that students who use marijuana get lower grades and are less likely to graduate from high school, and heavy users suffer impaired intellectual functioning even after 24 hours without the drug. Marijuana affects the brain's ability to learn and remember information—a particular concern for boys, since they are at higher risk for learning disabilities.

Toolbox

The subtitle of a White House Drug Czar press release dated April 25, 2007, reads: "This isn't your father's marijuana." The release reports findings from a 20-year analysis of marijuana potency. The results? The pot your son is exposed to is twice as potent as what you might have inhaled in the mid-'80s. As kids get more and more of "the good stuff," the drug is getting more of them addicted. Go to www. whitehousedrugpolicy.gov/news/press07/042507_2.html for more information.

Everything Is Fine in La-La Land

When his vocabulary gets reduced to "fine" or "good," it's easy for us to coast as parents. He's spending more time with his friends; he can drive himself around; and he's not reporting any problems. Party time!

Exactly. To envision their son smoking or drinking or inhaling or worse is extremely difficult for parents. And he makes it very easy for us to stay in comfortable denial. Even when we try to probe—or *especially* when we try to probe—he's not likely to give us much. But then, why would he?

It's hard for us to swallow the fact that the boy who once looked to us for everything now wants us to look away. If he's doing something we don't want him to do, it's in his interest to keep us in the dark. And in some ways, it's in *our* interest to stay in the dark where our fantasies can keep him young and innocent. But we know better. The question is, how do we continue to know *him*?

The Courage to Know

Parents tend to be very protective of their girls, but are often more willing to let a teen boy take on renter status (minus the rent). He often has the apartment-style room/living space in the basement, and he may have his own car. The irony is that our "independent" boys are more likely than girls to get addicted, arrested, and suspended for the high-risk behaviors they naturally crave.

In order to get the facts, we need to *want* the facts. That means being prepared for surprises, good and bad. It means asking him the hard questions. And sometimes it means *not* relying on trust.

This is a tough one for me (Laurie) because, as a therapist, I place a great value on trust. But I know too much. I'm the one teenagers tell about how wasted they got at the party or how they regularly smoke weed behind the school. And these are *good kids* with *good parents*. I left la-la land a long time ago.

Keeping Him Safe

If you ask where your son is going and he says "Out," bring him back in and lock the door. He needs to know that *you* need to know where he is at all times. This means telling you where he's going, informing you of any change of plans, and keeping his cell phone on at all times—though he is *not* to answer it when he's driving. Cell phones are a great help in keeping tabs. Our oldest snuck out one evening, and as soon as I figured it out, I called his cell phone. He had the good sense to answer it, and when I ordered him home, he was back in five minutes!

In addition to his check-ins, you can check in by calling his reported location and verifying (1) that he's there and (2) that a supervising adult is on the premises.

If you discover he's lied to you, make the molehill into a mountain. If there's one lie, there's more where that came from. Let him know that he now throws everything into question. You now have *carte blanche* (actually you always do, you're the parent) to check his cell phone log, his messages, his room, and anywhere else he keeps his secrets. I cringe as I write this, but if you have cause to read his personal notes or journal, do so.

Toolbox

Let your children know that Mom and Dad provide a 24-hour, on-call taxi service. Drill into your son: if he is *ever* in a situation where he has consumed alcohol, *do not drive*. And if he is *ever* relying on a ride from a friend who has been drinking, *do not ride*. Assure him that he can call you from anywhere at any time and you will come and get him, no questions asked.

Reining Him In

Just as you scooped him up as a toddler when he tried to run out into the street, you need to pull your teen boy back from time to time. Sure, restricting his freedom is punishing for him—*and* for you. And regardless of what he did to warrant the sentence, he'll respond as if you are alien parents with a twisted and very foreign idea of justice. This should affirm to you that the consequences *might* be adequate.

It is not easy to discipline a teenage son. And the worst part is not the fact that he may be taller than you (a friend of ours makes her son sit down in these situations), but he's also become very smart. He will display to you his skills in debate, logical reasoning, and drama, adding that nice little edge of aggression his testosterone supplies. But you *can* stay strong and provide him the parenting he's trying to avoid but clearly needs.

Staying Grounded

Before you sit down with him, sit down with each other. You're probably feeling a mix of anger, fear, disappointment, and shame. Be kind to yourself—it's common for parents to feel deflated when a son has slipped up. Some of these feelings have little to do with him but instead go to our sense of competence or concerns about what others may think. But what really hurts, perhaps more for Mom, is the sense of separation you feel—the recognition that you don't know your son as well as you thought you did. The boy who looked to you for the answers is now hoping you'll look away.

The irony is, this awareness of *not* knowing him is the beginning of true understanding. Make room for your feelings, but don't bring them all into the room with him. Talking it out as co-parents helps you sort out your reactions, but it also helps the two of you establish what your values are, what boundaries you are willing to enforce, and what the consequences of his behavior will be.

Take the time you need to get calm and clear; then sit down with him together. He'll know something's up, and he'll be set to defend himself. Boys defend when they feel attacked, so don't go there. Here are some tips for "the talk":

◆ Keep a level, "matter-of-fact" tone of voice throughout the conversation.

◆ Make it easier for him to tell the truth by asking "loaded questions." For example, if you have a pretty good idea that he's used weed, don't ask him if he's used. Ask him, in your calm voice, "How often are you smoking weed?" This exempts him from the concern that the truth will shock you, and exempts *you* from his too-easy "no."

◆ Work from most to least. Imagine the most extreme version (within reason) of his truth, and question from there. Teenage boys are masters of the sound byte, giving you just enough to fulfill your curiosity without busting their cover. So instead of asking who was involved in the unsanctioned party, tell him you are assuming all of his friends were involved. *Then* he's likely to give you specifics, such as "No! Jerry doesn't drink, and Lisa was out of town."

◆ Avoid fear tactics or propaganda. Research has shown that fear tactics—i.e., showing a graphic image of a car crash to inspire good driving—don't work. And inaccurate propaganda on the effects of drugs or alcohol will just turn him off.

◆ Respect his intelligence by acknowledging the complexity of the choices he needs to make, while making it clear what you expect of him. Be prepared for him to ask you what you did at his age. Your honesty not only gives you more credibility but can also open up a rich discussion of what you have learned and help him feel less alone with the pressures he's facing.

◆ Express confidence in his ability to do better. Affirm his healthy habits and behaviors, and identify friends who bring these out in him. Restrict access to troublemaking friends.

◆ Ground him.

Grounding Him

When you temporarily restrict your son's freedom and keep watch, you are grounding him emotionally as well as physically. When he's "out there" too far, he loses contact with his moral base and starts to judge his behaviors in relation to peer norms rather than what he's learned at home. So if he's at a party where everyone is smoking weed, an invitation to the "meth" room may feel exciting and dangerous but not necessarily out of the question. The standard consequence of grounding puts him in the position of seeing his behavior in relation to family norms.

When you ground him, be clear about what that means. Usually grounding means cutting him off from contact with his peers by taking away the keys, his phone, and access to IM communications on the

computer. Also be clear about how long he'll be grounded, and stick
to it. Often grounding also includes added household responsibilities
as a way of compensating for his disruption to family life. Chances are
you've had to make phone calls, take time to address his behavior, and
be home more to monitor him. His help with the laundry and lawn can
give you some relief and help restore the relationship.

The Perks of Pulling Him Back

If you have a teenage son, you're probably a fan of the cartoon *Zits*.
I recall a strip that shows Jeremy telling a friend that his mom used the
"F" word on him. His friend is horrified, and it is soon revealed that
the expletive is "Family Time." Family time is something a teenage
boy loves to hate, but you will find that grounded time can be secretly
enjoyable for both of you.

We have experienced a predictable cycle following the few "incidents"
we've had with our son. First there's the "crazy parents" smokescreen
mixed with shame, half-truths, and horror over the consequences. After
we investigate what actually occurred (or hear the "word on the street")
and come prepared for the real conversation, our son reluctantly acknowledges the truth and answers our loaded questions. Knowing we
know at least *most* of the story, he actually seems grateful that we are
being civil, and he accepts the consequences.

As parents, our cycle runs parallel to his. We feel horrified to catch
him doing something that we assumed he was "above" and suffer the
requisite shame and self-recrimination. Then we face the music and
face him, and we, too, feel a sense of relief that we can talk about it.
Most recently our son expressed gratitude that we had talked. We could
tell that it had been harder on him to cover up his infraction than to
have us come down on him. And we also are literally "closer" because
his world and our world have momentarily collided.

The last phase of the cycle, enforcement, can be rather sweet, and not
just because we get the house cleaned. A sense of wholesomeness is
restored; we share simple tasks and pleasures; he's there more for his
brother; and he's reminded that home, and even "Family Time," is not
so bad after all.

Of course, these perks are interspersed between periods of anger, sullenness, and attempts to IM his *real* friends. When we endure through the rollercoaster of his—and our own—feelings, home may be less "perfect," but it will *include* him. And that's the biggest perk.

The Least You Need to Know

- Teen driving accidents usually happen when it's dark or when passengers are in the car.

- Compared to girls, boys who drink heavily as teens are at significant risk for drinking problems as adults.

- Marijuana, which is more often used by boys, impairs learning and school performance.

- Don't expect him to tell you everything, and prepare to be surprised.

- Punishing him is hard, but it puts him back on safer ground and can bring you closer.

Chapter 20

Teenage Boys and Family Identity

In This Chapter

- ◆ Home is where a boy's heart is
- ◆ Routines he can count on
- ◆ Shouldering responsibility
- ◆ Vacationing with the family
- ◆ The importance of rituals

Teenage boys spend a lot of time not talking to their parents. They are content to gather with friends, talk to friends, IM friends, or withdraw to the computer or bedroom.

As a parent, you should realize the distance your son puts between you is natural, and yet your relationship is still important to him. You want your teenager to explore within a wider set of boundaries. And, you want your boy to enjoy a home life that provides stability to his springboard of adventure.

In this chapter, we discuss ways to keep connected to your son and reinforce the value of family time, chores, vacations, and ritual.

Boys Need a Home to Complain About

One constant for teenage boys is the lamentations about their family and home. As boys are gaining their own identities, standing out—way out—from their family is one sure way to gain recognition as a unique individual.

Your son may subject you, the parent, to contempt, ridicule, or castigation. He may barely conceal this derision, or he may throw it right in your face.

The home you provide may be inadequate as well. Even if it is a grand mansion, your house may likely be inadequate in some indefinable way that requires your son to spend time elsewhere. So let's take a closer look at the plaintiff to see if we can help explain some of these behaviors.

The Myth of Masculine Self-Sufficiency

Popular culture offers up great films of strong men defying the odds and defeating evil all by themselves. It's hard for a boy to turn his head away from watching cowboy Clint Eastwood repair his dislocated shoulder by jamming it back into place. The message is clear: here's a man who knows how to take care of himself.

Boys can and should be encouraged to consider heroism a virtue, but it is a virtue born from the recognition that adults need other adults, men rely on other men, and boys rely on their parents.

The brave responders in 9/11 perished heroically as part of a team of selfless public servants. Those colleagues who survived needed each other to deal with the grief.

Real life for your son must provide a counterbalance to the images he is provided. Mom and Dad show their love for each other. But Dad needs to show his son that he has male friends whom he looks to for a full adult life.

Your son, when he is feeling low, must come to appreciate that it is not only okay but also normal to want the comfort of a parent or a friend. Many researchers believe boys talk much less than girls. Others refute this argument and claim boys are not statistically different from girls in their use of language. However your son communicates his feelings, it is important for him to know that emotions fade and strong men look for and accept help.

Toolbox _____

For boys without fathers, there are specific programs that seek to initiate boys into responsible lives as men. *Boys to Men* is an organization of volunteer mentors created to guide boys 12–17 to responsible manhood through encounter weekends and other experiences. Check out www.boystomen.org and www.boystomennw.org.

Rolling His Eyes with a Smile

Take a minute to listen to your son's complaints. For boys, pro-social teasing is a common way to playfully interact. If you immediately jump out of your skin every time he takes a shot at you, you'll miss the times when he is just having fun.

He may not even verbalize his tease but may react with a roll of his eyes or a look that says: "You're giving me the clean-my-room speech for the one millionth time."

Because humor is one of the most effective parenting tools, your use of humor will hopefully help instill a playful side to your son's outlook on life. And parents can also take themselves too seriously at times. If your son teases you or rolls his eyes when lectured, give yourself the chance to appreciate whether he is picking up on a valid and humorous side of your interaction. Taking a tease shows you have a thick enough skin and a sense of humor—two qualities you'll want your son to learn or inherit.

Things He Can Count On

Shifting friendships, lost love, erratic homework schedules, and the highs and lows of his own increasing intense emotions can really throw a teenage boy. When boys are infants and toddlers, parents intuitively offer them a home that is secure and nurturing. And boys want some semblance of this warm embrace even as they age. Your son may not say he wants to eat with you, but rest assured, he will appreciate having a reliable meal in the presence of his family. So work to maintain an environment that is boy friendly, even as your son seems less friendly to you.

Dinnertime

When I (Barron) spent time on my grandparents' farm in South Dakota, the Alcester town whistle would signal to everyone for miles around that it was time to gather the family for a noon meal. If I was with my grandfather in the fields, we would head back to the farmhouse where Grandma had prepared fresh vegetables from the garden and a host of other great food. Pass the *real* butter, please.

In my immediate family, my parents made sure we stayed well fed. Our mealtimes were not as constant as those on the farm, nothing was, but our family greatly enjoyed eating together, especially when Mom prepared ribs or chili or steak. Her best dessert was a lemon bar, and the eating of those bars was essential to the midwestern diet.

Sadly, the noon whistle no longer blows in Alcester, and the passing of this tradition of community mealtime is a loss.

However, the tradition of a regular family meal is something every boy can cherish, whether it is a simple meal of white beans and cornbread or the latest California cuisine. Make shared meals a regular part of your family life. This calm in the middle of a storm may be the one place your son can feel freed up enough to reconnect with you that day. And as you already know, boys love to eat. Even if your son is a picky eater or watching his abs, a platter of good food will keep him glued to his dinner chair. And you'll have some valuable face time.

Downtime

Boys who run and run and run need downtime as much as they need a shower. Setting boundaries about how long your son can spend with his friends is necessary. Our younger son was sleeping over so much with his buddies we needed to enforce a lengthy downtime just to keep him from getting sick.

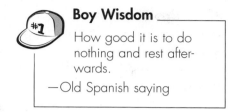

Boy Wisdom

How good it is to do nothing and rest afterwards.

—Old Spanish saying

A boy who learns to spend some time in quiet will learn the virtues of quieting his mind, from stress reduction to book reading, to discovering a new idea for fun. However, if *you* are the one who needs the downtime, make sure you let him know that he needs to help you out by going outside, to his room, or up the street to a friend's house.

Take care not to overschedule your son with too many activities. It can be counterproductive. Remember the story about the two lumberjacks who cut wood all day? The first took a break every hour, and the second one never stopped chopping. At the end of the day, the first lumberjack had cut more wood. He had taken the time to sharpen his axe. Think of rest for a boy as brain- and body-sharpening time.

Private Time

Boys enjoy having a private space to call their own, where they can shield themselves from everyone and everything else. Parents provide this place by assigning him a private bedroom if at all possible. Time for personal solitude is particularly important for introverted boys. These boys draw energy from being alone. Respect your son's private time and treasure it as a resource. If your son is seriously withdrawn, talk to him first to find out why he likes to be alone. Only after you are convinced he is avoiding society because of fear, as opposed to simply preferring to be alone, should you consider that his behavior needs further attention.

Family Time

As your family unit spends less and less time together as a group, make time to reconnect outside of just eating together. One way is to find an entertaining show to watch. New entertainment options like Tivo and Netflix make it much easier to sit down on a moment's notice and watch a fun show.

Many adults remember watching *The Brady Bunch* or *The Carol Burnett Show* as a family. *Wide World of Sports* was a big hit, too. Today the options for family shows are much deeper, so sit down with your son and ask him what he would like to see. Then order the DVD. Of course, a challenging movie may be a more interesting option for a teenager. Older boys in high school may relish the chance to see an R-rated movie with their parents that tackles a subject such as war or racism. Your son and you can then talk about the movie at the local coffeehouse.

Concerts and theater are excellent options for family time with older boys. If his siblings can join him, all the better. Family time can also be as simple and inexpensive as a picnic, a trip to the library, or a volunteer effort for a local charity. The point is to be together. For boys, that time together will be more enjoyable if your family is involved in a shared activity.

Doing His Part

Teenage boys are sheltered in North American urban culture. While parents correctly emphasize schoolwork, many boys get a pass on helping around the house.

To instill a sense of greater personal responsibility, a parent of a teenage boy needs to allow her son to shoulder some family obligations, teaching work as a value and not just as a chore to be accomplished.

Chores Prepare Him for Life

A boy sees popular images of a man on TV as a breadwinner, a soldier, and an athlete. He also sees the grocer when you go shopping, the postman on his rounds, and the pastor in the pulpit. Hopefully your son has learned that men can and do serve in many roles.

What your son may or may not realize is the work and discipline that each diligent adult male puts into his job. The soldier trains for years; the clergyman struggles with just the right phrase for a sermon; and the postman drives though rain, sleet, and gloom of night on his appointed rounds.

Chores, the routine and necessary work that attends daily living, teach discipline that will later serve your son in whatever profession he chooses. The simple task of taking out the garbage every Tuesday and Saturday will teach your son how quickly work accumulates and how necessary cleanliness is to an orderly home. If he doesn't do his job, the house quickly turns unpleasant—not the kind of home one likes to display to his friends.

Give your son more than one chore to do, and make sure he does them. An occasional failure is excusable, but disregard demands correction. For the life of them, our sons could not remember to take the empty garbage cans off the street and return them to the side of the house. It was as if they had a blind spot with regard to this chore. However, reduced allowances finally corrected this bad behavior for the most part.

It is easier, though, to emphasize the good. "It sure is nice to have fresh, clean clothes, huh?" "Thanks for emptying the recycling; it makes the kitchen so much more pleasant when I can quickly put the plastic away." Positive reinforcement will remind your son of the benefits of getting the work done as opposed to the relative horror that awaits a job failed. A boy who wants to do a good job and understands the benefits of a job well done will be prepared to work as an adult.

Chores also feed the real desire in boys to be seen as competent. A boy may grumble at a chore, but if he does it well and is complimented, he will swell with pride. A boy growing into a man wants to see and feel along the way that he is making progress, to see that he is growing into a man, not at some later date, but right now.

Your son's shoulders are getting bigger and his back broader. Handing out chores and telling him truthfully when he is doing a good job will let your son know that you know he can carry whatever load the family needs him to bear.

He Needs to Feel Needed

The larger the family, the more potential for a son to feel marginalized. As we mentioned in Chapter 6, chores impress upon every family

Toolbox

Chores such as laundry, food shopping, and cooking provide a boy with practical skills needed for life on his own. He may even discover he enjoys cooking and consider a career as a chef!

member that he is a contributor to the family's welfare. Your son needs to feel needed. He wants to be part of what is important.

If your son is lazy and shiftless, it's time to put your foot down and tack up a list of chores for him to do. Give him time to do the work, and make sure you show him *how* to do the work properly initially. Be kind, too; some work that seems obvious to adults is not so obvious to boys. Showing your son how to do a chore well will avoid the "You didn't tell me to do that" argument that will follow your appraisal of his inaugural work.

Family Vacation

Families have many classic vacation destinations such as Yellowstone, Mount Rushmore, Disney World/Land, Grand Canyon, and the beach to choose from. Also there are the routine trips to see family members who live elsewhere.

As your boy ages, he may travel better. He may even be able to help with the driving or tolerate the inconveniences without whining. Of course, a teenage boy who is displeased on a vacation will likely just sulk. Maybe these ideas will help your whole family enjoy time on the road.

Boys, Adventure, and Memory

Although parachuting was one suggestion our boys offered up for one vacation, this wish has yet to be fulfilled. Vacations are wonderful in their own right and do not necessarily need a signature event. Just camping for a week at a state park, or visiting another city, any city, may do. The memories of each trip will flow from your interaction with each other, and, of course, the disasters that follow any family—the blown tire, the sister vomiting in Times Square, the lost camera.

Parents can enhance any trip by picking a unique experience to partake in. Our boys particularly enjoyed touring Fenway Park, climbing a cliff in Acadia National Park, watching the Cubs at Wrigley Field, and renting a cabin a couple hundred yards from Old Faithful. They also remember Ground Zero, the changing of the guard at Arlington National Cemetery, and the Monet exhibit. Involving your teenage son in planning a vacation will help him build anticipation for and enjoy his vacation time with you.

Away from Peer Pressure

Another benefit of the family vacation for teenage boys is the chance to be free of the dominating presence of his peers. He can—but likely won't—wear a new fashion. He can also goof off more with his siblings and generally act more like a kid.

Vacations can bolster the influence you have to counter the negative influence of some peers. Vacations are more than a wonderful respite from the sameness of daily life. They are a valuable tool for developing healthy boys.

If he is missing his friends while on vacation, you can encourage him to pick out a small gift to take back home to them. Our youngest son was the recipient of many cool key chains. According to the giver's dad, these gifts required *long* shopping excursions. Our son delivered handmade bow and arrow sets to his friends after a trip outside the country.

Boys Count on Rituals

Ritual. The word seems archaic in a modern world, but for boys ritual is anything but archaic. Rituals are foundation blocks for a stable life.

The fact that your son is now a teenager is not a reason to abandon time-honored rituals. It may be time to modify some rituals, but before you give up on one, think long and hard.

Bedtime

A teenage boy runs on changing circadian rhythms or an internal body clock. He can stay up way, way late if permitted. He can also sleep 'til past noon. Scholars know this shift as a "phase preference." What causes this shift is undetermined. Getting up and going is known as *morningness*; active evenings are known as *eveningness*. More eveningness has been associated with rule-breaking behavior in boys and relational problems in girls.

For parents, the important thing to realize is that your son still needs lots of sleep. Getting by on a few hours may be necessary once in a while, but a consistent sleep schedule is vital to an energetic day. He'll also be more alert on the road driving to and from school.

Provide a ritual for bedtime even when he is a teenager. Besides demanding that he brush his teeth, bring him a small glass of water, say prayers, turn down his bed, give him a hug and kiss, or do all these things. Your son won't want this attention when he has friends over, but he will likely crave it when he is home alone. Also, the water, or kiss, delivered at the same time will trigger a recognition that it is, in fact, bedtime. His body can start winding down.

Holiday Traditions

Our boys never gave up the demand for an Easter egg hunt or a Thanksgiving weekend trip to cut down a Christmas tree. Of course, we looked forward to these traditions as much as the boys. They were important seasonal markers for each passing year. There were numerous other reminders as well, such as the Halloween decorations, the countdown on New Year's Eve—no matter how much Dad wanted to go to bed!

Keep your teenager connected with traditions. If he's never helped decorate before, include him. If he's never shopped with you for the special smorgasbord food, take him to the store. Get him in the kitchen to prepare the turkey at 8:00 A.M. Make him chop some wood for the fire. In other words, merge his childhood revelry with some adult responsibility. In a few years, he'll be cooking you the holiday dinner, and *you know* you want him to prepare the holiday dishes the old way.

Inventing Rituals

And you can start new rituals, too. Some families in the North, who were sick of the winter snow and cold, started celebrating Christmas in Florida. Our younger son loved the Christmas village sets you can buy piece by piece, so we introduced a little display. The village soon needed a planning commission to figure out where the new construction was going in.

Teach your son to respect rituals and to understand that he has power to affect the rituals as well. He can start a new one if he wants. Why not? As long as the ritual has meaning, then your son can only benefit from developing his ideas.

Not Too Old

Before you say to your son "You're too old for that," stop and think why you're saying this. It's possible that as a parent you're feeling a little tired and would just as soon skip the celebration. If you're feeling that way, well, you've got a lot of company. But also remember a tradition is more than just an activity the family does; it's a connection to a living family history for your son. Most likely, if you don't put up a menorah or hang the Christmas lights, you'll beat yourself up about it later.

Your teenage son needs ritual, even if he appears to sulk at the thought of dinner with the relatives. Beyond the family obligations—showing up for dinner—invite his participation if it will help him enjoy the tradition. If not, then don't push too hard, and try to enjoy yourself as much as possible. Of course, try not to humiliate your son either. Sticking him at the short table with his first-grade cousins during a holiday dinner will not create a memory to cherish.

I (Barron) hang a stocking on the fireplace mantle every Christmas season. It's the same stocking I've had for 40 years. The ritual of displaying it with the stockings for Laurie, Bjorn, Josh, and Coco (our golden retriever) warms my Christmas spirit.

Toolbox

As the years roll by, you'll most likely find that your son has come to rely on the traditions of your family and will actively remind you when you've delayed or ignored the ritual schedule. Ritual is a family embrace that your son can carry with him.

The Least You Need to Know

◆ Even though it may feel like there's some distance between you, teenage boys need parents who are still present and who know the value of humor.

◆ Requiring your teenage son to contribute chores keeps him connected and readies him for adult responsibilities.

◆ Teenage boys benefit greatly from regular family meals and proper sleep routines.

◆ Vacationing with a teenage boy is fun and serves to counteract peer pressure.

◆ Rituals create a lasting bond of love.

Chapter 21

Launching Him

In This Chapter

- ◆ Deciding on college
- ◆ Graduation and other rites of passage
- ◆ When he doesn't fly the nest
- ◆ When he moves out—and comes back
- ◆ Recognizing that he has his own life
- ◆ Matters of the heart

Boys are now in the minority when it comes to attending college. This trend developed rapidly over the last 40 years and is partially attributed to the fact that boys mature later and experience more behavioral problems than girls. Boys still lead in the math and sciences and enjoy better test scores in these areas. Yet boys make up only 42 percent of the student body.

Your boy, of course, may not wish to be an engineer or mathematician. While the playing field has leveled, nontraditional choices have opened up for boys, too. Helping your son figure out the next step after high school can be a daunting task. In this chapter, we bring dreams together with reality so you can find that just-right answer.

We also look at practical ideas on how to parent young men who return home after facing the first challenges of adult life. In addition, we prepare you for life with a future mate in the picture. Finally, we celebrate loving and relating to a child who has grown to be a man.

You've done a great job with him. Put your feet up and watch his new adventure unfold.

College Considerations

What motivates an older teenage boy to pick one school over another is frequently hard to understand or explain. Boys have unique fears about making it on their own, fears that are heightened in boys who were not frequently challenged. The choice often just comes down to "feel." So how can we help our sons prepare for and find the college that feels right?

Home or Away?

Colleges are short on men these days, so much so that some, such as Seton Hall, are starting football teams and bending admissions selections to men. Savvy college recruiters are putting more pictures of men on brochures. College student centers feature climbing walls and activities boys find attractive. So when it comes to choosing a college, boys these days have many entertaining options beckoning them with a warm embrace.

Boys, then, need to decide: home or away?

The ideal distance to college from home seems to be a two- to three-hour drive—close enough to come home for the occasional meal and laundry service but far enough away to discourage the 'rents from showing up uninvited. Many boys flee to the "U" in the big city, and some metropolitan sons run to the small four-year colleges that surround large cities like eighth-ring educational suburbs.

We cannot underrate the importance of visiting colleges and universities. The "feel" of a campus may be just what motivates your son to dream and plan. High school counselors can recommend colleges, and you can read *U.S. News & World Report* until the staples fall out, but a weekend road trip will help him see and feel out his options.

Your son, like half of transitioning teens, may choose to go to junior college while working and living at home. A gradual entry into college life works for many boys tentative about the big question of "what am I going to do with my life?"

Academic Goals

Boys can become disengaged with their goals and life when left without firm guidance and armed with few social skills. In Japan, this recent concept is known as *hikikomori*, young men withdrawing to their rooms and away from an active social life. Parents used to worry about boys who partied too much—think *Animal House*. Fat, drunk, and stupid is certainly no way to go through life, but neither is caffeinated, isolated, and addicted to playing video games 10 hours a day. College residential advisors and counselors see way too many college boys these days wasting away and dropping out because of such addictions and withdrawal.

Concern among educators on the growing gender gap in college has sparked the launch of the Boys Project at boysproject.com. It asks: Why are young women soaring in college attendance while young men are stagnating?

Some boys, of course, seem to know at an early age what they are going to do. They lock and load an ambition and don't let up until they are being quoted on a national news program as an expert. Most boys, though, find their way gradually. Goal setting in the meantime is still important, even if your son has not found his ultimate ambition. Help him plan the next semester classes instead of waiting until the day of registration at the junior college. Encourage him to work at an entry-level job in an industry he *might* be interested in instead of just working somewhere.

> **Keep Out!**
>
> Boys are more likely than girls to withdraw from college. By the end of the undergraduate years, 100 women will have earned a four-year degree compared to only 73 men. Boys need extra encouragement to both enter and remain in college.

Exposing high achievers to successful men in their chosen field is also helpful for boys in identifying and setting academic goals. "Lessons learned" by those who have gone before can help your son set concrete goals. What is a concrete goal? It's a goal with a date attached to it.

Your son will also benefit from talking with students who are taking the course of study he has chosen. An e-mail correspondence, set up via a professor, may be very useful in helping your son set goals for his first year in college. Professors will be more than willing to discuss expectations, too, but just be prepared for some blunt language. They see many students who are unprepared and may want to express their frustrations to you.

As your son is trying to identify his desires, help him avoid the male trap of choosing to be just like Dad, because, well, he doesn't take the time to think of anything else. Men easily fall victim to the idea that "I'll just be like the old man." Dad may very well be someone to emulate because of his values or community image, but healthy parents want their sons to choose their own paths purposefully and after mature consideration. A father wants a son, not a clone.

Cost

The options for paying for college are numerous. As costs have risen dramatically against inflation, parents have become more discouraged about paying for college. Yet studies consistently show that the earning capacity of college grads far exceeds high school graduates. Black men with just some college experience earn 36 percent more than black male high school graduates. White men with professional degrees earn 262 percent more than white male high school graduates.

In other words, college is a good investment. Your son is going to be 22 years old anyway, better that he reaches 22 with a college degree.

Savings, grants, loans, work-study, and military benefits are the traditional ways of paying for college. Expecting your son to work to save at least for living expenses is reasonable as well. Many states have guaranteed or, like West Virginia, free tuition programs. You can use a Coverdell Education Savings Account and limited tax credits (Hope Scholarship; Student Loan Interest, etc.). Remember to fill out early the free application for financial aid (FAFSA) form at fafsa.ed.gov and check out savingforcollege.com as well.

As costs have risen, there has been an adjustment in the number of years boys expect to study before graduating. Also, boys who work (particularly in medium to large corporations that depend on a stream of new hires), have a significant leg up on recent graduates who spent all their time studying and no time looking for a job. Costs can be managed over time with a steady stream of income, and the more closely the income stream is tied to post-graduation work, the better.

Who Decides?

Boys, whether they are boy monkeys or boy humans, take more risks than girls. They also consistently overestimate their abilities while girls underestimate their skills. Most drowning victims are male. Why? Because they overestimate their ability to swim, and once they're caught in the current, it's often too late. Men also get more raises in the workplace because they are more likely to take a risk and *ask* for a raise. With risk comes reward as well as hazard.

Take the time to have a realistic conversation with your son about his academic skills and study habits. He may be overestimating his abilities to handle the academic currents of a university several hours from home. So, as far as where your son goes to school, an honest conversation about desires and costs will prompt a decision.

You may wish to suggest a few places to help narrow down the choices and then let your son choose where he wants to go. In the end, he is going to have to choose whether he is motivated to attend college and do well. Your choosing for him will do little good other than delay the natural progression of his ambition. If you cannot afford where he wants to go, that's a different problem. Do not exclude his first choice without having a long talk with the financial aid office. Sometimes, aid officers can "find" money when they know the applicant is very committed to the placement.

Rites of Passage: Old and New

Standing together after graduation, my (Barron's) friends and I discussed our 20-year reunion. At that moment, the magnitude of graduating struck home. The magnitude of *his* graduation may strike you even harder. But with a little help, you can enjoy and manage your son's graduation and his move away from home.

Graduation Day

Hopefully your son will reach graduation day along with the other 65 percent of boys who take home a high school diploma. Graduation day, though, is bittersweet. It's both an end and a beginning. He may not realize it, but this day will be the last he will see many old friends for some years to come.

Modern society has few male rites of passage for boys about to change their social status. What many schools do offer is a co-ed high school graduation and a co-ed party. Hopefully, the school will have a party that most kids will attend in safety.

Parents need to take a moment to pat each other on the back, as well. Damn fine job! Excellent parenting! While he is out celebrating, pull out the baby book and marvel at what you have done. You did this. You created this wonderful, accomplished, imperfect, loving son.

He is your greatest work, and he is still in progress.

Helping Him Move

Teenage boys are not big checklist makers. You need to help by teaching him how to move if he'll be attending a college away from home. Having been in his room for the last 18 years, he may dream about moving, but he still does not realize what he needs to move. Download from his college an unnecessarily long list and prioritize. Assemble several different-size boxes. Check with the school to see if he can have a mini-fridge and mini-microwave. He will want both, and they are an excellent way to make a room feel homey.

Can't ship it all? Some moving and storage companies are offering mini-containers for moving one room's worth of stuff. The company drops off this roughly 8×8×12 or larger container; you fill it; they pick it up and deliver it; you empty it; and they pick it up. (Check out doortodoor.com, pods.com, or gominis.com.) Cool!

Toolbox _____

Check with the college to see if they allow building a lofted bed. This bed maximizes floor space by being placed on a wooden frame near the ceiling. Lofted beds are the first real must-have item at college that freshmen do not plan for. Check out kit suppliers like collegebedlofts.com. Or if you plan to build the bed yourself, you'll need supplies and tools: a sketch, lumber, saw, drill, lag bolts, washers, nuts, etc. Don't plan on more than a space for a twin bed. Get to the campus very early to allow for construction. If you can, stay in town the night before, and be one of the first to arrive at the dorm.

When He Doesn't Move Out

Graduating means your son is considered ready to try flying outside the nest. However, many young men ages 18 to 24—some 56 percent compared to 43 percent of young women—live with their parents after graduation. Some need another several months, or even a few more years, to sort out their ambition. When takeoff does not appear imminent, you can still enjoy your son's presence while encouraging him to make the big leap.

A Dream with a Deadline

We need to be honest with ourselves and recognize the ripe smell that arises from our son's repeated statements about his plans to move on and move out. A dream becomes a goal *with a deadline*. Expecting him to write down a deadline and post it on the refrigerator is meaningful and fair—fair to us and fair to him.

Start with some short and midterm goals that he can easily reach. Asking 110 percent effort is pretty much a recipe for failure. It sounds good in Hollywood sports cliché movies, but in reality it tends to work less effectively than asking for a 90 percent effort. Set reasonable and measurable goals (number of applications, number of interviews, number of networking contacts, a resumé or business plan).

Then, follow up. Try to meet over a meal and discuss your son's progress in a pleasant manner. If he still can't decide what he wants to do and you absolutely need him out, set him up in an apartment and pay his initial rent, making sure he understands that this is the last rent payment you will make. Remember, boys respond to firm discipline better than girls, and firm action on your part may be just what he'll respond to.

Sweat Equity

If the reality is that he needs to live at home, your son can still contribute in concrete ways—painting, cooking, cleaning out the storage room, digging or weeding a garden, and so on. He may be cash-starved, but he is chock-full of potential industry. He will likely both appreciate and feel a little guilty about continuing to live at home when his buddies have moved out, so his valuable work will let him share the financial burden. Also, helping out will help *him* feel more competent and confident. An improved self-image may be just what he needs to feel accomplished and ready to take on the world.

Rent Is Due on the First

If Junior is busy with work or perhaps you don't want little Dagwood to repair things, establish a rent that is fair to him and you. Give him a due date, just like a "real" landlord. However, real landlords don't tell their tenants they can't have sex, or choose what music can be played, or set curfews. If you want to set some house rules, that's well and good, but don't expect him to pay the market rate for his space.

A final note: the presence of young adult men in the home is the reality in economies where mortgages are not common. For example, in Syria, nothing is remarkable about generations living together, and young men work for years to save enough to afford a separate small residence.

> **Toy Box**
>
> I recently met a man and woman who had been married for fifty years and they told me a story ... Their forty-six-year-old son had just moved back in with them, bringing his two kids, one who was twenty-three and one who was twenty-two. All three of them were out of work. "And that," I told my wife, "is why there is death."
>
> —Bill Cosby, *Bill Cosby on Fatherhood*

In America, we may see young men living additional years with their parents for a variety of reasons.

When He Moves Out and Moves Back!

Prodigal or no prodigal, whatever you are feeling when your son lands back home, it most likely feels worse to him. Ah, life. Here's how to help your son survive that first, painful body blow.

Lost His Job/Girlfriend/Ambition

Ouch. That look on his face says it all. He may shrug and say "I don't want to talk about it" (a classic!), but you can still feel his pain. Maturity brings many things, and one is the knowledge that light follows darkness and that every life has significant, necessary losses. Unfortunately, our maturity is fairly useless to a young man who has gotten fired for the first time, had his heart ripped out by his first "serious" girlfriend-roommate, or has decided that his dream of making "nationals" is not going to happen.

A few days of quiet and some nice home-cooked meals may put him into a better disposition. After that, you can have a talk about what it means for him to live at home again. Right now, he needs some company and familiarity. He needs to know that there are some reliable things in this world. He has come home to you! Good old Mr. and Mrs. Reliable. (He has edited out the previous thousand times he yelled at you and said he wanted to live his own life, blah, blah.)

Fortunately, while not claiming to be perfect in any way, shape, or form, you have managed to accomplish raising this wounded young man to the point where he knows what's good for him. Home. He may just stay for a night, a few days, or until he gets back on his feet. But still, he needs to be at home.

Solving, Not Judging

After the requisite open wound-licking time has passed, encourage your son to sit down and begin seeking solutions. If it's a job, then it's time to realize that employment certainly is important. Have him pull out his resumé and update it, or help him create one. If it is matters of the heart that are the big concern and long talks with Mom or Dad aren't cutting it, a therapist can help him sort out his feelings and move on.

When he becomes upset, avoid the temptation to solve the feeling away (for example: "You just need to get out, son"). Also resist telling him the *solution* to his feelings. Simply help him identify his feelings. Tell him: "I can tell you are really angry/sad/confused." Then, be quiet for a few minutes. The feelings will fade in intensity, and the conversation will continue. This mix of empathy, emotional intelligence, and problem solving will permit your son to work though this difficult time.

He's Got a Life

Your son is becoming a man, yet he still looks to you for approval and love. Adults disagree and yet still communicate. Parents and adult boys who disagree still need to hold each other close. The boy behind the beard will be learning more from experience than guidance; that is, he'll be learning as he makes his own way. When he wanders back, he'll know the door and your heart are always open.

Eye to Eye

The power we had when our sons were younger dissipates as they age and gain strength to make their own decisions. This is as it should be. Resist the very real impulse to feel *personally rejected* when he disagrees with you. The expectations we have for our children must eventually, and sometimes painfully, yield to their autonomy. As an adult, he can change political parties, decide that the Cubs will never win, or wear whatever ugly clothing fashion he decides is hip. This is not your son rejecting you. This is your son making up his own mind and becoming a man.

Adult Activities

To be concerned about your son's safety is natural as he is in your heart at all times. Unfortunately, while you hold him close, he is out living it up and taking all the risks that come with life. Try to sort out your concerns, and thus your need for communication, into a rough list of "none of my business" and "some of my business."

Who your adult son chooses to befriend is pretty much none of your business. Until your son starts to get serious, he needs to experiment and date a variety of people. Later, you can discuss openly your appreciation for his future mate.

Of course, if any person is putting your son at serious risk (drugs, drunk driving, violence), you can and often must act. Spending time together doing things he likes (he still eats, right?) may be even a better way to short-circuit destructive behavior.

> **Toolbox**
>
> Now that your boy is grown and gone and you can finally afford it, buy season tickets for his favorite team sport. You'll see him more often and have a great conversation starter.

He's in Love

When your son's future mate arrives on the scene, strange and potent emotions rise. A huge dose of empathy is called for here. Maybe she is not your choice, but you don't get to choose. Here's to real love.

The Joy of Loving

We get to drink at 21 and, around the same time, we often become intoxicated with real love—not puppy love, or spring break lust, but real, honest, I-want-to-make-you-breakfast-in-bed-and-spend-the-rest-of-my-life-with-you love. The concept of committed companionship can be both comforting and frightening to him. It is pure joy for your son to recognize his desire to love deeply and the person deserving of that love. For him to consider that he might lose such joy to disease, accident, war, crime, or another person is frightening. Commitment in the face of fear, having the courage to love even knowing the risks, is a quality we can help our sons find in themselves.

Losing a Son?

When a mother and daughter-in-law-to-be discuss the wedding, a palpable sense of tension may fill the room. Outsiders feel this undercurrent as part of the tidal transition that must take place when a young man chooses a mate.

Mom, who has birthed and nurtured this gift, must now hand him off to another female. She will no longer be the central woman in her son's world, and it's natural for her to grieve the transition. The son's bride can feel threatened as well. After all, Mom was the first woman in his life and will always be a part of his world.

It is appropriate for your son's new partner to be protective of her new relationship. There is room for everybody, but it is up to Mom to show some restraint.

"Gaining a daughter" is an attitude that helps mothers open themselves to having more rather than less. As a son's relationship grows into a real love, we as parents can help by first staying out of the way. Pestering him as to when and if he is going to "make a commitment" is not what he needs. Certainly we can be available and offer to help him sort it out, but the best thing parents can do is to continue to model healthy adult relationships.

As for welcoming his new love, Mom and future daughter-in-law can go shopping or spend a day together when Dad and son go off to a game. Eating meals together and hearing about their day is a wonderful way to connect, too. Of course, you will eventually want to invite her parents for dinner, if possible. You are gaining a daughter; they are gaining a son; and perhaps, just perhaps, you'll get some grandchildren out of the deal.

Embracing Your Blessing

Before and after the very necessary rule setting and cajoling, may we all choose tenderness. Let's embrace our sons throughout their lives with the depth of thankfulness and love we felt when we first held them close in that small, warm blanket.

The Least You Need to Know

◆ Boys need additional encouragement to choose college and to remain in college.

◆ Men who attend college earn significantly more than men who have high school degrees.

◆ When your son moves back home, offer him encouragement and kindness, and help him set goals with deadlines.

◆ If your young adult son shows the gumption to disagree with you, he is becoming a man.

◆ Welcome your son's future mate and console him tenderly if his first serious relationship fails.

◆ Continue to love your son the way you did when you brought him home from the hospital as a newborn.

Resources

If you'd like to learn more about raising boys, these books and websites are a good place to start.

Books

Barkley, Russell A., and Christine M. Benton. *Your Defiant Child: 8 Steps to Better Behavior.* New York: Guilford Pub., 1998.

———. *Taking Charge of ADHD: The Complete, Authoritative Guide for Parents.* Rev. Ed. New York: Guilford Pub., 2000.

Barry, Dave. *Dave Barry's Complete Guide to Guys.* 1st Ed. New York: Random House, 1995.

Brazelton, T. Berry, and Joshua D. Sparrow. *Touchpoints Three to Six: Your Child's Emotional and Behavioral Development.* Cambridge, Mass.: Perseus Pub., 2001.

Brinley, Maryann Bucknum. *Oh Boy! Mothers Tell the Truth About Raising Teen Sons.* 1st Ed. New York: Three Rivers Pub., 2004.

Cosby, Bill. *Fatherhood.* Garden City, New York: Doubleday, 1986.

Drexler, Peggy, and Linden Gross. *Raising Boys Without Men: How Maverick Moms Are Creating the Next Generation of Exceptional Men.* Emmaus, Pa.: Rodale, 2005.

Elium, Don, and Jeanne Elium. *Raising a Son.* 3rd Ed. Berkeley, Calif.: Celestial Arts, 2004.

———. *Raising a Son: Parents and the Making of a Healthy Man.* Hillsboro, Ore.: Beyond Words, 1992.

Goleman, Daniel. *Emotional Intelligence.* 1st Ed. New York: Bantam Books, 1995.

———. *Social Intelligence.* 1st Ed. New York: Bantam Books, 2006.

Gordon, Jay, and Maria Goodavage. *Good Nights: The Happy Parents' Guide to the Family Bed (And a Peaceful Night's Sleep).* 1st Ed. New York: St. Martin's Griffin, 2002.

Gottlieb, Andrew R. *Sons Talk About Their Gay Fathers: Life Curves.* New York: Harrington Park, 2003.

Gray, John. *Men Are from Mars, Women Are from Venus: The Classic Guide to Understanding the Opposite Sex.* 1st Quill Ed. New York: Quill, 2004.

Gurian, Michael. *The Wonder of Boys: What Parents, Mentors, and Educators Can Do to Shape Boys into Exceptional Men.* New York: Putnam, 1996.

Hallowell, Edward M., and John J. Ratey. *Driven to Distraction: Recognizing and Coping with Attention Deficit Disorder from Childhood through Adulthood.* 1st Touchstone Ed. New York: Simon & Schuster, 1995.

Harrison, Harry H. *Father to Son: Life Lessons on Raising a Boy.* New York: Workman Pub., 2000.

Jensen, Peter S. *Making the System Work for Your Child with ADHD.* New York: Guilford Pub., 2004.

Marcovitz, Hal. *Teens & Gay Issues.* Broomall, Penn.: Mason Crest, 2005.

Meurer, Dave. *Boyhood Daze: An Incomplete Guide to Raising Boys.* Minneapolis, Minn.: Bethany House, 1999.

Miedzian, Myriam. *Boys Will Be Boys: Breaking the Link Between Masculinity and Violence.* 1st Ed. New York: Doubleday, 1991.

Nikkah, John, and Leah Furman. *Our Boys Speak: Adolescent Boys Write About Their Inner Lives.* 1st Ed. New York: St. Martin's Griffin, 2000.

Pollack, William. *Real Boys: Rescuing Our Sons from the Myths of Boyhood.* New York: Owl Pub., 1998.

Real, Terrence. *I Don't Want to Talk About It: Overcoming the Secret Legacy of Male Depression.* New York: Scribner, 1997.

Rich, Jason. *Growing Up Gay in America: Informative and Practical Advice for Teen Guys Questioning Their Sexuality and Growing Up Gay.* 1st Ed. Portland, Ore.: Franklin Street Books, 2002.

Savin-Williams, Ritch C. *The New Gay Teenager.* Cambridge, Mass.: Harvard UP, 2005.

Sax, Leonard. *Why Gender Matters: What Parents and Teachers Need to Know About the Emerging Science of Sex Differences.* 1st Ed. New York: Doubleday, 2005.

Shaffer, Susan Morris, and Linda Perlman Gordon. *Why Boys Don't Talk—and Why It Matters: A Parent's Survival Guide to Connecting with Your Teen.* New York: McGraw-Hill, 2005.

Sommers, Christina Hoff. *The War Against Boys: How Misguided Feminism Is Harming Our Young Men.* New York: Simon & Schuster, 2000.

Strong, Susan. *The Boldness of Boys: Famous Men Talk About Growing Up.* Kansas City, MO: Andrews McMeel Pub., 2003.

Taylor, John F. *Helping Your ADD Child: Hundreds of Practical Solutions for Parents and Teachers of ADD Children and Teens (with or Without Hyperactivity).* 3rd. Ed., Rev. Roseville, Calif.: Prima Health, 2001.

Websites

www.aclu.org   Website of the American Civil Liberties Union. Information on civil rights and getting a printable card for your son to carry in case he is stopped by the police.

www.boystomen.org and www.boystomennw.org   Regional organizations devoted to training boys during weekend retreats on how to be responsible men.

www.clubpenguin.com   A fun social networking site for children.

www.collegeboard.com   College entrance exam testing authority that provides helpful information to parents and students.

www.doortodoor.com, www.gominis.com, and www.pods.com Companies that can provide drop off/pick up moving containers for college students.

www.driversedge.org   A crash course in *not* crashing, taught by race car drivers.

www.fafsa.ed.gov   Standard financial aid application required by colleges.

www.gsanetwork.org   Group that connects the Gay/Straight Alliances together.

www.health24.com   Health information site from South Africa.

www.homeschooling.about.com   A reference website for homeschooling.

www.mindstorms.lego.com   A toy that combines Legos, computers, and robotics.

http://music.yahoo.com/lyrics   A site used to review music lyrics.

www.nais.org   Website for the National Association of Independent Schools: a good site for parents considering private schools.

www.nces.ed.gov   Website for the United States Department of Education, National Center for Education Statistics.

www.netlingo.com   A website for learning computer slang.

www.netnanny.com   A software program used by parents to block porn and other offensive material on the Internet.

www.nytimes.com   Leading newspaper in America that offers excellent reporting of health and education issues related to boys.

www.outproud.org   A resource for boys who are gay or are questioning whether they are gay.

www.pcworld.com   A website/magazine with link to free software that can protect your computer from spam, viruses, etc.

www.pflag.org   Website of PFLAG (Parents, Families and Friends of Lesbians and Gays), a national organization promoting the health and well-being of gay, lesbian, bisexual, and transgender persons.

www.runescape.com   An online, interactive, and free fantasy gamesite popular with boys.

www.scouts.com   Website for the Boy Scouts of America.

www.usankf.org   Website for the United States National Karate Federation.

www.usfirst.org   Website for FIRST (For Inspiration and Recognition of Science and Technology); it sponsors national robotics contests.

www.wiredsafety.org   WiredSafety provides help, information, and education to Internet and mobile device users of all ages.

Index

fears, 6
  fear of failure, 219-220
  locker room fears, 164-165
  self-consciousness, 172-175
feelings, sharing, 240-241
female friends, 189-190
"feminine" gift, responding to, 54-58
  creativity, 56-58
  gentleness, 55-56
  relationships, 55
fighting concerns, 218-219
FIRST (For Inspiration and Recognition of Science and Technology), 124
FIRST LEGO League. *See* FLL
FIRST Robotics Competition. *See* FRC
FIRST Vex Challenge. *See* FVC
fishing, 117-118
flirting, Oedipal Phase, 33-34
FLL (FIRST LEGO League), 124
For Inspiration and Recognition of Science and Technology. *See* FIRST
FRC (FIRST Robotics Competition), 124
Freud, Sigmund, Oedipal Phase, 32
friendships
  female friends, 189-190
  first friends, 47
  handling wrong crowd situations, 196-198
  importance of, 188-189
  middle school boys, 146-148
  online friends, 192-195
  opening home to friends, 190-192
  play experiences, 48
  pleasure, 188
  puberty challenges, 167
  social and emotional skills development, 133

verbal concerns, 49
video games and, 195-196
FVC (FIRST Vex Challenge), 124

G

games, skills development, 71-72
Gardner, Dr. Howard, multiple intelligences theory, 93
gay. *See* homosexuality
Gay-Straight Alliance. *See* GSA
gender (male identity images)
  heroes, 40-43
  strength concepts, 44-46
  teaching son to act heroically, 43-44
gentleness, responding to "feminine" gifts, 55-56
gifted programs (school issues), 92-93
girl issues
  aversion to girls in middle school, 148-150
  friendships, 189-190
  relationship issues
    conversation concerns, 200-201
    dating, 201-203
    falling in love, 208
    handling breakups, 208-209
    media influences, 204-205
    sex education talks, 205-208
    understanding what girls want, 203-204
  welcoming future mates, 281-282
goals
  academics, 273-274
  setting, 228-229
goofiness stage (middle school boys)
  enjoying the silliness, 152-153
  playing along with, 153
graduation day, 276

U–V

W–X–Y–Z